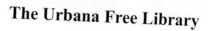
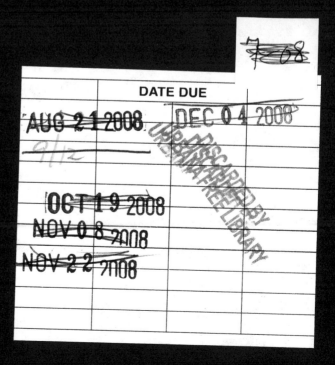

GOD WILLING

GOD WILLING

My Wild Ride with the New Iraqi Army

CAPT. ERIC NAVARRO, USMCR

Potomac Books, Inc.
Washington, D.C.

Library of Congress Cataloging-in-Publication Data

Navarro, Eric, 1975–
  God willing : my wild ride with the new Iraqi Army / Eric Navarro.— 1st ed.
    p. cm.
  Includes index.
  ISBN-13: 978-1-59797-169-0 (alk. paper)
  1. Iraq War, 2003—Personal narratives, American. 2. Navarro, Eric, 1975- 3. Marines—United States—Biography. 4. United States. Marine Corps—Biography. I. Title.
  DS79.76.N38 2008
  956.7044'345092—dc22

                                                      2007042745

Printed in the United States of America on acid-free paper that meets the American National Standards Institute Z39-48 Standard.

Potomac Books, Inc.
22841 Quicksilver Drive
Dulles, Virginia 20166

First Edition

10 9 8 7 6 5 4 3 2 1

CONTENTS

PREFACE

From the outset, my time spent living, training, and fighting with the Iraqis was completely surreal. Even though I was only a lieutenant on his first deployment I knew I was living in interesting times, and I set out to keep a daily journal. I distinctly remember telling one of the Marines who served with me that I was going to write a book about our tour advising the Iraqi Army. I don't know if he believed me or not. I didn't care. I knew in my bones that I was going to do it and that our story was an important one to tell. Even with the passing of time, my perspective on the events described and dissected in the pages that follow has barely changed.

Ultimately, the book attempts to capture my and my fellow drifters' reality in Iraq.

Thus, I should write a few disclaimers. First, I have changed nearly everyone's name except my own. I did this not because I craved the spotlight but because I wanted to protect my friends from undue attention and respect their privacy. If they want to come forward with their own experiences, they can do so on their own and in their own way. Second, any opinions offered are mine and mine alone. I do not represent the U.S. Marine Corps. I have simply collected evidence during my own experiences and through hearing about the experiences of people I served with. I have examined the evidence and come to certain conclusions. I have decided to impart to the reader those conclusions in an effort to both pay tribute to all the advisers who have worked with the New Iraqi Army and bring to light the difficulties associated with building up a foreign country's military from scratch. I have also shared a few recommendations and lessons learned in the hope they may be of use to any service people who take part in an adviser mission in the future.

Once again, all of the words and opinions contained herein are my own and do not reflect the opinions of any other Marines, or Americans for that matter.

Third, this book is the result of a process. I kept a daily journal during my Iraq tour. I then turned the journal into a narrative using the words I had written and my own memory of the events. During the writing and rewriting process, I had time to think about everything that had happened, and I was able to provide a more objective analysis of the events. Everything I write about actually happened and has not been embellished. Any small discrepancies are merely the upshot of faulty memory. Ultimately, I stand by my work.

Finally, it is impossible to thank every single person who has made major contributions to my life and to the publication of this book. However, several key figures stand out. Bing West, a former Marine and now fellow author, was kind enough to help me from the beginning of my quest for publication. I thank him for taking the time out of his busy schedule to read my work, offer support and criticism, and point me in the right direction. Kevin Smith, who was working for another publisher at the time, saw enough talent in my writing to go ahead and recommend me to Potomac Books. There's not much I can do to repay such a kind act except to say thank you in these pages. Don McKeon and Don Jacobs at Potomac Books were good enough to see potential in my story. They also endured my ceaseless e-mails, which should probably put them in line for some kind of award for patience.

Speaking of patience, I could not forget to thank my family. My parents, especially, have been nothing short of amazing. Lord knows I have tried my best to make their lives difficult over the last thirty-three years, and yet they have never failed to be there when I needed them. Their love and compassion is unending and inspiring. My brother and sister have never let me down, and I hope they can say the same of me. I may have beat them up a couple of times too many, but isn't that what big brothers are for? The rest of my family and friends, especially my grandparents, need to know that they too have made such meaningful contributions to my life that without them this book would not have been possible. For their support, I thank them.

I also have to thank the Marine Corps for helping to shape me into the man I am today. An old recruiting commercial shows the Marine Corps taking a fiery piece of metal and through force of will and craftsmanship honing it into a sleek sword. At one time I was that piece of metal. Now, I believe, the Corps has shaped a sword.

Finally—I have to save the best for last—I thank my beautiful wife, Dorothy. She is, without a doubt, the finest person I have ever known. Forget for a second that she is gorgeous, her loyalty, dedication, and courage have helped me become a better person ever since I met her. In this world, these three qualities are rarities. I am blessed to have found them and to have found her. She, like so many wives in today's America, had to endure the emotional, gut-wrenching experience of watching her husband leave for war. Yet she stood tall and held on while I was risking my life for my country. Her strength was and is nothing short of incredible. She doesn't hear it enough from me or from the people around her, but she needs to know that she is among the best we have in this world. She is my hero.

FIRST HOUR, FIRST CONTACT, FIRST IMPRESSIONS

"Insha Allah."

This phrase translates as "God willing" or "If God wills it."

When you live with Iraqis for nearly eight months, you become numb to those two words. They invade every conversation. Their meaning hangs in the air around you during every military mission. The words act as a password, a way to tell who has been a U.S. adviser and for how long. But you don't need to have been an adviser to gain an understanding of the significance of the words. Not only does the idea embodied by the two words form the backbone of the Iraqi faith and culture, but it describes perfectly the reason the United States faces such difficulties in endeavoring to bring democracy and stability to the cradle of civilization.

"Insha Allah" cuts through the fog of war, the politicians' cynical speeches, the media doom and gloom, and the Muslim posturing. It took me a while—a little over two hundred and ten days, to be exact—but I finally realized that the words lie at the heart of the problem in Iraq. In fact, they *are* the problem.

"Insha Allah," "God willing," "If God wills it"—they are all phrases that mean everything and nothing. However, any examination of this Arabic phrase and of our mission to train the Iraqis to restore order in their country requires more than confident declarations. It requires specific conclusions supported by experiential evidence. Fortunately, or unfortunately, depending on one's point of view, it didn't take long, as I

1

spent time with the New Iraqi Army, for the experiences, the evidence, and my own conclusions to start piling up. My examination of that phrase, "Insha Allah," and our mission with the Iraqis began in my first hour, during my first contact with the enemy, and, of course, it started with those ubiquitous two words.

"Insha Allah"—it was the first time an Iraqi ever said this to me. The time and place was such that I did not realize the phrase's symbolic significance yet. I was too busy trying to get my situational awareness up. I knew very little about the Iraqi people and even less about our mission.

"OK, so then do we have enough water or not?" I exhaled, long and loud. I was exasperated. I had been talking to this particular Iraqi for nearly twenty minutes trying to get an answer. I waited. The Iraqi looked like he was thinking hard.

"Insha Allah," he said, with a smile and a shrug. The rest of the Iraqis who were gathered around us nodded in agreement with their leader.

His name was Major Ali. He was the commander of the 2nd Company of the 9th Battlion of the 2nd Regiment of the 1st Division of the Iraqi Intervention Force (IFF). The company was a mixture of holdovers from Saddam Hussein's old army and raw recruits who were lured by the promise of a steady paycheck in a country suffering from crippling unemployment. The IFF was a part of the New Iraqi Army, which was being stood up in the wake of the decision to disband Saddam's old army forces. It was supposedly designed to go into the cities, whereas other portions of the New Iraqi Army focused on other areas. I never understood the reason for the separate force because the majority of the fighting had been taking place in Iraq's cities, but over time I realized that the Iraqis simply loved titles. They loved making up new and colorful names for themselves. Hell, even the insurgents couldn't settle on one name.

Major Ali was not an insurgent. At least, I didn't think he was when I first met him. He was too nice. He smiled a lot, nodded in respect, and deferred to me throughout our initial meeting. I knew I probably could not discern whether an Iraqi meant me harm based on these courtesies, but I thought

I had a good sense of the man. He was short, no bigger than five feet six inches tall, and older than most of the other Iraqis. From his shortly cropped white hair to the grey beard that covered his wrinkled face, I estimated him to be well over fifty years old. He had only a few cracked yellow teeth left in his mouth, and he didn't understand a word of English. Because our higher headquarters personnel, whoever they were, had decided they couldn't spare a single interpreter, the language barrier was posing an obvious problem for us collectively and for me, in particular.

I was one of ten men attached to the 9th Battalion as what was then called an Adviser Support Team (AST). We were ten American Marines assigned to live with, train, and go into battle with approximately more than five hundred Iraqi soldiers. Our team comprised one major, who acted as the officer in charge of the entire team; one first sergeant, who was the senior enlisted man on the team and who would team with the major, as in all Marine units, and act as his adviser on administrative and enlisted issues; a captain; two gunnery sergeants; four staff sergeants; and me—one lone lieutenant. I was there filling a captain's billet because apparently there weren't enough stray captains hanging around to get plucked for this mission.

The intent behind our selection for this team was clear. The powers that be had decided they needed experienced men. Every member of the team, except for me, had been deployed multiple times, both in Iraq and elsewhere, and, in theory, could rely on their great wealth of experience during our time with the Iraqis. Of course, combat usually dictates that the opposite of what you expect to happen will indeed actually happen. Thus, within the first hour of our operational deployment with our Iraqi battalion, I, the least experienced Marine, was first introduced to the phrase, "Insha Allah." And not long after that I came up with my own interpretation of those words.

It was December 19, 2004, during the mop-up stages of Operation Phantom Fury—"The Push"—the battle to retake Fallujah, a city located in the heart of the Sunni Triangle and at that time the center of the insurgency. The media was focused on the city. So, too, were the politicians. I thought at the time that I was charged with the most important mission of all of our forces in country: training and standing up the New Iraqi Army. Both the U.S. president and secretary of defense had intimated as much during speeches made just prior to our entrance into Fallujah. They said that creating the army had become our most pressing mission. I bought the party line, hook, line, and sinker. I thought that if we could get the Iraqi forces up and running then U.S. forces might have a chance to build a better Iraq. Once the Iraqis were good to go, then we Americans could start going home. As a result, it felt as if all eyes were on us. The advisers were the tip of the spear. These delusions of grandeur, however, had to take a backseat to more immediate concerns: did the Iraqis have enough water and where were they going to take a shit?

We were in the middle of a small courtyard in an abandoned mosque on the corner of two streets called Katie and Evan. The 9th Battalion had taken root in a collection of buildings to form a crude set of battle positions. The Iraqi battalion commander, his staff, and what was supposed to be the Headquarters and Service (H&S) Company occupied a big house one block away to our northeast. First Company was across the street from us in an abandoned hospital, and 3rd Company was due north up the road in an empty palatial mansion. Second Company was ordered to take up a position inside the mosque compound to help protect the southeastern portion of our perimeter and also to control a key intersection. The Iraqis had their machine guns set up in positions that pointed down the main avenues of approach, and they had guards at certain key points along the back edge of the mosque so that no one could sneak in and cut our throats during the night.

The mosque was empty when we took up residence. Blast and bullet holes speckled the sides of many of the outer walls. A wall made of HESCO—cubes used to erect walls quickly— partially protected the front entrance to the mosque compound. The cubes were staged and then filled with dirt, like giant building blocks. They provided the only protection for the front of the mosque.

I was standing in the courtyard facing east. Over my left shoulder was a tall tower, a minaret, from which the sermons and prayers normally would have been broadcast, but on that December day there was nothing but silence, sometimes broken by the idle chatter of confused-looking Iraqis. At the base of the tower was a small rectangular mound of dirt and about ten cats constantly made their way back and forth from the mound. A body had been buried under the dirt, the remains of one of the insurgents who didn't get away. The insurgent's comrades, the ones who escaped, had taken the time to give him a hasty burial, probably to ensure that he made it to the afterlife and the seventy-two virgins that supposedly awaited the jihadists. I don't know if he made it to that sexual heaven, but he did make a nice meal for the cats. Each one would rush up, kneel, take a nibble of flesh, and then rush off.

To my right was a large room. The Iraqis used sign language to let me know that it was the prayer room and that, because I was not a Muslim, I was not allowed inside. From my vantage point, I could see that it was a square room with a high ceiling, which allowed worshipers to look up toward Allah. There was no furniture. It was just a room for the Muslims to kneel on their rugs and bow down in. The word *Islam* means submission (to the will of God). Bow down. Or suffer. Although no prayers were heard on that December day, there had already been plenty of suffering.

Fallujah was like a corpse. It was the meat that was left over when the body's life was extinguished. There was rubble everywhere. Whole buildings laid in ruins. Bullet holes were everywhere. There was no running water. Raw sewage spilled into the streets. Burn marks, resembling black scars, cut across the faces of the abandoned houses. There had been a fierce battle here, and many people had died. Most, if not all of the bodies were gone. Mortuary Services did a superb job of erasing all human evidence from the scene.

Although Fallujah had been cleared by our forces and was virtually empty, residual enemy activity remained high in the area. Plenty of insurgent stragglers continued to hide in the corners of alleys or in hidden spots inside the closets of some of the houses nearby. They were waiting for some unsuspecting

American patrol to stumble onto them. They wanted one last attempt at killing Americans before they were sent to the bliss of the afterlife.

In addition to the remaining enemy presence, there was the fact that we were out there on our own. An American unit was stationed down the road, but up until that first hour we had had no contact with them. I wasn't sure if they knew we were there. Hell, no one knew we were in the area except the enemy. When we first arrived, one hour earlier, I could feel the enemy watching us. For the first time in my life I felt hunted. It wasn't a feeling that was hard to understand. We were ten Americans accompanied by more than five hundred Iraqis. Who knew how many insurgents were out there? And who knew how many of the IIF Iraqis were insurgents themselves?

The feelings of isolation and constant danger stayed with us throughout our mission. The determinations we were continually asked to make were complex, a reality that sank in almost immediately. By the time I spoke to Major Ali about the company's water supply, I had a good sense of how dire the situation was.

My boss, Major Lawson, decided to split up the AST and attach us to specific companies. We would work with the Iraqi company leadership and help them manage the company. That plan, however, didn't take into account the Iraqis' reception of us. Would they listen to us? Would they attack us? Would they run away, as some stories had it? These ideas rolled around in my head as Major Ali jabbered on in Arabic.

Each line company, 1st, 2nd, and 3rd, had two Marines assigned to it. Each pair included a senior AST member and a junior AST member. I was assigned as 2nd Company's senior adviser. As the senior adviser, I was to take the lead when dealing with Major Ali. Staff Sergeant Turner was the junior adviser working with me. He sat back, observed, offered advice, and, of course, kept his eyes peeled for any threats.

Turner, a black man with a big ass, was in his mid thirties. He was a black belt and had a low, mild-mannered voice that hid his killer's instincts. While Turner was a seasoned staff noncommissioned officer (NCO) and an Iraq War veteran already, he was not without his faults. He took his time talking and expressing his opinion. He was polite almost to a fault, and this came back to bite me almost immediately.

Staff Sergeant Turner and I waited while Major Ali talked to one of his lieutenants about the setup of our position within the mosque compound. The city had no running water, and we had to figure out how many water bottles we had, how many we needed, and where the troops were going to go to the bathroom. The Iraqis had special needs when it came to water. They used it in a variety of rather interesting ways. Obviously, they needed enough water to drink. But drinking water was the least of my worries. By observing the soldiers milling about in the courtyard of the mosque compound, I learned that the Iraqis liked to wash their heads and hands, and even their bare feet, incessantly. As I had my first discussion with Major Ali, I could see the Iraqi soldiers going about their hygiene routine behind him. They took the bottles of water that were supposed to be used for drinking and poured the water over their heads; then they washed their feet. The fact that we were operationally deployed inside the city of Fallujah didn't seem to matter. Considering we had just occupied a battle position inside a city that was yet to be cleared of enemy fighters, there were far more important things to worry about besides cleanliness. The threat of impending death was the most obvious concern. And this didn't even take into account the fact that our water supply was limited or that we didn't know when our next resupply would arrive.

The final factor in the water calculation was the most important. How many bottles of water did an Iraqi use when he went to the bathroom? You see, the Iraqis did not use toilet paper. I had learned this when we arrived in East Fallujah Iraqi Camp (EFIC), a small camp outside of the main Marine base Camp Fallujah, where we had waited for the 9th Battalion of the IIF to arrive, shortly before we deployed into the city. Instead of the elevated toilet common in most Western countries, Iraqis use a squat toilet—basically a slab of porcelain even with the ground and with a hole in the middle. The user positions his feet and squats over the hole, tries to hit the bull's-eye, and then pours water down his ass crack, using his left hand—only his left hand—to splash water into those hard to reach areas. I'll save a dissertation on the hygienic values of such a practice for later, but until then, suffice it to say, this method of ass cleaning was going to be a major problem for us while we lived in a confined space with over five hundred Iraqis and had no running water.

At no time in my Marine training was I ever prepared for such a situation. When we reviewed tactical decision-making scenarios, the one about where the Iraqis were going to shit and how much water they would need to wipe their asses somehow never came up. The old saying "What now, Lieutenant?" wasn't going to cut it on the sarcastic scale for this situation.

Nonetheless, I was expected to make and/or advise Major Ali on these sorts of decisions. So, I attempted to work through this particular issue with him during our first face-to-face conversation. I had already tried to impress upon him the seriousness of the situation. We didn't know how long we would be in the mosque, and the thought of spending weeks in a place where shit and shitty water were pooling around made both my stomach churn and my brain scream out words like *cholera* and *dysentery*.

As Turner and I waited, Ali spoke to Lieutenant Ahmed about this point. I was using Ahmed as a crude interpreter. He knew some English but thought he knew much more than he actually did. This made him a little dangerous. I had been warned that Iraqis were easily offended, and Ahmed was no exception to this rule. It was important not to embarrass him in front of the others, especially since he was an officer and many of the basic soldiers had gathered around to listen to their leaders' conversations. To me, this practice made the soldiers look like American teenage girls, but I never said as much to any of them. Again, I was trying to put forth a respectful yet powerful image. They had to know I was not there to tell them what to do, but they also needed to know that, if I had to, I would take charge and would take control of the situation. It was a delicate balancing act.

Ahmed was making that balancing act a little more difficult. While Major Ali was pleasant mannered and seemed to defer to my judgment, Ahmed looked at me cross-eyed. It was clear he didn't trust me. He was still sizing me up—this strange American Marine who stood before him. I would have to work hard to win him over. In the short time I interacted with Ahmed, however, I knew that no matter how much effort I put into changing his perceptions of me, he would remain a problem. He had a sneer on his face whenever he talked to people, not just me but also his own soldiers. He carried himself with an air of self-importance—not an admirable quality to have as an officer. Instead of leading, he was more interested in ordering his soldiers around. If I were to trust this initial impression of the man, I would have to keep an eye on him. And that is what I did the most of during those first few cautious exchanges with the Iraqis: I formed initial impressions and tried to figure out who was a friend, who was a foe, and who was in the middle.

One soldier who I knew immediately was not only going to be a valuable asset to the company but also a friend was a man named Mohammed. I remember thinking, when I saw him the first time, "Wait a minute. He's not an Iraqi." First of all, he was bigger than almost all of them. He was about six feet tall, a little shorter than my height, and he had some muscle tone to his body. While all the others were tiny, scrawny, or both, Mohammed looked like he was in the military. He also carried himself as such.

Near where Ali and I were talking, a gaggle of lesser soldiers were sitting around doing nothing, with their helmets and flimsy flak jackets and AK-47s all off to the side. Some were washing their feet, others smoking cigarettes. All of a sudden Mohammed came stomping through the group in a confident gait and started barking orders at his fellow Iraqis. They either respected the man or feared him because they stopped what they were doing and gathered their gear and moved along. When I found out he was only a jundee, or private, the lowest level of soldier and not even an NCO, I laughed out loud at the oversight. Word was that many of the officers and NCOs in this new version of the Iraqi Army had bribed their way into a higher rank. Corruption was a way of life in this desert country, and obviously Mohammed didn't have enough money to reach the station he most clearly deserved.

Mohammed approached my meeting with Ali and Ahmed. As he walked toward us, again I noticed his confident walk and command presence. The rest of the soldiers clearly looked to him for guidance. And it turned out he could speak some English—better than Lieutenant Ahmed. He said he learned it from watching movies.

"Marhaba, ani Mulazem Awal Navarro," I said, using my limited Arabic to say, "Hi, I am 1st Lieutenant Navarro." I stuck my hand out. Mohammed smiled widely when he heard my Arabic. I could tell by the mutterings from the audience of other jundees that I had won some points by trying to speak to them in their native language. I could earn their trust by treating them with respect, even if I couldn't get the thoughts of water bottles out of my head.

"Good morning, Sir. Ani Jundee Mohammed," he said, shaking my hand and then placing his hand on his heart. This was a common sign of respect, and I hastily tried to copy the motion, even though I still wasn't sure what it meant.

With Mohammed on board and proving to be a much better interpreter than Lieutenant Ahmed, I patiently worked my way through the discussion with Major Ali. We went through the amount of water he thought the company needed and settled on a number. We agreed that Major Ali would first try to secure more water through his own chain of command. If that didn't work, then I would step in and talk to Major Lawson and the rest of the advisers attached to the Battalion Staff and try to make something happen.

Once the water bottle problem was settled, we moved on to discuss our position's current security situation, which was less than ideal. We had to make sure our heavy weapons were pointed in the right directions. On this judgment Major Ali seemed to agree with me completely. I had the feeling that Major Ali was there only to go through the motions and collect a paycheck. He was simply a little too old for war at that point in his life. Still, I had no choice but to work with him.

I went point by point over where our weapons should be positioned and what other measures we needed to take. There was arduous pointing and gesturing and making sure Mohammed was communicating the ideas correctly, and Major Ali kept nodding in agreement. I hoped he understood.

"Now, Sir, I go make sure jundee with the PKC, OK?" The PKC was the Iraqi medium machine gun. It was similar to our 240 Golf. I nodded in approval and Mohammed was off.

I concluded my first meeting with Major Ali with handshakes all around and smiles and all the rest. Staff Sergeant Turner and I stood together in the open courtyard.

"Well, what do you think, Staff Sergeant?" Turner had remained silent throughout the exchange with Ali. He looked at me and struggled to find the words, until events interrupted.

Suddenly we heard whistling. Louder and louder. It sounded like one of our jets. But it was too loud, too close. And it was getting closer.

Boom! The explosion hit just on the other side of the wall I was facing, about ten meters from my head. Smoke and dust flew into the air. The Iraqis immediately started scurrying all around. Many of them were running around barefoot. They were not wearing helmets, were holding their AKs by the triggers, and were frantically jabbering on in Arabic. One of them raised his rifle into the air and fired. Bam, bam, bam! A three-round burst to nowhere.

The crackle of gunshots was all around. Was it the enemy trying to overrun our position? Was it friendly fire? Where was the enemy? Where were they shooting from? What were my forces doing? How could I get control of this situation and react to the enemy's fire? What was going on? All of these considerations flashed through my brain in a nanosecond. It was the normal fog of war. But the Iraqi soldiers were complicating matters by running all around me, panic stricken. My vision was still blurry from the blast when one jundee bumped into me.

"Mister, Mister." (That's all most of the Iraqis could say to me.) His eyes were wide and white. His helmet was on backward. His teeth were yellow and cracked. He had no shoes on. His AK was pointed right at me. He was terrified. One wrong move and I was dead.

"Mister, Mister . . . wahhabi!" He pointed to the sky. They

all called the terrorists wahhabis. Our jundees were primarily Shiite, and they knew that most of the insurgents were not like them. It was their way of distinguishing themselves. They were very protective of their image. Wahhabis equaled bad guys. I nodded yes and moved on. I had to get a handle on the situation or it was going to spiral even more out of control.

I pushed past more frightened Iraqis. There was no military-type response from any of them. I turned just in time to watch one of the Iraqi machine gunners start running down the street. He had his machine gun, a fairly heavy weapon, at his hip, and he was firing a long two-hundred-round burst right down the street at no one.

"Drifter Two, this is Drifter Six," my radio crackled to life. We dubbed ourselves the drifters because we had no real unit. We drifted between the world of the Americans and that of the Iraqis. Neither side actually wanted us there to begin with. I was Drifter Two because I had been assigned to 2nd Company. Drifter Six was Major Lawson. He was advising the Iraqi battalion commander.

"This is Drifter Two, send it."

"Uh . . . yeah . . . what's the situation over there?"

"At least one indirect fire impact approximately from the east. Attempting to regain control of the situation and assess the damage and or casualties, Sir."

"Roger . . . yeah, it might be a good idea to go ahead and do that. It's probably not the best thing to have that machine gunner running down the street like that."

I had to laugh to myself. His sarcasm, under the circumstances, was impressive. It was that kind of laid-back approach that would serve him and the rest of the team well during our asymmetrical deployment.

"Roger, Sir."

Other radio calls came in from the other companies, which only made the situation worse, more confusing.

"Drifter Two, this is Drifter Three. I think those rockets came from the north."

"Drifter Three, this is Drifter Five. Did you say there were multiple rockets?"

"Drifter Five, this is Drifter Diamond. I am getting reports from the Iraqis. They are saying they saw two bad guys running across the street to the east."

"Drifter Diamond, this is Drifter Six. Where are they saying the enemy went?"

"To the east, across the street."

"Across what street?"

"No impact. No idea, Sir."

My head was spinning. Now we had two wahhabis—a possible rocket team—running around, defeating our defenses. Maybe that's whom the Iraqis were shooting at?

Soon after the radio exchange, a pair of up-armored Humvees came racing down the road out of nowhere. I had no idea who they belonged to, but I was glad to see them.

Some of the Iraqis, those who were still standing out in the open making easy targets of themselves, pointed the Humvees in the direction they supposedly saw two bad guys run, down an alley on the side of some irregularly shaped houses, about fifty meters from our position. The Humvees responded; the gunners up in their turrets turned to position their weapons and blast away.

Bam, bam, bam! A burst from a Mark 19 grenade launcher sprayed high explosives into the alley and presumably into the bodies of the two insurgents who had attacked us. The Iraqis joined in by shooting off hundreds of rounds. At whom I had no idea. Clearly we would have to work on fire discipline, if we ever made it through this initial madness.

I ran off to investigate the rocket's point of impact. We had set up a defensive position in the vicinity not twenty minutes prior, and I was afraid we had taken casualties. Mohammed was one of the soldiers I sent to that spot. I feared the worst, as I ran up the stairs. I knew the position was in one of the rooms of the school part of the mosque compound that formed one side of the courtyard. The room was full of smoke and dust.

"Mohammed? Mohammed? Where are you? Are you all right?"

Out came Mohammed with his small, squinting eyes and his big nose, covered in dust.

"Mohammed, Shlonek [How are you]?" I asked.

"Oh is good. Is good," he responded in English. I looked out of the window to where the rocket must have hit. I realized we were lucky. The rocket must have hit an outer wall first before impacting the main part of the building. Otherwise, Mohammed would have absorbed a lot more of the blast. It was a close call for all of us.

I ran back outside to find Staff Sergeant Turner. He was standing in our original spot. He hadn't moved the whole time.

"Staff Sergeant, are you alright? Are you hurt?" He didn't answer, just grunted. "Well, what do you suggest we do to get control of these nutjobs?" I screamed to be heard over the deafening gunfire and explosions.

He just stood there, saying nothing. I watched his eyes, and it looked like he was stuck in reboot mode.

"Staff Sergeant?" Nothing.

I looked around, at the Iraqis, down the street, up around all the buildings from which a sniper could possibly take a shot at me. I walked out from behind the HESCO wall that was protecting me and out into the fray. A group of maybe twenty Iraqis were on the other side of the wall, shouting and shooting their weapons at nothing.

"Hey! Hey! Stop! Awgif! Awgif! Stop!" I tried to get their attention.

One or two of them stopped and looked at me, but the rest kept on shooting. Those who had initially stopped seemed to acquiesce to herd instincts and soon rejoined their friends. The firing continued.

I walked with a purpose to one of the machine gunners, who appeared to be causing most of the problem. He was on full automatic and wasting ammo. And the Iraqis with AKs were trying to keep up with his rate of fire. I made sure I did not cross any of the Iraqis' fields of fire. By then I realized they did not understand fire discipline, and I knew if I walked in front of any of them I would take several rounds to the back. So, I dodged and weaved my way to the machine gunner. I had my right hand on the handle of my rifle in case I had to use it. I used my left hand—my free hand—to reach out and grab him. He looked startled. I thought for a second he might swing around, while still firing, and launch about ten bullets into my stomach.

"Stop! Awgif!" I stared right into his eyes, trying to get my point across. I thought I could send the right signals directly into his brain through ESP. He looked at me. Blank. No recognition. I pointed sharply back toward the mosque. I felt like I was disciplining a dog. The Iraqi cowered accordingly. But he was just one of many. It would take too long to approach each individual soldier and explain the meaning of one shot, one kill.

I had to find a better way to gain control of this mob. And that's when lesson number one dawned on me. It was an elementary conclusion, but it took the heat of flying lead to remind me that to control the body, I had to control the head. I had to find one of their leaders. I needed an Iraqi who could take charge. I looked and found the only officer around. He was a meek-looking lieutenant who was about to shit himself. I grabbed him. I remembered that his name was Khalil and that he understood some English.

"Go out there and get them to stop!" I screamed at the top of my lungs. The whole sordid display had gone on long enough.

"I'm . . . sorry . . . please . . . re . . . peat. . . ." He struggled with the words.

"Go!" And I pushed him toward his troops. He took one look at me, and my hand on my rifle, and finally started to grab his men. I joined in to help him. This all would have been easier if I had a no-shit interpreter, but they were considered a luxury. There I was, assigned as an adviser to a foreign military unit, and I had no formal means of communicating with my soldiers. I would've laughed at the situation if my life and the lives of my fellow Marines hadn't been at stake. The time for such gallows humor would come later, but the time to assess where we presently stood was definitely at hand.

I was angry and frustrated—emotions that would surface again and again throughout the deployment. Whose cruel joke was this? What type of mission were we actually engaged in?

I needed to be able to talk effectively to Major Ali so he

would control his men. I needed to effectively tell all of the soldiers that we had taken care of the threat, if there ever was one, and that they had no reason to waste their ammo. But, given the circumstances, all I could do was point and gesture toward most of them and hope they understood me. Billions of dollars spent, and all I could do was point in a time of crisis? I thought there had to be a better way to build the New Iraqi Army.

This was my first taste of combat, and it was an unmitigated disaster. Why do I highlight this anecdote? Because I had spent a mere one hour operationally deployed with the New Iraqi Army before I witnessed that first example of what was meant when the Iraqis said, "Insha Allah."

According to an Iraqi, the only reason we didn't die during those events was because it was God's will for us not to die. Our survival had nothing to do with the enemy's actions, nothing to do with our own actions, nothing to do with whether the Iraqis could exert control over their emotions and manage their weapons efficiently, and definitely nothing to do with whether or not the Iraqis could shoot straight. Picture an entire country that believes that God controls everything and that the citizens have no control over their own destinies. Picture an army that believes that God and God alone determines whether it wins a battle and that the soldiers and generals have no say in the matter of whether they live or die.

Given my deployment as adviser to just such an army, it was only a matter of time before I came up with my own interpretation of those two words, "Insha Allah."

Shit happens.

IRAQI PSYCHOLOGY 101

Truth be told, when Major Ali let loose the phrase "Insha Allah," it was not the first time I'd ever heard it. When the AST arrived in theater, our first stop was Camp Virginia in Kuwait. We stayed there for three days waiting to catch a C-130 flight into Baghdad. During this short layover we received an important briefing from a man named Dr. Chung. He was of Asian descent but grew up in America and identified himself as a psychologist who worked with the Central Intelligence Agency (CIA). When he ran down a long list of his accomplishments meant to impress us, the one item that caught everyone's attention was that he was one of the people assigned to compose a psychological workup of Saddam Hussein himself. This dovetailed nicely with the main thrust of his presentation: an examination of the Arab mind and its contrasts to the American psyche.

During our time in Kuwait, our team was jet-lagged from the long trip across the Atlantic, and thus, we paid less attention to the details of Dr. Chung's briefing than we should have. It wasn't until we met our Iraqi counterparts that observations from the brief started to click. As we spent more time with the Iraqis, more of Dr. Chung's points began to make sense.

Dr. Chung is the one that introduced us to the title phrase, "Insha Allah."

"You are going to hear the phrase 'Insha Allah.' It means,

'As God wills it' or just 'God willing.' Muslims will use this phrase to explain away the terrible events in their lives. They believe everything, the good, the bad, and the ugly is decreed by God and, therefore, must be accepted. Believe me, you will here this again and again. You must try and learn to understand it."

To illustrate the concept he described an Iraqi who doesn't shoot straight: "If an Iraqi misses a target, he believes that God himself did not want him to hit the target. He believes his miss was literally Allah's will. It had nothing to do with a lack of training. It had nothing to do with whether that soldier, that jundee, practiced marksmanship. No, it is not that Iraqi's fault. It is God's fault." I snorted to myself. I have to admit now that I didn't believe Dr. Chung at the time. I couldn't. My American way of thinking wouldn't let me. Of course, my American notions of personal responsibility were dispelled rather quickly during that first hour in Fallujah.

How could an entire country, an entire people, live their lives believing that free will does not exist? How could they walk down the street thinking that whatever happened to them was the will of God and not a result of their own choices and actions? How could a country run on fate and fate alone? I should've asked Dr. Chung these questions, but I did not consider them at the time. It took experiences such as that first contact with the enemy, the Iraqi reaction, and many more instances of Iraqi insanity to drive home Dr. Chung's original point.

"You, as advisers, are going to have to understand the Arab mind-set," I remember Dr. Chung saying. "It is very different from how you or I think." This was an understatement, to say the least.

"I was asked, by who I will not say, to interview and come up with the psychological profile of Saddam Hussein. I sat inches away from the man. He is not stupid. He is ruthless, cunning, a master of deceit. In the Arab world these are signs of strength. Strength can only be met by strength here. You have to understand this."

A few questions, should have been asked of our strategic policymakers at this point: Why was this lesson being given to those on the tactical level? And, more important, was this lesson being shared with the true decision makers? Far be it for me, a simple lieutenant at the time, to question strategy and the implementation of a prescribed course of action, but it struck me as wrong to address these points to a group of advisers who were going to be attached to only one Iraqi battalion. Shouldn't a briefing of this sort have been disseminated across the American leadership spectrum to facilitate better understanding of our Iraqi partners?

While I do not deny that this sort of educational material aided me and my fellow AST members in subsequent dealings with our Iraqi counterparts, it would probably have proved even more effective for our higher headquarters to have undergone the same cultural training. As will be proved in additional examples of the coordination and logistical deficiencies that we encountered during our deployment, a great deal of our difficulties as an AST resulted from the American higher headquarters' disengagement on a cultural level from the Iraqi higher headquarters. In short, our bosses on the American side clearly did not understand the Iraqis they were supposed to be working with, and this led to a lack of understanding throughout the chain of command, with disastrous consequences for our mission.

Even my fellow AST members had varying degrees of understanding concerning the Iraqi mind-set and its effect on our interactions with the Iraqi soldiers. Some of the advisers understood they had to treat the Iraqi leadership with respect in public and never make fools out of them in front of their troops. They also understood that the Iraqis would say one thing in a private conversation and then say something contradictory once they were in a more public setting. In addition, these advisers knew that not all Iraqis were created equal. Not all of them wanted to be in the military but it was the only job readily available to them, and not all of them appreciated the United States being in their country, although there were many different factors that contributed to such an attitude. Some advisers understood that we had to distinguish those who wanted to work with us from those who couldn't stand us. All of these psychological issues, coincidently, were concerns Dr. Chung warned us about.

Other AST members didn't or couldn't understand. A key point to remember is that our team was purposefully filled with experienced Marines. All had been in the service for at a minimum eight years. While much of their experience would serve them well in a combat situation, it would also prove a hindrance in adviser work because many of them, especially several of the staff NCOs, were set in their strict Marine Corps values. When an Iraqi platoon sergeant, clad in a T-shirt and trousers, with a huge gut hanging over his belt, yelled at his men to get their gear on, it simply riled the Marine SNCOs to no end. The SNCOs would give the Iraqi sergeants tongue-lashings that ultimately served no purpose. The Iraqi would not fight back; he would shut down and not listen to the American.

Over time, I learned that to take effective corrective action in a case such as this, an adviser had to bring the Iraqi platoon sergeant over to a private area, away from his men. Then, and only then, could the Marine advise the Iraqi that when issuing orders to his men he should also strive to set an example. In some such cases it was preferable to wait until later that night, to sit down and break bread with the Iraqi counterpart. During the course of the meal, an adviser might offer words of wisdom on how best to lead a platoon.

Another possibility, the technique I found most effective, was to take the Iraqi on indirectly. As Dr. Chung had warned, Iraqis did not like confrontation. They thrived on deceit or actions taken behind a face of calm. Using my technique much advice would go unsaid, but the Iraqis were always watching. They were keenly aware of everything we did, and they would emulate or even copy exactly what we did. So, I would simply slip my points into a conversation and make innocent comments. In the case of the sloppy Iraqi platoon sergeant, I went to his room at night and struck up a conversation.

"Tisbah Alhair [Good evening]," I said. The use of a little Arabic was another key as it implied the proper respect. We talked about all manner of things until I could steer the conversation where I wanted it to go. A jundee walked by without his helmet on. I shook my head in disapproval as the platoon sergeant watched.

"Jundee, mui zain [Soldier, no good]," I said. The platoon sergeant concurred in English, "No good." I pointed to my own helmet and flak. "Ani guli zain [I am very good]." The Iraqi platoon sergeant nodded up and down. I then looked him up and down. I made sure he could see my eyes tracing his body from the feet to the top of his head. I did not say a word. Then I moved the conversation to an unrelated, neutral topic such as where he was from. He answered with a city's name, "Mosul" or "Basra," where most of the battalion was from. We exchanged a few more pleasantries before parting ways amicably.

Not twenty minutes later, I walked by the same room, and wouldn't you know it, the platoon sergeant was walking around in full gear. The technique, which we later called the Jedi mind trick, had worked. I was able to change an Iraqi's behavior without humiliating him and without the help of an interpreter. All it took was a few carefully placed words and setting the proper example.

Encounters such as this one, and the lessons borne from them, were exactly what Dr. Chung was trying to teach us about. And it was exactly these types of lessons that our own American higher headquarters never seemed to learn. Time and time again I witnessed an American colonel or other high-ranking officer either ignore his Iraqi counterpart or simply try and tell him what to do, instead of showing him what to do by setting the example. Either those officers never received Dr. Chung's briefing or simply ignored it. This disconnect, I surmised, was the result of poor training and a lack of understanding. Such was not a wholly inconceivable conclusion given the state of our so-called pre-deployment training.

All AST members were first introduced to the parameters of our mission at the Security Cooperation Education and Training Center (SCETC) on the Marine Corps base in Quantico, Virginia. We instantly nicknamed the place SKETCHY because it was located in a far-off, nondescript corner of the base and no one had ever heard of it before. Once there, we were supposed to be trained in preparation for the complexities of adviser duty. One interesting element of our time at SKETCHY must be brought up during this discussion of Iraqi psychology.

A reasonable person, on hearing that a team of Marines was going to be assigned as advisers to a foreign military, would assume that the bulk of the team's pre-deployment training would consist of coursework on the specific language and culture of the foreign military. In order for advisers to even begin to train both the basic soldiers and the leadership of a foreign force, they would have to learn how to communicate with the foreign force. How could a group advise a military if the group's members could not communicate effectively with the foreign soldiers?

With this in mind, I began studying the Iraqi dialect of Arabic on my own. I read as much as I could about the history and culture of Iraq as well. I expected these pursuits to be merely a primer for my formal adviser training at SCETC. Those expectations were proved incorrect on the first day at SKETCHY. It seemed our language class was cancelled because of a scheduling conflict.

What caused the scheduling conflict? We had been slated to go to the Virginia International Raceway to partake in a two-day stunt-driving course. We learned how to drive around corners at high speeds. We learned how to use a car as a battering ram. And, finally, we learned how to drive at night without using headlights. All of this was, for lack of better term, the coolest training any of us Marines had ever received while on active duty. But there was one problem: it had absolutely nothing to do with our adviser mission.

SKETCHY offered the racetrack training, it seems, because our instructors believed we would be driving around Iraq in small convoys by ourselves, with limited-to-no backup and we should know how to escape danger in such a situation. The reasoning made sense until you weighed two important conditions. First, the actual deployment proved them wrong. While we did end up driving around in small convoys, not once did any of us employ any of the techniques we learned at the stunt-driving course. Second, and most important of all, the resulting scheduling conflict left us without any formal language and culture training. This was a critical oversight.

Couple lack of language skills with our lack of qualified interpreters at the beginning of our deployment and anyone can
see why many of us thought that someone had tried to sabo-
tage the mission. Either that or they were playing a sick joke
on us. Hell, we would have laughed if our situation wasn't set
within the context of bringing Iraq back from the brink of
oblivion.

Context was the pivotal point in this matter. Our team of
ten Marines was given fewer than six days to pack up our
things, say good-bye to our families, and report to Quantico.
Once at the base we received nonsensical pre-deployment
training that didn't prepare us for our mission. After over
three weeks of PowerPoint presentations about basic infantry tactics that we were all proficient in already, we were
sent to Iraq. When we arrived in Iraq—Taji to be specific—
we were greeted by a colonel we had never met before, who
said he was our boss and told us that we could expect almost
no logistical support from his group once we deployed with
our Iraqi battalion.

Following that cheerful salutation, we were convoyed from
Taji to the EFIC. Surprisingly, we traveled in an unarmored
civilian bus and were given only twenty rounds of ammunition for the trip, down one of the most dangerous roads in
the country. After we arrived at the EFIC, we had to wait for
about ten days before our Iraqi battalion convoyed up from
Numeniyah with the AST we were replacing. In the interim,
we begged, borrowed, and stole whatever gear we could find
from adjacent American units. This included an armored
Humvee and some handheld radios, which became our principle means of communication for the duration of our deployment. Remember, our own higher headquarters had
already disavowed themselves of our support. We were on
our own.

When the 9th Battalion of the IIF arrived, we met the AST
that we were replacing. Its members were all Army reservists,
and from their appearance they were on their last nerve. First
Lieutenant Saint Maria was the first soldier we spoke with.
His exact first words to us were, "Sorry we're late gents, we
had a vehicle rollover on the convoy up here. Apparently one

of our drivers fell asleep and crashed the vehicle. The problem was the soldiers in the back didn't listen and were riding in the back with stockpiles of gear and supplies along with them. Oh, and they weren't wearing their helmets. We lost three soldiers. When the vehicle rolled over two were crushed and killed instantly. The third is in pretty bad shape. We got him back to Baghdad for surgery, but they don't think he's going to make it. So, the rest of the battalion is pretty shaken up about this. I would tread lightly with them right now."

He took a look at the reaction of our group and smiled. "Believe me when I say this gentlemen, this is just another day in the Iraqi Army." He finished with this rather prescient line, exhaled, and then crashed on a bunk to sleep off the twelve-hour ordeal he had just endured. He left us newbies to ponder our situation.

The 9th Battalion received two days of urban warfare training given by Marines from 3rd Battalion, 5th Marine Regiment (3/5), one of the adjacent Marine units. The training consisted of learning how to clear a room in a house and how to hold a rifle the right way. We advisers had nothing to do with this training. We had not even met our Iraqi counterparts yet. We simply watched as one Iraqi after another walked by holding their AKs pointed right into the back of the Iraqi in front of them.

Finally, my team of Marine advisers, along with the 9th Battalion, packed up and convoyed into downtown Fallujah on orders. The Iraqis rode in unarmored, open-backed Russian-made Ashook Leland trucks. We had a couple of armored Humvees but not enough to fit all of us Americans. Consequently, some of us, including myself, had to convoy into a combat zone in an unarmored Nissan pickup truck. Picture five geared-up Marines, squeezed into a tiny Nissan with our rifles sticking out of the windows in a futile attempt to provide a hard target for the enemy.

We arrived in the city; took up positions in an unoccupied mosque, other unoccupied buildings surrounding the mosque, and relieved an Iraqi unit and their U.S. advisers in a separate building; and set about trying to figure out exactly what we were expected to do with our Iraqis. We had no official interpreters, limited supplies, little to no contact with any adjacent friendly units. And, as described in chapter 1, we had to repel an enemy attack less than an hour after our arrival.

Does this sound like a well-conceived, well-executed plan of action on the part of the American military, which was attempting to follow through on the orders of the U.S. president, to stand up and train a New Iraqi Army? Of course not. When viewed in context, this effort was perilously close to a complete dereliction of duty on the part of those commanders who were discharged with seeing that the president's intent was carried out and that his end state was achieved. Not only were U.S. servicemen and women in greater danger than they had to be in, not only were Americans not provided with the proper training and resources to accomplish the mission, but all this happened at a time when the American public was being told that training the New Iraqi Army was the main effort of the entire Iraq mission. At this point the secretary of defense was saying that training the Iraqis and preparing them to fight the insurgents would not only result in victory but also provide the means to begin withdrawing our own forces from the country. The American people were basing their continued support for our overall involvement in Iraq on this calculus.

In this context, my fellow Marine advisers and I were individually augmented, brought together as a team, and sent over to live with, train, and go into battle with a battalion from the New Iraqi Army. In this context, our initial lack of support must be judged, and judged harshly. The link between the president's aims and the military's execution of those stated aims was bent, if not completely broken. Given the evidence from our early days in Fallujah, I could see some of the flaws in our adviser mission. However, it was this question of context—the context of our mission within the larger operation and its impact on our ability to deal with the Iraqi battalion—that remained with us throughout our time with the Iraqis.

Dr. Chung, during his initial briefing, warned us about the importance of the concept of context in dealings with the Iraqis when he said, "They have no sense of time. It is a polychronic sense of time. Because in the desert it is either hot or it isn't."This quote struck me as particularly important. Dr. Chung had further explained this idea by pointing out that the Arab culture was still, as it had been for centuries, basically tribal in nature, a fact we Americans had not taken into account when we decided to topple Saddam. Living in the desert, the Iraqi people originally lived in nomadic tribes and did not keep time or communicate in the ways Western-ers did.They did not keep time in a linear, chronological man-ner but rather in a "polychronic," or literally, "many times," manner. In addition the tribes relied heavily on oral tradition as a means of communication. What developed from these two cultural traditions was a reliance on placing people and their deeds in the proper context in order to convey the proper meaning. This reliance on context permeated all of our interactions with the Iraqi soldiers.

The easiest way to explain the role context played in the Iraqis' lives and in our lives as advisers is to tell a story. Lieu-tenant Saint Maria, the Army reservist adviser we first spoke with, told us that the Iraqis had a tendency to shit everywhere. This was a problem that would remain a major concern throughout my time with the New Iraqi Army.

"OK, so we finally had the Iraqi colonel—not the current one but his predecessor—order the jundees, during a battal-ion formation, to stop shitting in all the rooms on our base down in Numeniyah.And it worked, sort of. We actually got them to shit in the shitters and not leave piles in the corners of abandoned buildings.The only problem was that when we had to move the battalion to new barracks, the shit hit the fan all over again—literally! We started finding piles everywhere. I don't even want to tell you what they did to one set of toilets. It was like a bomb went off. It was like they had for-gotten everything they had learned in the previous location. Like, once they left a place, they also left the lessons learned at that place.

The Iraqis were governed by the context of their situa-tion. The rules that applied to them in one environment did not necessarily transfer to different environments. Given the Iraqis' surroundings and cultural development, the preeminence of context was understandable. If you were a tribesman, traveling through the desert, where one hot, sun-filled day melded with the next, the only way you could tell time was to place each new encounter or each new village you came across into its own particular context. It would be difficult to clearly distinguish among events or places or people without remembering them within a larger mosaic. However, the consequence of such thinking became obvious to us advisers, when the context was changed. The Iraqis' entire train of thought was thrown off until they could construct a new context. They would not apply anything they learned in their old context to this new situation. Instead they would apply only what they learned anew within their new context.

All of this psychology was overly complex for most of us advisers. What it boiled down to was that it took us many days to teach the Iraqis the same lessons over and over again. If we moved locations or if something changed from lesson to lesson, we had to go back over old training. So, for every two steps forward, we ended up taking one back.

We, as Marines, were almost prepared for these types of challenges. We were used to persevering in the face of frustration and adversity. However, were we prepared for the consequences of totally immersing ourselves in the Iraqis' culture? That question lingered for me. How would we Americans be affected when placed in the Iraqis' polychronic world? Would we lose our own linear, chronological thought process? Would we begin to think like them? If the answer was yes, the result was disconcerting: we would come to live in a world where "Insha Allah" made sense. That thought made my Western mind cringe.

3

THE NINJA SHITTER

The Iraqis' psychology was truly important for my AST's purposes. Understanding the reasons behind the Iraqis' behavior was critical when trying to shape or change the way they conducted themselves as a military unit. However, sometimes even the most detailed analysis could not help us explain the rhyme or reason behind the Iraqis' actions. Sometimes it seemed reason had nothing to do with it. One such case occurred the day we arrived, after the initial attack.

I had just witnessed an entirely unprofessional and absurd Iraqi military response to an enemy attack. Shooting wildly in any and all directions was not an acceptable reaction to contact with the enemy for any country's military. Perhaps this tactic would make sense if it were used during a last stand, when all hope was lost. However, for the Iraqis, it seemed to be the first and only line of defense. When in doubt, shoot.

The Iraqis' employment of this deadly tactic was only the tip of the iceberg. I could understand where the Iraqi soldiers' shoot first, ask questions later mentality came from. It was clearly the result of a lack of military discipline and of proper training in both tactics and basic weapons handling. Given that most of the jundees had prior experience in Saddam's army, the fact they were still lacking in these areas pointed to an obvious failure of overall leadership and command and control. All of the AST members, as American Marines, had confidence that in time we could instill in the jundees the necessary discipline. This was a basic military calculation. This made sense to us.

Even when Major Ali decided, as a way to make sure our position was safe from future enemy attack, that it would be wise to send his entire company out on one patrol, and even when that company-size patrol left the rest of us, perhaps ten men, behind in the mosque compound all alone, I was able to give him a pass. "OK, so Major Ali did not understand what the term 'troops to task,' meant," I said to myself. That misconception, a problem military in nature, was easy enough to fix. This also made sense to me. But no one in our chain of command, and probably no one back home, could make sense of some of the other phenomena we encountered. The problem of the Ninja Shitter comes to mind immediately.

To understand the rather disturbing case of the Ninja Shitter one has to understand the situation. Following the initial attack on our position and the ensuing Iraqi reaction, the entire battalion was on edge. I had been able to get a hold of Major Ali and his lieutenants and some semicompetent staff NCOs. Through them, we were able to gain some sort of control of the jundees. But the mosque compound was still astir. Danger hung in the air. I could almost smell it. The Iraqis themselves remained frazzled. They moved about the courtyard in hurried steps. Some lost their purple flip-flops here and there. Others just stood, dazed, eyes darting back and forth.

I tried to remind myself not to make any sudden movements. The jundees were too spooked. They might shoot at anything. It was important for me to keep my composure on the outside. The Iraqis had to see me remain calm. If they followed form, they would try and emulate me.

Of course, I too had the rocket fuel of adrenaline still pumping through my veins. My heart was pounding like a war drum against the inside of the small arms protective inserts (SAPI) plate I wore on my chest. But the Iraqis could see none of this. The only emotion I allowed to seep through was anger, and I let it through purposefully. My knowledge of the culture was coming in handy. I knew that the Iraqis respected strength and could be kept in check with a degree of respect and fear for those in a leadership position.

I used my anger to project power over the soldiers. Relying on the mental discipline of my Marine training, I was able to control the anger and direct it towards the Iraqis in a meaningful way. I was angry at the way they had behaved, and I wanted to make sure they knew that without coming across as out of control. I stomped my way through crowds of jundees. I stood erect and conspicuously kept my hand on my rifle's pistol grip. I took confident steps, almost stalking past them. When their eyes met mine, I did not look away but instead looked right down into the bottom of the individual Iraqi until my sheer willpower forced him to look away. It must have worked because I could see out of the corners of my eyes as I passed the jundees trying to straighten themselves out. They stood more erect and tried to wear their gear more correctly. The crowds of them parted as I approached to allow me to walk through.

I was satisfied with my display—until, of course, Major Ali and I discussed the need to patrol the area for additional insurgents. He thought a "patrol" required walking the whole company out the front gate and down the main avenue in a column. That was about the time I started truly understanding why the Iraqis found those two words—*Insha Allah*—so enticing. But, let's not think on that yet. The Ninja Shitter is a more instructive example of the obstacles we drifters faced in our mission to train the Iraqi Army.

Following Major Ali's decision to leave his battle position virtually unguarded, Staff Sergeant Turner and I decided it was as good a time as any to figure out where the three of us Americans were going to bed down for our first night in downtown Fallujah. I say three of us because we were joined by one of the old AST members for a night or two as part of a half-hearted turnover of mission.

The old AST member was Staff Sergeant Tewilliger. He was a U.S. Army reservist from Tennessee, and he had spent almost an entire year with 2nd Company. He was there when the 9th Battalion stood up, and you could tell the experiences of the previous year had worn on him. The attack less than an hour before couldn't have helped matters either. He wore bifocals that made him look older than he actually was. His

eyes were bleary behind the glasses. He smoked a new cigarette every two minutes. His hair was thinning. His nerves
were fried.

"Sir, where are we going to rack out tonight?" he said in a
deep Southern twang. And he would be sleeping in the same
room as me. A perfect setup.

The layout of the mosque compound was such that many
small rooms were hidden around corners or at the ends of
windy corridors in the rear of the buildings. The Iraqis had
already taken up all of the rooms in the front of the compound. Given the events of earlier that day, all three of us
wanted to put some distance between ourselves and the
Iraqis. So we began surveying the rooms in the rear. At the
very far corner, lying just past the room that had been designated the latrine, we found a semisecluded room that I decided would make a good place to sleep. In retrospect, the
decision was a disaster. I can't remember what I was thinking at the time. My exhaustion must have already kicked in.

The room was a small eight by eight square. It had previously been part of the kitchen area, and pots and pans were
strewn about the floor. The entire area was covered in dust
and grime. Assorted bugs and roaches creeped and crawled
from one corner to the next. There were two entranceways
into the room. One led through a series of maze-like halls
back to the courtyard; this was the entrance we had used.
The other led right into an alley and eventually to the city
streets.

At the time we were thinking that this rear exit could act
as a solid emergency escape route. The doorway was situated
near the alley. If the enemy decided to attack from the main
complex, we could get out in time to rally a proper defense.
Or, if the enemy tried to sneak in through the back alley we
would be able to repel their advance. The plan seemed fool-
proof at the time. However, the Iraqis had a way of poking
holes in even the best-laid plans.

The bedroom had two parts that were separated by a curtain of some sort. The first part was the small eight-foot square
that we squeezed into. It was simply a box with a window.
The three of us Americans grabbed our gear and set up cots

with our sleeping bags rolled out on top. The second, adjacent part contained the doors that lead to both the hallway and the alley. This part also had an open ceiling. The people upstairs could look down and see into this part of the room, and the Iraqi soldiers took to speaking to us from overhead.

"Mister, Mister." They would lean over the railing and wait for us to appear.

"What?" I was annoyed. This was the third time this particular Iraqi had called out to us.

"Batteries?"

"No, I do not have any batteries." I was done playing this game.

We decided to wall ourselves off in the dirty kitchen area to get some semblance of privacy. But before we could gather material to create the wall, I heard the commotion of the whole company returning from their patrol. I could hear the soldiers spreading through the compound. Several of them tried to come into our room. They walked in unannounced, seem startled by the three giant Americans staring back at them, said "Excuse me" in Arabic, and left. This must have happened five different times before we were able to barricade the door with some metal and wood we found laying around. The barricade didn't last long before it was pushed in and fell with a loud clang and thud to the floor. Some Iraqi was pushing the door open as hard as he could.

"Whoa, whoa, whoa there, little fella," Staff Sergeant Tewilliger said.

The Iraqi jundee stood there smiling. He could not have been more than five feet tall. He was built like a child but had a thick black mustache and the wrinkles of an older man. His helmet almost completely covered his eyes and fell to one side of his head. His uniform didn't fit him: the sleeves fell past his hands. The AK he was holding was almost as big as he was. When he smiled, he revealed about three or four yellow teeth.

He didn't say anything. He looked around the room, then back to us, then back to the room. He seemed especially interested in a specific corner. His nose twitched like he was sniffing the air.

"Can we help you?" I finally asked him. Nothing. Just a wicked smile.

"Alright, alright, that's enough. Out you go. Out you go." Tewilliger had had enough. He shooed the curious Iraqi back into the hallway and reinforced the barricade.

The light of the day was disappearing, and the air was getting colder. The day had been long, and we were eager to turn in for the night. The three of us dealt with the stress of our predicament in three distinct ways. Tewilliger tried to sleep with his pistol in his hand. He laid down as soon as he could and forced his eyes to squeeze shut, but I could tell he wasn't sleeping. Turner snored as soon as his head hit the cot. He didn't budge the entire night. I was in the middle. I kept my weapons on the floor underneath my cot. This way, if someone came for us I could reach down while still on the cot and bring the weapon up in little time. It seemed like a good system. I practiced several times before I felt comfortable enough with the motion, and then I tried to get some sleep. My body was exhausted from the day's events. It had started with a drive into downtown Fallujah in an unarmored Nissan pickup truck that I would try never to think of again, and ended with a hundred-man patrol. It was time to sleep.

Unfortunately, after having been shot at and after dealing with the Iraqis, my mind simply would not cooperate with my body. It didn't help that as the night grew darker and the Iraqis quieted down, the city came alive in different ways. My ears became my eyes in the pitch-black room.

First there was this constant mechanical whining sound, which reminded me of a running lawnmower engine. It was one of our unmanned aerial vehicles (UAVs), designed to use its infrared cameras to find the enemy at night. It was not much more than a big model airplane, but it cost over a million dollars. The noise it made never went away. It just kept burrowing its way into my dreams.

Then more sounds rattled me out of near sleep. Bang! Bang! Bang! Shots rang out in the distance, outside somewhere. The shots were followed by the hollow booms of mortars responding. It was a deadly song. I was keenly aware of each note.

I could hear Tewilliger sit up in his cot. I could hear his pistol, at the ready, shaking in his hands. Turner kept on snoring. He sounded like a rhino. He was so loud I started to worry we wouldn't be able to hear anyone coming. Or maybe he'd give our position away.

All of a sudden, I heard more strange sounds: meows. Tens of cats meowing down the alley, their mews echoing eerily.

"Are you fucking kidding me?" I said under my breath.

"No, sir, that there be the felines of the neighborhood. They eat the bodies." Tewilliger's Southern twang was so thick he started to sound like Yosemite Sam. I started to laugh at the absurdity of it all. He chuckled nervously along with me.

Turner let out a roaring, suck-your-last-breath-in type of snore, as if to punctuate the insanity. I couldn't take it anymore and started to laugh heartily out loud. This whole place was ridiculous.

Bam! It sounded like someone was trying to get in the adjacent room past the barricade. Tewilliger heard it too. I heard him jump up off of his cot. Bam! There it was again. I couldn't tell if the enemy was coming from the alleyway or from inside the mosque complex. The bangs were echoing from all directions. I reached down and gripped my pistol. I also grabbed my pair of night-vision goggles (NVGs). I fumbled about trying to put the goggles and their harness on as fast as possible. I flicked the switch and the green light of night vision soon bathed my dilated pupils. I could see the entire room. Turner was still lying on his cot, fast asleep. I turned to see Tewilliger sitting there, shaking, his pistol pointed in front of him toward the curtain we had put up to separate us from the adjacent room. His eyes were wide and shined bright green. He was looking back and forth not sure what to do. He was scaring the shit out of me.

There were sounds in the next room as if someone was still trying to come in.

"Staff Sergeant, I've got my NVGs on." I whispered as low as possible.

"Alright, Sir." He whispered back.

"We're going to have to clear the next room to see who that is. OK?"

"OK." I was watching him in the green light. He couldn't see me.

I slowly got out of my cot, one leg at a time. I was trying not to make a sound. I didn't want to tip off the intruder to our presence. Bang! I accidentally kicked Turner's cot and winced. I could see Tewilliger wildly swing his pistol around toward the new sound, toward me. Turner kept on snoring.

"Sorry." I offered. I could see Tewilliger was still pointing his weapon in my direction. That wasn't going to work for me.

"Staff Sergeant, are you ready to get this guy?" This snapped him back toward the intruder.

"Yes, Sir." I crept closer to him. We would have to be on the same side of the opening to avoid shooting each other. One of us would have to pull the curtain back as fast as possible while the other one would be the first into the adjacent room and the first to face the intruder. Since I had the NVGs there was no point in pretending who was leading the way.

"Staff Sergeant, you pull the curtain back. I'll go first. You come back behind me and cover my six. Got it?" I was whispering the whole time, but I thought he heard me. He definitely didn't protest me going first.

"I'll be right behind you, Sir." He whispered back.

Our attack plan was set. We crouched together at the right side of the curtain, weapons drawn. Turner still hadn't budged.

"Ready, on three." I took one last look around through the green lens of the NVGs. Tewilliger had one hand on his pistol and the other ready to pull the curtain.

"One." The UAV still whirled in the air above us.

"Two." I could hear Tewilliger's breath catch in his throat.

"Three!" I screamed this last number out and whipped open the curtain. I rushed into the room, my pistol in front of my eyes. I was ready to kill. I was going to survive.

But, there was nothing. No one was there. The room was empty. The barricade was still in place, unmoved. All of a sudden my NVGs went bright green, as if a giant green sun had burst into the room with us. Partially blinded, I ripped the goggles off my head.

"Goddamn it!" I screamed—too loud. Some of the Iraqis upstairs started to stir. Squinting, I saw Tewilliger standing there with a bright flashlight beaming from his other hand.

"Sorry, Sir." It was all he could muster.

"Mister, Mister. Shinuu? Shinuu?" I assumed they meant, "What happened?"

"Maku. Maku shi [Nothing]." My limited Arabic came in handy again.

The Iraqis grumbled back to sleep while Tewilliger insisted on inspecting the entire room. He couldn't believe no one was there. I could. We had been driven mad by our surroundings and by the Iraqis. The place was getting to us. We were chasing ghosts.

Eventually, Tewilliger made his way back to his bunk. I watched him with my NVGs for a few moments to make sure he'd be OK. His pistol never left his hand, even as he drifted off into a fitful sleep. And my role model, Turner, lay in the same position. He had not budged the whole time. My mind had finally had enough. I decided it would be quite alright with me if I died in my sleep that night. At least I wouldn't feel anything.

I dreamed of a city ruled by giant man-eating cats, with flying noise machines, jolly green giants roaming the streets, little rat soldiers crawling all around me, and Death, calling me with just a whistle. In short, I dreamed of Fallujah.

The next morning arrived way too quickly. I must have gotten an hour of solid sleep. The Iraqis were already jibber-jabbing back and forth, probably about whose turn it was to make the *chi* (tea). Turner, obviously well-rested, was the first to dress and be ready to go. Tewilliger and myself, on the other hand, ran a little behind.

I had just gotten my boots on when Turner opened the curtain.

"What the fuck is that?" he bellowed out.

I looked to see him standing in the center of the adjacent room.

"What?" I didn't see anything. He pointed to the near corner. Sitting in that dingy corner, next to a half-empty water bottle, lay a big pile of dark brown human shit.

"Oh no. What the hell?" I jumped up, and we all stood there, marveling.

"Are you kidding me?" Tewilliger added.

"Take a good look, gentlemen. This is what we are up against," I declared.

Turner shook his head. We didn't know what to say. Tewilliger looked confused. He was looking all around the room, and then up to the upstairs room. "I don't get it. It doesn't look like he could have done it from above," Tewilliger said.

"No, the angle is wrong." I was examining the trajectory it would have to have taken to land in that corner. "Besides, he couldn't have bent over that railing up there." It was physically impossible. "Could he?"

"No, Sir. It had to be that little guy," said Turner. He had to be correct.

"You're right, Staff Sergeant. He was eyeing that corner the whole time."

"Probably marking his territory."

"Well, he must've liked what he saw there."

"I'll say. You see the size of that thing?"

"I don't even know how a person that small could make that."

We stood there in wonder and amazement. But something was still bothering Tewilliger. He kept shaking his head back and forth.

"There's just one thing I don't get."

"*One* thing?"

"Yeah, if it was him and the barricades haven't been moved, how the hell did he get in the room, take this huge shit, and then get out of the room all without being discovered by any of us?"

No answers came to the three of us. It took awhile, but finally, Staff Sergeant Turner, the black belt instructor of the group, broke the silence.

"I don't know how he did it. But, I'll tell you what, I would love to meet him. I wouldn't even be mad. I would just want to shake the man's hand."

"Yep, that guy is 'the Ninja Shitter.'"

The moniker, and the story attached, lived on in infamy for the duration of our time with the Iraqis. Many of us treated the little jundee like a celebrity.

The emergence of the Ninja Shitter was more significant than it initially seemed. As previously stated, many of the Iraqis' problems could be considered a result of a lack of military training and discipline. With time and effort, one could see measurable improvements in the demeanor of the jundees and their leaders. But the Ninja Shitter represented a much larger problem. The Ninja Shitter was the embodiment of a previously unaddressed issue that threatened our entire endeavor in Iraq.

Remember, a human being, Mr. Ninja Shitter, sneaked into the room next to us in the dead of night and decided he had to defecate in the corner of the room. Not only that, but he had made the determination hours prior that there was a specific corner, in a specific room, that he was going to target. Plus, this target of his was in the room right next to the room the American strangers were sleeping in. The only conclusion we could reach was this man was indeed marking his territory. He was, for all intents and purposes, acting as an animal.

The implications of this conclusion were profound for me. I did not approach these implications lightly, nor were they something I had expected when embarking on this mission. Initially, I had understood the ideas of "Insha Allah" and "the polychronic mind-set" to be merely cultural idiosyncrasies that I had to understand and translate into a Western grammar. Even after the experiences of the initial hours, I had hope that a bridge could be formed between the two disparate cultures. All we drifters had to do was find the material to build that bridge. But, what if the chasm between the two cultures spanned many hundreds, if not thousands, of years? What if the gulf was too wide?

How was I supposed to understand the concept of a grown man marking territory with his feces? In this world of political correctness, where we are taught that every single person is not just equal but the same, was I even allowed to make judgments based on the event that I witnessed? Was I allowed to state emphatically that any man who shits in the corner of the room in order to mark his territory is less of a man than I am? And, if I do make such judgments, what does that mean for our collective efforts throughout all of Iraq?

Were the Iraqis less civilized than us? Was it even more than that?

I was not prepared to draw these conclusions. I could not bring myself to accept the idea that the Iraqis were less civilized and the consequences it would have for our mission. I was not ready to abandon hope. I couldn't accept it. But the prospect became harder to ignore each time I passed the Ninja Shitter. I was most troubled by the way he smiled, like a satisfied rodent. His feral grin might've been our own impending failure smiling at us.

INTERACTIONS AND MOVEMENTS

Whether failure was staring us in the face remained to be seen on that second day in Fallujah. It was still too early to come to such a conclusion. Whether the Iraqis were uncivilized mattered less at that moment than how I was going to interact with them. Our interactions with the Iraqis were perhaps the most important aspect of the adviser mission. On a day-to-day, minute-to-minute basis we drifters had to navigate a social landscape that contained a myriad of forces working in different directions. Let's break these forces down for purposes of examination.

First was the obvious Iraqi versus American cultural dichotomy. The Iraqis had a different set of beliefs, which included the Insha Allah concept, than we did. They also had different cultural mores, including not using toilet paper and having many wives. The key to dealing with this dichotomy for us was to know a great deal about the Iraqi culture and to treat it with respect. The respect did not necessarily have to be genuine. We Americans merely had to feign respect for the Iraqis. In fact, the Iraqis themselves seemed to feign respect for one another some of the time. They did this primarily to avoid causing their peers and superiors public embarrassment. What was said behind an Iraqi's back need not be talked about in public.

Within the two main groups of Iraqis and Americans were many different subgroups, based on rank, experience level,

41

and ethnic background, that I had to be aware of. For example, I might take a different approach with a basic jundee than I would with Major Ali. With the jundee, I could be a little more informal. I could ask him about his family, joke with him, try to make him laugh. When talking with Major Ali, I might be more guarded. I wanted him to know that I knew what I was talking about. He needed to take me seriously. I was a mere lieutenant with less than three years experience in the Marine Corps, and he was a major with over twenty years time in the Iraqi Army. Despite that difference, he needed to respect me enough to follow through with my suggestions. So, I had to be more direct and professional when discussing troop movements and the status of our water supply with him.

Even among Americans, I spoke differently to Marines of differing ranks. But, I also conversed differently with Marines who were not advisers than I did with my fellow drifters and other AST members from other Iraqi battalions. Advisers simply had a set of experiences that separated us from Marines who lived on a base outside the city such as Camp Fallujah. We even had experiences that were different from those of the infantry Marines who had just pushed through the city and now acted as its occupiers. They were there to kill the enemy. We were there to get the Iraqis to kill the enemy themselves. We had different mentalities.

Culturally, learning where a man came from was a good way to try to understand his motivations. Most of our battalion was Shiite. They came from the southern part of the country, near the city of Basra. Knowing the history of the country, I knew that the Shiites had been deprived of much of the country's wealth during Saddam Hussein's reign. Hussein shared his power with his fellow Sunnis. As a result, the Shiites in the south seemed to be less educated. Many of them couldn't read or write. They came from simple farms. Many of the Sunnis in the battalion seemed much more sophisticated, in relative terms. The Ninja Shitter, not surprisingly, was a Shiite.

On the American side, cultural differences played out as well. Knowing where the different drifters came from helped me know how to approach them. Someone from the South was distinctly different than I was, as I came from the New York City area. A black Marine had a different way about him than a white one did.

In addition to these unchanging cultural characteristics, I had to keep in mind the setting or occasion of an interaction. Remember, I was not only training and going on missions with both the Iraqis and my fellow drifters; I was also living with them day and night. So, during an operational meeting, my tone was more serious. During the down times, especially later in the deployment, I could have an informal night with the Iraqis. We could watch a movie together and try to hold a conversation about our respective lives outside the military.

All of these different social situations took place one on top of the other. Just when I finished a meeting with Major Ali about needing to patrol the area, some jundees would corner me to ask about America. Then I would be called over to meet with the rest of the AST members to discuss the disposition of our forces. But, of course, right after our meeting we would share stories or talk a little about home. Thus, I lived in a constantly changing cultural mosaic that challenged my ability to communicate and understand the world around me.

One of the mission's principle goals was to bridge the gaps between all of these different parties. I needed to be able to coax a Sunni to take orders from a Shiite or a jundee who was a first sergeant in Saddam's army to listen to a lieutenant whose father bribed people at the Ministry of the Interior for his son's promotion. I needed to get a Marine from 3/5 who spent the last month fighting house-to-house to retake this city, killing all on sight, to sit down and discuss a battle plan with an Iraqi officer who looked just like the insurgents that Marine had been killing. Needless to say, negotiating my way through these experiences was challenging, frustrating, and hilarious, in a gallows humor sort of way.

The morning following the Ninja Shitter incident, Tewilliger, Turner, and I agreed that the dark, dirty, and cold room we had called home that first night was not going to work for us going forward. Not only did the room have lingering bad vibes from the night before, but upon further review, it also didn't make any sense militarily. Looking back on it, I had made a mistake. I had positioned us in the rear of the compound, too far from the main Iraqi body to control it in the event of an attack. Plus, we were too close to the alley. Any insurgent intruder could sneak up close enough to throw a grenade into our laps before we even knew he was there.

Having decided to move, we walked into the courtyard to scope out a new location. The Iraqis had colonized every nook and cranny of the compound. It wasn't unusual to trip over a jundee who had made a random corner his bedroom. The only items most of the soldiers had with them were a couple of uniforms, a weapon, maybe a pack of some sort, and a bedroll. Most of them had piled into a room—as many as could fit, sometimes more—dropped their roll, and called that spot on the floor home.

The three of us Americans surveying the setup from the courtyard drew the requisite curious stares. We found a room that was the closest to the main gate and situated directly across the courtyard from Major Ali's room. This would allow us to communicate better with Ali and the rest of his leadership and, thus, to control the Iraqis better. No more wild shoot-'em-ups, I thought. Plus, in the event of a frontal attack by the enemy, we could meet the assault immediately. I trusted our fighting skills much more than those of the two Iraqi guards who were lounging in chairs at the front gate.

The major drawback of the room, though, was also the location—right near the front gate. A wall of HESCOs, the dirt-filled cubes designed to provide cover, blocked direct fire from the street, but still, we were right there. If a rocket-propelled grenade (RPG) made it over that front wall somehow, our room would be the first to go.

I weighed the options and decided the risks could not be avoided. Proximity to Major Ali was the determining factor. I had to be able to influence the leadership in order to influence the entire company.

The room was big enough to comfortably fit the three of us. The Iraqis had crammed about ten of their jundees into the square. They were almost stacked on top of one another. When we poked our heads in, those who were awake were surprised by us Americans. We were like aliens to them.

"Mister, Mister, chi?" or "Hello, hello, Mister."

"Sabbah Alkhair [Good morning]," I said. They smiled whenever I attempted to speak to them in Arabic.

"Sabbah Alnoor," they responded, continuing to smile their yellow-toothed smiles.

"Shlonek?" one of them asked. He was a fat, older guy with a thick, black Saddam moustache and a belly that hung over his already loosened belt.

"Zain, zain. Winta? [Good, good. And you?]" I responded.

His grin widened with each correct Arabic word I spoke. I was scoring a lot of points. I was not coming off as the usual, rude American. I treated them with respect and, in return, earned their respect. This paid dividends in later, more difficult times.

"Uh, we Amreekis," I said, pointing to the three of us, "we want this room." I tried using hand gestures to make my point. The Iraqis looked at me, confused. Either they had no idea what I was saying or pretended not to understand because they didn't want to give up the room.

"Sir, it'd probably be easier to go tell Major Ali we need this room," Tewilliger advised. He was right. I found Major Ali and told him, through Lieutenant Ahmed, that we wanted to be closer to him so we could work together more. I pointed to the room we wanted. Almost immediately, Lieutenant Ahmed went to the room and started yelling and screaming in Arabic to the jundees in it. About two minutes after that, the room had been vacated.

"Shukran [Thank you]," I said and nodded in appreciation to Ali. He nodded back.

"You're ... wel ... come," he squeezed out in English.

"Oh, good Inglise, good Inglise," I offered in praise. He beamed back at me. We were making headway.

Tewilliger, Turner, and I set about moving our gear from the back alley room that had provided so much drama the night before. The Iraqis watched us intently. It felt like we were on some sort of stage.

As we began the move, Staff Sergeant Sullivan, another drifter, came stomping into the compound. The guards greeted him with the obligatory "Mister, Mister." He growled back at them. Sullivan was short and wiry. His face was creased and his skin was coarse. He was an infantryman by trade, and he had been in the Marine Corps for over twenty years. When he walked, he walked with his feet pointed outward, like a duck. He reminded me of Burgess Meredith as the Penguin from the 1960s *Batman* TV series.

"What are you doing here, Staff Sergeant?" I asked innocently.

Sullivan stood there grinding his teeth for about two full minutes before blurting out, "Sir, the geniuses up at battalion have sent me here."

"Alright. What for?"

Again, he gave us a dirty look. "I guess I'm going to be with 2nd Company from now on."

"Well, who're you switching out with?" Tewilliger's time with these Iraqis was coming to end. He was with us for a couple of days to act as a bridge between the Iraqis he had been working with and us. This left Staff Sergeant Turner as the only possibility.

"Fuck if I know, Sir. You officers are the ones with all the answers." Obviously, this was one of those situations during which my ability to interact with different types of people was being tested.

"Alrighty then. Get your gear and throw it in that first room over there." I pointed to our new hooch. He took one look at the location of the room, scanned the surrounding area, then looked back toward the front gate and the street behind that.

"Sir, are you fucking crazy?" I thought he was joking, but one look into his gritty eyes told me differently.

"What the hell are you talking about, Staff Sergeant?"

"That room!"

"What about it?"

"It's right by the front gate. An RPG could take us out in one shot!" Sullivan, I learned over time, did not have a power lever. He was stuck in high gear at all times.

"Staff Sergeant," I said, stressing his rank to make sure he knew who was in charge. I did this not out of some sense of personal entitlement; rather, I knew that if I let anyone run over me, I would be out of the leadership business. The Iraqis were watching how I dealt with my fellow

Americans. "Staff Sergeant, I am aware of the risks. But we have the HESCO wall over there to protect against a direct shot. Plus, we are right near the Iraqi company commander. And, finally, this is the only room left. Take a look around. All of the other rooms are either too big, or too small, and all of them have been filled with Iraqis already."

Sullivan was still stewing. He had the most combat experience of anyone on the team. He knew what he was talking about. And he was right, according to the book, but as we were all learning, this mission did not fit nice and neat into our definition of combat operations. All of us, including Sullivan, needed to learn to adapt.

"So, I hear what you are saying, but this is where we are staying," I finished.

Staff Sergeant Sullivan took a long, grizzled breath, then stomped into the room. Soon, he was busy sweeping the dust out of our room. Once a course had been set, he went about accomplishing his mission.

The Iraqis never stopped watching us. Dr. Chung had told us that with the Iraqis we would always be on stage. Setting the example was critical. And he was right again. Once the Iraqis saw us start to clean our room, before putting any of our gear in, all of them were sweeping their own rooms. They were copycatting our every move.

Once the room was semiclean, we started to reload the room. Soon, a crowd of Iraqis started to form behind us. At first they simply stood there and watched. It was unnerving to say the least. I tried to ignore them, but then they started asking questions.

"Mister, Mister. You Army?"

"No. Ani muushat bahreeyeh [I am a Marine],"

"Ahh, Mar . . . rine."

"Marine very good. Army no good," I said, laughing. Tewilliger hadn't heard.

"Yes, yes, Marines good."

"Mister, Mister. Madame?" I didn't know what the Iraqi was asking me.

"He wants to know if you're married. If you have a wife back home," Tewillger helped decipher.

"Oh, oh. Madame. Yes," I nodded affirmative.

"America?" The Iraqi pointed off into the distance. I guessed he meant, "Was she back in America?"

"Yes, yes. Madame. America."

"Mister, Mister. Baby? Baby?" About twenty of them were now surrounding me, eager to hear my answers.

"No, no baby."

"Leish [Why]?" they asked. I shrugged. What I wanted to say was, "Because I am over here helping the New Iraqi Army learn to shoot straight," but I didn't know how to say that in Arabic.

"Mister, Mister, wayn America?" I knew *wayn* meant "where." I guessed he wanted to know where I was from back in America.

"Oh, New York." Of course, they instantly recognized these words.

"New York. New York. Ahh . . . " With each response they turned to converse with their friends in Arabic and discuss my words. I must have heard New York repeated ten different times. I kept waiting for a September 11 reference. I wondered if they had even heard about the attacks. Most of them were illiterate, and they relied on an oral tradition. I was sure they had heard stories. Did they know that 9/11 was the reason we were in Iraq? Did they care?

"I go America," one of them said in his best English. Others nodded behind him. It seemed many of them had the same dream. Their eyes were filled with wonder. They talked about America as though it were some magical other world. I guess, to them, it was. They had only heard about it or seen pictures. Some of the more educated must have read some books about the United States. They started naming different places: "California, Texas, New York." They all had hope for the future. I wasn't about to tell them that most of them would never make it outside their own country.

"Mister, Mister, America, you take." They pointed to me and then to themselves. They wanted me to take them back to America with me. I tried to laugh it off. "Money, money." I rubbed my fingers together. Even they understood what made the world go 'round.

Still, their questions kept coming. They wanted to see my rifle, which I kept with me at all times. They wanted to see my bayonet, and then compare it to their own. A newcomer would join in and start asking about my wife or America. I tried to ask them questions too.

"Wayn?" I said, trying to ask where one of the Iraqis was from.

"Mosul," he answered. Another said, "Najaf." Still another said, "Karbala."

"You, Fallujah?" I asked one.

He shook his head. "No, no. Fallujah no good. No good, Mister." They all kept repeating that. "Fallujah no good. No good Fallujah."

I soon learned that Iraq was broken up into different tribes and that each tribe either benefited or suffered from Saddam Hussein's influence. Fallujah was a place that housed many of Saddam's allies. Because most of the jundees were Shiite, they associated Fallujah with Saddam and the repressive policies that kept them underdeveloped for so many years. Every interaction was instructive for me.

I tried my best to answer their questions for the better part of an hour, but eventually I was called away to the battalion house for a meeting with Major Lawson. The rest of the battalion advisers were there, along with the senior advisers assigned to each line company. We were all there to receive new marching orders and to listen to a situation report on the state of the city. Major Lawson prepared to start. His style of leadership was laid-back, matter-of-fact, but serious when need be. He looked serious when he opened his mouth for the first time.

"First things first. Just got word from 3/5 that they're going to start letting civilians back into the city in a couple of days. With cars."

Silence. What a way to open the meeting, I thought. "They can't be serious," I blurted out. Judging from the looks of the others, I was speaking for the group.

The potential for chaos was obvious to all of us. First, how could we prevent the enemy from sneaking back into the city with the normal civilians. One couldn't tell who was an insurgent and who wasn't. Second, the addition of cars to the equation in Fallujah was particularly troubling. The car bomb was probably the most deadly weapon in the enemy's arsenal. In short, we were playing with fire.

"Word is that the Iraqi government, the Ministry of the Interior or some shit like that, they are the ones pushing this. So, it's going to happen. We're just going to have to deal with it," Major Lawson explained. This was not the last time we were at the business end of a decision made by the Iraqi Ministry of Interior. Considering that evidence that the ministry was corrupt and probably infiltrated by the insurgents later started piling up, one has to wonder if allowing vehicles back into the city was part of an insurgent plot to infiltrate our defenses.

"So, we have a couple of days to link up with 3/5 and set up our forces appropriately." The 3/5 Marine battalion was in charge of the northern part of the city. We had taken up position in an area controlled by their India Company. India Company would be our American partner unit.

"Company 1," the Major pointed to Gunny Gonzalez, the company's senior adviser, "you are going to head out to the Jolan Park. They're setting up a humanitarian assistance area, and they want to put an Iraqi face on that operation."

"Lieutenant Navarro," he said, turning to me, "you and your company are going to link up with India Company at their position. You will be the first to conduct joint patrols throughout the area."

"Company 3 is going to remain with the battalion as firm base security."

"Excuse me sir, excuse . . . " Gunny Babineaux, the senior adviser for Company 3, interrupted. "Exactly what firm base are we talking about here." His eyes were blinking the whole time he talked. I wondered if he had Tourette's syndrome.

"I'm getting to that, Gunny." The major was annoyed. "The battalion headquarters unit will set up a new firm base right here." A giant map, an overhead satellite image, of the city was located on a wall behind the major. He used the map to point out a new location where this Iraqi battalion was going to move. Where these orders were coming from, no one knew.

"Sir?" Babineaux interrupted again.

"Yes, Gunny?"

"Uh, do the Iraqis know about this? Because I don't think Captain Akeel knows. And I've got no terps to tell him. So . . . I was just wondering. . . . Because, you see, I thought we were here to help them, but I didn't think we were in charge."

"Right after this meeting I'm going to sit down with Colonel Mehgid."

"Oh, I see." For a man who had been in the Marine Corps for over twenty years, Gunny Babineaux seemed to have a problem with authority. This quality proved more troublesome as the mission progressed.

Shortly after the meeting adjourned, I went outside to survey the landscape.

"Mister, Mister." A tall, lanky Iraqi soldier was standing at the top of the front steps. He was smiling from ear to ear and giving me a weird look.

"Hello. Marhaba."

"Ah, Mister, good Arabee. Good, Mister." He kept looking at me with these strange eyes. What did he want? He took one finger, his index finger from his right hand, and pointed it toward me. What was he doing? Then he took the index finger from the left hand and pointed right at me. I shook my head, not understanding. He kept smiling. "Mister, Mister." The soldier brought his two fingers together and started rubbing them on the sides. "Fikki-Fikki," he said with his eyebrows bouncing up and down as if to say, "You know now what I'm talking about?" And I finally thought I did.

"Is this guy hitting on me?" I said to myself aloud. I was in shock.

The jundee kept rubbing his index fingers together, like, I thought, two people lying next to each other. "Fikki-Fikki," he said again, still smiling wide.

I left the scene even more confused about the Iraqis than I had been before. An hour later, back in our room at the mosque, that particularly disturbing interaction was still bothering me.

"I can't fucking believe it. I come all the way around the world, thousands of miles from home, just to get hit on by some gay Iraqi soldier!"Tewilliger laughed. We were all in a circle, heating our meals ready to eat (MRE) dinners on a new kerosene heater.

"Yes, Sir. Women are for children. Men are for pleasure," Tewilliger explained.

"But I thought it was against their religion." I said, incredulous.

"Well, a lot of things are against their religion. Drinking. Porn. They still do it."

"So, what you're saying is their religion, all this high and mighty shit, is just a front?"

"You said it, Sir, not me."

"Yep, they're just like all the rest of us," Sullivan added rather matter-of-factly.

"They believe in God, or Allah, when it suits them," I said aloud, but the comment was more for myself. Were the insurgents the same way? Was the enemy gay? If so, did that mean they were using religion as a front for propaganda purposes? And where did Allah come down on all of this? I was more confused than ever. The Iraqis seemed to operate outside the world of logic and reason.

As I was considering this, a group of Iraqis came knocking. "Mister, Mister. Batteries. Tape. Tape."

"Why do they always want tape? What do they do with it?" I asked as Tewilliger stood up and rummaged through a pile he had made of all the items Iraqis asked for. He'd been through this all before.

"Fuck if I know, Sir."

"Hey, you," I said, pointing to one of the Iraqis. "Are you all gay?" They didn't understand what I said.

"I think, Sir, the word is 'doodeki,'"Tewilliger offered. As soon as he said the word, the Iraqis started laughing.

"Doodeki?" I pointed to one of them.

"No, no. Mister, no doodeki!" He denied it, but the look in his eyes was a little less certain. Maybe he was embarrassed to admit it.

"You doodeki?" I turned and pointed to another one. He said the same thing. But they were all laughing, saying "doodeki" over and over again, and then pointing to each other and smiling. The whole scene was ridiculous. It was not my finest moment.

The next day, as ordered, I took 2nd Company down the street to link up with India Company, 3rd Battalion, 5th Marine Regiment. Maybe *took* is the wrong word. I herded the company together into a loose formation. We tried to make sure we had every member of the company by counting each Iraqi individually.

"Seventy five, seventy six—hey, you! Get back in formation!" The Iraqi had no idea what I was saying, but he conjured the meaning from my angry stare, my finger pointing directly at him, and the hand that never left my rifle's grip.

Every time I went through the counting procedure one of the jundees would just walk out of the formation. Then two more would appear out of nowhere and join the group. This would force yet another recount. Sullivan, Tewilliger, and Major Ali were all doing their own counting for accuracy purposes.

"I've got 120," I exhaled, happy to be done.

"Sir, I count 117," Tewilliger said.

"One hundred nineteen here," Sullivan added. I shook my head. Wasn't it the Arabs who gave us our system of numbers?

Major Ali was finishing up. If he came back with the same number I had, I was going to go with it. Ahmed translated. "One hundred twenty-eight." I threw up my hands. The Iraqis started laughing. "Ah, Mister, Mister. Amreeki," they said. They rambled on among themselves even as we started the count over.

The number that we settled on was somewhere around 125. The breakdown between officers, noncommissioned officers, and soldiers was not clear, but we didn't have time to do any more counting. We had to board the Leland trucks and get to our new position down the street.

The Iraqis packed all one hundred and whatever members the company currently had into a handful of the medium-size trucks. The officers rode in a pair of the Nissan pickup trucks. Sullivan and I were the only Americans going along for the ride. We said our good-byes to Tewilliger and hopped into an armored Humvee. At least we'd have some protection this time around, unlike during our initial Nissan pickup ride into the city. Our Humvee trailed behind the convoy to prevent any stragglers from falling too far behind. Another Humvee, carrying a few of the drifters assigned to the battalion, acted as the lead vehicle.

We were moving only a few blocks west of the mosque but that was more than enough distance for the Iraqis to lose their way. We were not two blocks into the convoy when one of the Nissans and a Leland truck turned down a side street. It took twenty minutes to get the wayward Iraqis back into the convoy's main body. Once reorganized, we continued on. We finally arrived at India Company's position, an hour late. In Iraq, that was considered on time.

India Company had taken part in some of the most brutal fighting of the entire war in Iraq up to that point. Operation Phantom Fury had claimed the lives of over one hundred Marines in the past month. These Marines were battle hardened. They had just finished fighting many insurgents, men who looked a lot like the jundees now stacked in trucks, sitting at India's front gate. The Marines at the front guard post must've flexed their trigger fingers a little bit when those Leland trucks and Nissans, with machine guns in the flatbeds, first approached. The look on the young Marines' faces when we drifters approached them was classic. Their eyes asked me, "Who are you? And what are you doing with the enemy?"

"How ya doing, Marine?" I said.

"Good morning, . . . Sir."

"We're here to link up with you guys."

"Uh, all of you, Sir?" He was looking around at the over one hundred armed Iraqis sitting in the Leland trucks.

"That's right."

"Wait one." He went inside his post and used his radio to call up his superiors for guidance. Clearly, this Marine had not received the word about the company of Iraqi soldiers coming to live with him. After a few garbled radio transmissions, the Marine came back.

"Alright, Sir, go ahead. Our XO [executive officer] will be there to link up."

We drove through the gate and into the complex. The camp was just another series of confiscated houses. Concertina wire was strewn in a square to mark the boundaries. Sandbagged guard posts were situated in the four corners and on top of some of the different houses to provide better fields of fire.

We had the Iraqis park in the main clearing in the center of the camp. Some of them started hopping out of the truck beds, RPGs and machine guns still in their hands, even before the trucks stopped moving. Trying to get them all together in one cohesive unit was more difficult than herding cats.

The Marines who were outside watched us with a mixture of amusement and mistrust. To them, any and all of these Iraqis could be or were, in fact, part of the insurgency—the enemy. And I couldn't blame them for feeling that way.

A Marine lieutenant was standing in the clearing, wearing a pair of mirrored sunglasses. I went up to him to introduce myself.

"Hey, how are you? I'm sorry we're a little late." I extended my hand.

"No one ever said anything about this many!" he said as he shook my hand.

"Well, I don't know who told you what. All I know is I was told to take this company to link up with you. And that we'd be conducting joint patrols starting ASAP. As far as numbers, we don't have an exact count, but we've got about a hundred and twenty with us."

"That's way too many. We don't have room for them. Or food." I was not surprised that there had been a miscommunication. It was becoming commonplace.

"Well, I don't know what to tell you. We're here, so, if it's alright with you, I'd like to link up the Iraqi company commander with your company commander and get this ball rolling."

"For right now, I need you to take them into that building over there." He pointed to a small brick house in the far corner of the complex. We were getting shooed away already.

Once the Iraqis were crowded into the small house, Staff Sergeant Sullivan and I made contact with India's company commander to figure out when we were going out on patrol. Tomorrow was the short answer, which came quickly after making our introductions. The timing was not up for discussion with the Iraqis. Major Ali had no input in how his troops would be used. I had not anticipated the mission going this way. I thought we were supposed to be helping the Iraqis stand up their army so that they could go and fight. As an adviser I was told I was not in charge of the Iraqis. Apparently, the Marines of India Company were under no such restrictions. This put me in a difficult position. I was the bridge between the Americans and the Iraqis, but I had no real power with either side. I could only influence events. My negotiation skills would be tested.

In this situation, however, I quickly recognized there was no room for negotiation. The Marines would tell the Iraqis what to do, at least for the time being. I would have to be the conduit through which the information was funneled.

When I told Major Ali what the plan was, he responded with a shrug of the shoulders. He was old and had seen it all. "Insha Allah," he said, simply. I was both used to and sick of those words by then.

I turned my attention away from the will of God to make sure the Iraqis didn't cause trouble and the Marines didn't kill any of the Iraqis. This was a difficult task. The Marines obviously did not want to get to know the Iraqis on a personal level. Their relationship with the soldiers was strictly professional. They had already seen several different iterations of the Iraqi armed forces: first the Fallujah Brigade, then the Iraqi National Guard, then the Iraqi Civil Defense Corps. Each one had failed to deliver serious forces. Each one had crumbled under the weight of corruption, incompetence, and desertions. These new soldiers looked no different.

In addition they felt "the muj" (mujahideen) factor. Every American felt it. Any one of these Iraqis could be the enemy. We could not know for sure who was on what side. Tales of rampant enemy infiltration had been spread among the Marines since the occupation began. Most were rumors, but one never knew whether some could be true.

All of this worked against us drifters. While some in India Company showed Sullivan and I courtesy as fellow Americans and fellow Marines, I could tell that others were keeping their distance. We were with the Iraqis; we were guilty by association.

After our arrival, we were given the rest of the day to break up the Iraqis by platoon and to assign them to a corresponding Marine partner platoon. After the Iraqis had been broken down, they were to help the Marines of India Company improve the defenses of their compound. Lieutenant Ahmed was assigned a platoon and told to help his partner Marines fill sandbags and build up fighting positions in case of an enemy attack. Unfortunately—and Dr. Chung had warned us about this—Ahmed, like many Iraqis, believed that an officer was something of a tyrant or slave master, who was above all menial tasks. Therefore, he didn't expect to do any heavy lifting of his own.

When the Marine platoon commander found Ahmed taking a nap while the rest of his platoon was out in the midday sun working their butts off, their relationship soured right away. A confrontation ensued and quickly ended, with Ahmed thrust backward into a nearby wall, an American hand gripping his throat. Ahmed was not used to this kind of treatment. He thought he was special.

"Lieutenant, we have problem," Ahmed said to me once he got me alone.

"You mean *you* have a problem, right?" He just looked at me. He didn't want to admit it. I could tell by now that half my job would be playing diplomat between the Iraqis and the Americans.

"I will talk to the Marines, OK?" I said. He looked satisfied. "But, you are going to have to work just as much as your men," I added. He didn't like that at all.

"No, no. This is no good. No good." He stomped off to plead his case to Major Ali. He was going to be a constant thorn in my side.

The cultural conflicts between the Iraqis and the Americans did not stop with Ahmed. There was no running water in the entire city, so the little outhouse toilets in all the houses' courtyards could be used for urinating only. The sewer system was still intact. The Americans understood the situation and set up tents as makeshift toilets for defecation. The Iraqis, however, continued to use the outhouses. Not even an hour had passed before angry Marines began complaining up their chains of command about the turds that were magically appearing in the pissers. I had to deal with this problem every time we moved the Iraqis. Throughout the deployment, the most vital question we had to ask our partner American units was, Where were the Iraqis going to shit?

India Company was forced to construct some sheds specifically for the Iraqis. To keep them out of the old, pre-existing outhouses, I enlisted the help of Jundee Mohammed to translate some signs we posted at the toilets' entrances. They read, "No shitting. For pissing only." We wrote the words in both Arabic and English so the Iraqis wouldn't think we were singling them out. Of course, all of the Americans knew who the signs were really for. The signs reminded me that I was no longer a Marine, I was the resident diplomat.

Patrolling

The patrol was the single-most important mission the Iraqis conducted while we were in Fallujah. The Iraqi battalion had limited logistical support from anyone in its chain of command, its leadership was weak, and the American units it was working with didn't trust the Iraqi soldiers or even engage the commanders. Still, the Iraqis had a few discernable strengths that came in handy during patrols. First, they provided the coalition forces with more manpower. Their presence alone eventually allowed us to increase the footprint of coalition forces throughout Fallujah. Second, the Iraqis knew the local areas and the population much better than the Americans did and could gather valuable intelligence by using this knowledge. Finally, involving the Iraqis in patrolling operations gave a boost to coalition public relations. Putting the Iraqi soldiers out there among the population, we hoped to score propaganda points by showing the Iraqi military and the Americans working together to bring security to the area.

Second Company had been ordered to link up with India Company of 3/5 and to start participating in joint patrols. Staff Sergeant Sullivan and I, as the advisers for 2nd Company, were there to facilitate a cooperative interaction between the Iraqis and the American Marines. We were also there to monitor the Iraqis' progress as they went through the patrol missions. The Americans had arranged for each India Company patrol to take a fire team of Iraqis—three soldiers and an NCO or officer—out with them. Over time, when we felt they were ready, Sullivan and I would take a whole squad of Iraqis out by ourselves. The goal was to start the Iraqis' training with the smallest unit possible, the fire team, and to build up their patrolling capabilities from there. India Company, in order to maintain security throughout the designated battle space, was conducting around-the-clock patrols. We planned to rotate every single Iraqi from 2nd Company through the joint patrols and to keep rotating them through until we judged them ready to conduct their own patrols independent of the Marines from India Company.

When we first arrived at India Company's base, the Iraqis were far from the point of conducting their own patrols. The key component of any transition from joint patrols to independent Iraqi patrols was the company leaders' abilities. Each NCO and each junior officer in the company was going to have to demonstrate an ability to lead their small units, whether fire teams or squads or platoons. The first joint patrol would provide a clear indication of the small unit leaders' current abilities.

The day after we linked up with India Company, I observed four Iraqis—three jundees and an areef, or sergeant—prepare for their first patrol. They were looking around at the squad of about ten Marines, trying to see what the Americans were doing to get ready. Dr. Chung's advice came into my mind once again. I had to set the example.

I readied myself in front of the fire team, so the Iraqis could copy me. I made sure I was drinking water. A couple of the Iraqi soldiers did the same. I checked my ammunition pouches. They followed. I made sure my weapon was loaded and on safe. They still had a long way to go on in terms of proficiency at this task. The areef, who was supposed to be leading the fire team, decided to check his weapon by looking down the barrel of his AK, not the ideal way to figure out whether one's weapon was loaded.

The situation in the city was still tense. We had received reports of enemy ambushes, especially at night. Needless to say, India Company was prepared for contact with the enemy. For example, on this first joint patrol, we would be accompanied by two M1A1 Abrams main battle tanks. As we prepped for the mission, the high-pitched whine of two turbine engines roared to life. Those metal behemoths were much appreciated. We would have some serious firepower out there in case the mujahideen assaulted us.

The two tanks used their tracks to grind their way into position. One would be at the front of the patrol. The other would provide rear guard. The mix of tanks and infantry was classic military operations in urbanized terrain (MOUT) doctrine. Tanks by themselves would be exposed to enemy fighters sneaking up with grenades and other explosives, whereas infantry alone lacked the firepower to deal with serious threats such as car bombs. Combining the two mitigated these problems to some extent.

When the M1AI Abrams rolled out, the Iraqis simply stood there in awe. It looked as though they had never seen an American tank before. Soon, however, they were startled out of their stares. We were off, on the move.

It was early in the morning, and the sun was still struggling up into the sky. The Marines took their positions in a standard column formation: two single-file lines, one on either side of the road, with each man spaced about five to ten meters behind the man in front of him.

A lieutenant's normal position in the formation was in the middle of the two lines, overseeing the entire formation. I was not performing the normal lieutenant functions, however. I decided it was best to act as one of the members of the formation. This way the nervous Iraqis could watch what I was doing and follow along. I made sure to keep enough space between myself and the Marine ahead of me, a precaution we took so that an improvised explosive devise (IED) or mortar couldn't take us all out in one blast. Also, I sucked down as much water as possible through the hose of my camelpak. I wanted to make sure I was plenty hydrated and that the Iraqis watching me were staying hydrated by following my lead.

In this kind of movement, every man was responsible for scanning his sector. I did my best to look down every alley, into every window, on every roof, anywhere an insurgent could be lurking. Whenever I came to a cross street I would raise my rifle to cover the next man, who in this case was an Iraqi, as he crossed the street. He would then do the same for the next man, and so on. To my surprise, the Iraqis picked the moves up quickly. They still looked terrified, however. It seemed like they didn't think they were ever going to have to do anything on this job. They must've planned to simply show up, do as little work as possible, collect their paychecks, and then go home. They didn't yet realize they were supposed to be our exit strategy. Regardless, they kept up with the India Company Marines fairly well.

Unfortunately, I wasn't impressed with the areef. He seemed to be in way over his head. He seemed too young to be in a supervisory position. He was also the first Iraqi to start slacking during the patrol. I caught him letting his weapon fall to his side, from either boredom or fatigue. I had to shake my own rifle to emphasize how he was supposed to be holding his not once but three times during the first thirty minutes of the patrol. I began to make mental notes concerning his performance.

Over the course of the patrol, it was easy to see that the Iraqis didn't yet have the mental stamina needed for this work, which required a steady focus over a long period of time. The soldiers had to be ready for anything at any time. Starting with the Iraqi areef, they all seemed to lose interest in the patrol quickly. Perhaps the rest of the fire team was following their areef's lead. Their laziness would have been interesting to watch were its consequences not potentially deadly.

The patrol afforded me the opportunity to get a clearer picture of where the city stood. It was not a pretty sight. Fallujah was in ruins. The Iraqi authorities had not started to let any of the civilians back in yet, so the streets were deserted. Raw sewage was pooled in the gutters. The stench of human waste and garbage was overpowering. Whole buildings had been destroyed, blasted by a bomb from the sky or blown apart by a surface missile, maybe an artillery shell or a tank's shot. Strangely enough, I occasionally noticed a house that had been reduced to rubble framed by houses left almost completely untouched. On one street a barbershop on the corner lay abandoned but was still completely intact. The red, white, and blue cylinder kept spinning in the breeze. But, right next to the shop was a two-story building that had been smashed. Its roof had fallen in and the entire building had collapsed on itself. Black streaks cut across a wall. Bullet and fragment holes were sprayed all over. Spray-painted symbols adorned the outside of every front door. Most were red Xs or circles with Xs through them. They had been used during the main battle to let follow-on forces know that the house had been cleared of enemy forces. It seemed some of the houses must not have stayed cleared for long. Some doors had two, three, sometimes four different symbols, probably meaning that those houses had been cleared more than once. Patrolling Fallujah reminded me that urban, house-to-house fighting was a brutal business. To emphasize this point, it seemed, stray dogs followed us during the entire patrol. I had the feeling they were waiting for one of us to fall, so they could pick the bones clean.

The patrol leader from India Company was a young, grizzled sergeant. His platoon commander was supervising the patrol. The sergeant was in good command of the formation, and he made all the radio calls to report his position to his higher command. I could only hope our Iraqis would approach even one-half this kind of leadership some day.

Every fifteen or twenty minutes, the patrol leader would raise his arm, palm open, to signal a security halt. During each halt, I would kneel on one knee and then split my time scanning the area and watching to make sure the Iraqis were doing the right thing. During one stop, I turned to see what the areef was doing. He caught my gaze and smiled from ear to ear, like this was all make-believe.

"Hey, Mister, Marines good," the areef said, holding up a raised thumb to signal his approval. I shook my head. We were a long way from building a professional military in this country.

One of the tanks whirled past me, and I noticed a series of posters that had been put up on many of the city's walls. One of these posters was not a foot from where I was kneeling. It was the color of flames and depicted an Iraqi man on his knees, with his hands to his eyes and his mouth agape in a cry of anguish. To top it off, he was kneeling between a picture of Abu Musab al Zarqawi, leader of al Qaeda in Iraq, on the left and Osama bin Laden on the right. The meaning was clear: Iraqis were burning in hell because of the two terrorist leaders. It was a well-done poster as far as artistry was concerned, but I knew it would not make a dent in the insurgency. Art could not trump religion or the will of the tribe or whatever was driving the insurgency.

We continued the patrol on along the main thoroughfare, which cut the city in half. We passed what used to be a park, in the Jolan area, which was going to be a humanitarian assistance center when the civilians started returning. A wheel, the kind kids used to spin around on, now circled—empty.

The patrol turnaround came and went, and we were soon on our way back toward India's camp. Unfortunately, the Iraqis realized the end of the ordeal was at hand. We Marines called this realization "smelling the barn." At the end of a patrol or operation, participants naturally become lax and lose focus. Usually you can rely on the professionalism of the Marines and the patrol leader to combat this urge to relax, but I had almost forgotten about the Iraqis.

We were not even two hundred meters from our destination, when I heard, Rat-a-tat-tat! Rat-a-tat-tat! The sounds of a burst of AK fire slammed into my ears from behind. I whirled around, my rifle instinctively coming up to press on my cheek. My left hand was gripping a handle protruding from the barrel. My right hand was holding the pistol grip, with my right index finger pressing lightly on the trigger. My eyes were looking down my sights, ready to pick out the enemy, center the red dot on his chest, squeeze, and kill.

I found the red dot. It was centered. But it was sitting on the chest of the Iraqi areef. He was standing there, holding his arms up away from his AK. "Excuse me. Excuse me. Mister, Mister. Excuse me," he kept repeating apologetically. He had been carrying his rifle by the trigger guard. Why? I would never understand. He had ended up pulling the trigger and firing into the ground at full automatic fire.

I looked around at the rest of the patrol and understood how close the Iraqi areef had come to being killed. Every

Marine, true to their training and experience, upon hearing the four-round burst of AK fire, had swung around and trained their weapons on the perpetrator, ready to kill.

"What was that?" I could hear the patrol leader's radio squawk. The patrol leader was burning a hole through the areef's chest with his eyes.

"Nothing. Disregard. Just an Iraqi."

"Roger, understood," the leader replied.

This was not the kind of first impression I was looking for from 2nd Company. The Iraqi areef in question had no business being in a position of authority. He was too young and did not take his position seriously. One look at him standing there, pleading for his life, confirmed this depressing conclusion.

The individual leaders of the Iraqi small unit were the critical vulnerability of the entire company. Their ability to lead a group of their fellow soldiers was going to make or break our mission. This fact was easily proved during the next few weeks. With each subsequent patrol, it was clear who were the strong leaders and who had no business leading a group of goats, let alone military men.

Following the first couple of patrols, I soon realized that we drifters, Sullivan and I, were not wanted around the India Company area. The Marines considered me to be a random lieutenant, clearly in charge of nothing and no one, and Staff Sergeant Sullivan tended to rub everyone the wrong way with his coarse nature. Everywhere I went, I was at the business end of strange stares and mumbled gossip. Our standing with the Americans dropped like a ton of bricks as soon as they caught us conversing with our Iraqi counterparts. It also didn't help that someone had misstated the number of Iraqis coming with us. All of a sudden, India Company was faced with a group of rowdy Iraqis over one hundred strong. They had been told to expect about forty.

Major Ali did nothing except set up his own room while over half of his company tried to squeeze into the two remaining rooms in the crumbling old house we had been relegated to. Lieutenant Ahmed was similarly unhelpful and fast approaching a meeting with an American fist. He was caught watching TV when he was supposed to be prepping for a patrol.

I didn't need a translator to tell me where all of this was leading. I made the call back to Drifter Base. We would leave India Company with the forty Iraqis they were expecting and take Major Ali, Lieutenant Ahmed, and the rest of the company back to setup positions within Drifter Base. From there, we would make daily linkups and conduct joint patrols.

"Mohammed, Major Ali and I are going back to battalion," I told the jundee. I broke the news to him instead of Ahmed because I couldn't stand the sight of the Iraqi lieutenant anymore. I already trusted Mohammed more than most of the Iraqi lieutenants. He demonstrated leadership on a daily basis, and the India Company Marines were even starting to like him.

"Why you go? You no like Mohammed?" He sounded sincerely hurt. The Iraqis seemed to bond with people rather quickly.

"No, no. I like you. Colonel Mehgid needs us back in battalion. Besides, I know you and Mulazem Khalil can do the job." I tried to pump Mohammed up. Khalil, the platoon leader, was a weak leader and very unsure of himself. I knew this particular contingent would sink or swim on Mohammed's ability to keep them together.

"OK, whatever you like. Insha Allah." Mohammed smiled broadly.

"Insha Allah," I replied instinctively. Was I going native? Was I actually starting to understand what they meant? The question remained with me until the end of my time with the Iraqis.

Once back at Drifter Base, we established a house in which 2nd Company would live and from which they would plan and execute their operations. We would be in close proximity to the battalion group, which included the Iraqi battalion commander and his staff, plus Major Lawson and the rest of the American AST members assigned to the Iraqi staff. We would also be close to the radios, which had finally established a communications link with the Marines of 3/5. This meant we could coordinate our joint patrols with India Company.

Second Company was still going to be the main force from the 9th Battalion to take part in the patrolling operation. Patrolling would be my focus for the foreseeable future.

We arranged for India Company to take care of the forty or so Iraqis who were still living with them so we could concentrate our energies on the remainder of the company, whom we lived with in Drifter Base. India Company would start its patrols from its own forward operating base (FOB) with a fire team of Iraqis imbedded within the American squad or platoon. The Marines with the embedded Iraqis would patrol the area between the two base camps, and once they approached Drifter Base, they would then link up with a squad of Iraqis from the remainder of 2nd Company. The two units would then continue along the predetermined patrol route as one larger unit. Following the conduct of that part of the patrol, we would circle back around, reenter Drifter Base, and drop off the Iraqi squad, and then India Company's patrol, with the original fire team of Iraqis still attached would continue back to its own base.

This plan was effective for several reasons. First, we were able to increase the number of Iraqis who were able to go out on patrol. Each patrol was like a live fire training evolution, with the only difference being that enemy combatants were actually out there trying to kill us. As far as providing a means to train the jundees and their leaders in the conduct of a patrol, nothing compared to real world experience in a semicontrolled environment. I say semicontrolled because the city was, at least at the outset of our patrol operations, still largely unoccupied. Thus, the only people out there were Marines, the Iraqi soldiers, and straggler insurgents. And the insurgents did not, for the most part, try to pick off Americans except under the cover of darkness. At this point, night operations were a complete impossibility for the Iraqis of the 9th Battalion for reasons that will be illustrated in a later chapter. Having said all of this, we were not attacked during those first joint patrols. Thus, the Iraqis had an opportunity to get their legs under them before they experienced any casualties. They conducted real world patrols under the watchful guidance of an adjacent American unit and their advisers, and they were able to meaningfully contribute to the security of their area of operations.

Second, these patrols were effective because the Marines were able to keep a fairly tight control over the new additions to their battle space by accepting them into some of their simpler missions. They knew when the Iraqis were leaving their base and when they were traveling through the area. By extension, the Americans' inherent distrust of the Iraqis' movements and intentions was alleviated.

Third, and most important from the AST members' standpoint, the interaction between the Americans and Iraqis was fruitful in not only developing a working relationship between the two culturally different military units but also in developing the Iraqis' small unit leadership skills. The American patrol leaders were able to link up with Iraqi NCOs and officers and, through an interpreter the Marines brought with them, go over the planned patrol route and any other coordinating instructions that were pertinent for the day's action. This allowed the Iraqi NCO or officer to be involved in the planning behind the patrol in at least a small fashion. As the advisers facilitating this interplay, we tried to instill a sense of confidence in the Iraqi NCOs and officers by having them talk directly to the American patrol leaders.

Sullivan and I coordinated the linkup of the Marine patrol with the second batch of Iraqi soldiers on our end. First, I talked to Major Ali through Lieutenant Ahmed, with, I hoped, limited language distortions. I asked Major Ali who was scheduled to lead the next patrol, and I made sure that the Iraqi patrol leader knew at what time the American Marines would arrive. Once I established the who and when, Staff Sergeant Sullivan and I prepared for the patrol. We had to accompany our assigned Iraqis on any and all major operations. I always got fully geared up in a public area of the 2nd Company house so that the Iraqis could watch how I prepared. This also allowed me to ensure that the soldiers were on time: I would get ready early enough so that when the Iraqis followed my lead they would be prepared in time to start the patrol.

Once the India Company personnel arrived, I was the first one to greet the Marine patrol leader. I went over the plan with him and then brought over the assigned Iraqi NCO or officer to make the appropriate introductions. I made sure the Marine went over the patrol plan with the Iraqi. After the review of the plan, we checked that the Iraqi jundees had all their helmets and flaks on and that no one was wearing their pink or purple flip-flops. Then, the patrol continued along its route.

One of us, either Sullivan or I, would accompany the patrol to check two things. First, we ensured the Marines were employing the Iraqis properly. Allowing a jundee to run up to a suspected IED and kick it, for example, was improper employment. Second, we monitored the Iraqis' performance. This was an essential part of our jobs. We were constantly evaluating the Iraqis and their ability to operate in an effective military manner.

As time went by, and after many joint patrols with India Company, I saw signs I never expected: signs of progress. The Iraqis actually looked to be learning. Well, perhaps *learning* was not the right term. They improved at mimicking the Marines and the Americans' conduct when on patrol. The only way, I surmised, we could test their actual learning of this behavior was to step up training to the next level: independent patrols.

The thought of a small unit of Iraqis walking around the area on its own probably gave India Company the creeps, but we were going to have to try it. In my eyes, the only way to create an effective Iraqi fighting force that could eventually take the place of the Americans was to force them to conduct their own operations. Of course, the Iraqis would not be completely unsupervised during these independent patrols. The drifters would provide the watchful eye over each patrol, meaning two lonely Americans joined each squad-size Iraqi patrol. Major Lawson ordered that no drifter go out on a mission alone. I felt like my compatriot and I were a pair of cops, with one partner watching the back of the other and vice versa. It was small comfort, but comfort nonetheless.

Picture two Americans walking around with a group of Iraqis through the streets of Fallujah. I had not been trained for this scenario. Reality in Iraq, however, had a strange way of throwing the unexpected at you, and the adviser mission seemed to be particularly marked with this type of uncertainty. That is why the most successful advisers were those men who could deal with uncertainty and remain flexible. Whether I was flexible enough for the demands of this particular mission, I didn't know. Regardless I never had a chance to opt out. The realities of our missions were not changeable. I simply tried, in my capacity as senior adviser, to focus on starting this new phase of company operations on the right foot.

My first step was to ask Staff Sergeant Sullivan, with his infantry expertise to be the hands-on patrol expert. This accomplished two things. First, it placated Sullivan. He was a crusty sort who had been in the Marines so long he thought he knew everything. I wanted to show him that I had confidence in his knowledge, at least with respect to this particular mission. This made him happy. He was in his element and took to it immediately. Second, it freed me to focus on the bigger picture as far as the company was concerned. I was able to supervise not only the patrol operations, but also all of the other things going on within the company such as resupply, improvement of our house defenses, and development of the company leadership. It was a win-win situation, and as a result, Sullivan and I started working well together.

Using a map at the house, Sullivan involved the Iraqi patrol leaders in planning their own patrol routes. Once the routes were set, we ensured that the company leadership assigned each individual jundee to a specific patrol with a designated patrol leader. In the hour prior to the patrol kickoff time, we made sure the patrol leaders inspected their men to ensure they took the proper gear and supplies. We also taught them to brief, at the very least, the patrol route to each and every member of the patrol. After a while the Iraqi patrol leaders actually started completing these tasks on their own, without prompting. Eventually, I could open my door and find an Iraqi standing over a big map in the main foyer of the house and showing each and every jundee where they were headed that day.

The AST members judged the Iraqis' progress during the

actual patrols. What I personally witnessed illustrated, as well as anything else that happened during our time with them, both the Iraqis' strengths and weaknesses. Forget for a second the actions of the individual patrol members. Some of them were better than others, and some clearly did not belong in a military organization. What was most interesting was the way each patrol leader exposed his abilities or lack thereof.

Take 2nd Company's three lieutenants for example. Lieutenant Ahmed, as I have already established, fit into the tyrant category. He felt he was superior to his soldiers and did not treat them well. They followed his orders only because they were afraid of him. While this worked for Ahmed in the short term, I knew that eventually one of his jundees would shoot Ahmed in the back. I judged him in the middle of the three. He sort of knew what he was doing but became bored and more lax in his attention to his troops as his patrols wore on. As an adviser, I had to supervise him continuously out of fear that he would try and slap one of his men. He feared me, and thus I was able to prevent any of his violent tendencies from manifesting.

The weakest of the three lieutenants was a man named Khalil. He made his weakness obvious from the way he carried himself to the way he controlled his men. Khalil was slight of build and overly polite to anyone he spoke to. He spoke in a soft voice and delivered his orders without a hint of aggression. His eyes always gave the sense that he was unsure of himself. His lack of confidence appeared during one particular patrol when he got the entire patrol completely lost. He was staring at the map when I went over to see where we were going. I found that he was holding the map upside down. Plus, he was holding the map out in front of him as he walked during the entire patrol. Any enemy sniper could have pinpointed him as the patrol leader in about a second. I was not impressed.

The third and final Iraqi lieutenant was Jalal. He was the most impressive of the group for a variety of reasons. First, he carried himself with confidence but he was not overly confident. He treated his soldiers fairly and also led them ably. He was attentive during our meetings with him, and he asked pertinent questions. Over time, we were able to rely on him more and more. We were also able to simply sit back and supervise when going out on patrol with him and his squad. We rarely had to step in to correct him. He had prior experience in Saddam's army, but he did not hold that up as a qualification for automatic respect. He earned it.

The images of these three young officers brought our entire adviser mission, and whether it would ultimately be successful, into full relief. By placing the responsibility in the hands of the Iraqi leadership, we would find out soon enough who was capable of organizing and leading this new army and who needed to be discharged. We were putting the country's fate back onto Iraqi shoulders, one patrol at a time.

For the first time I was encouraged by what I saw. Maybe there was room for some hope.

6

TWO WAHHABI

I learned over time that hope was a four-letter word in Iraq. The Iraqis demonstrated an unrivalled ability to turn promising results into failure after failure in the shortest of time spans. Riding the emotional roller coaster of their small successes versus their more numerous shortcomings proved to be one of the most difficult aspects of the adviser mission.

The most alarming consequence of their inconsistent performance, for me personally, was my own transformation. The Insha Allah concept began to invade my own thoughts and outlook on the adviser mission and our day-to-day lives with the Iraqis early on. The idea behind the phrase was not only making sense to me but was becoming a routine answer for all the troubles I encountered. I learned that in Iraq, caught among the natives, the only way to deal with the random events and the Iraqis' incongruous actions was to adopt a more fatalistic outlook on my situation.

When an Iraqi shot himself in the foot, and the Iraqis looked to me to find the soldier medical help, my instinctive reply was "Insha Allah." When Major Ali wasn't present for a company accountability formation, the same words came out of my mouth. Hell, even when conversing with my fellow drifters I noticed that all of us were using the phrase more frequently.

Knowing that the majority of one's life was completely out of my control was frightening to my Western mind, which thrived in a world of personal responsibility and free will. In reaction to this fear, I embraced the idea that a higher power controlled everything. I began to think that I could not change what happened around me. It was comforting to think that since I had no control, whatever was going to happen would happen no matter what I did. Perhaps I was beginning to understand why the Iraqis thought the way they did. Did everything happen according to God's will after all?

This question came up daily during my time at Drifter Base in Fallujah. While the patrols showed signs of progress, the Iraqis' behavior themselves within the confines of the FOB was more disconcerting than I could've imagined. Specifically, their conduct of the second-most important mission for the New Iraqi Army—guard duty—reminded the drifters of the many months of hard work we had left to do.

Drifter Base had been moved the same day 2nd Company had left the mosque compound to link up with India Company. The 9th Battalion's headquarters took over a position that Kilo Company of 3/5 had occupied for the last month or so, a collection of eight houses that had been confiscated and sealed off from the rest of the city with a flimsy fence line of concertina wire plus a couple of bulldozed piles of dirt and crushed concrete that formed makeshift barriers. A large clearing was situated in the camp's center and acted as the motor pool for most of the Leland trucks, the Nissan pickup trucks, a couple of heavy-duty Russian-made trucks called Razs, and a kitchen trailer that didn't work.

I remember when I returned from India Company's position and drove up to the new drifter base for the first time. I immediately noticed the guard posts. They were small wooden shelters, reinforced haphazardly with sandbags and shaped like irregular blocks, that had been built on the top corners of many of the houses. I could see the barrels of the Iraqi's Russian-made PKC medium machine guns sticking out toward the surrounding city. Two Iraqi soldiers were stirring in each post. That was a good thing. Overall security had been established, I hoped.

It was worrisome, though, that when we drove through one of the gates I saw only one guard and he was sitting down in a plastic chair with his helmet off and his rifle resting comfortably in his lap. He was waving to us as we drove by.

"Where the fuck is your helmet? And where is the other guard?" I yelled out.

He just kept waving. "Salaam Alaikum [Peace be to you]," was all he said in response.

The setup within the wire illustrated the way the Iraqis worked. Third Company, which stayed with the battalion headquarters group and was supposed to be in charge of base security, had seen fit to take possession of three of the houses. The Iraqi battalion commander, Colonel Meghid, had taken the best house available. Was he living in the same building as his American counterpart, Major Lawson, to facilitate the proper level of communication and cooperation? No, of course not. Colonel Meghid needed the biggest house, and it needed to be in the center of the camp. This requirement was indicative of the class system that had existed in the Iraqi military during Saddam's time in power.

Our predecessors, the Army reservist AST members we relieved, had explained to us how the system worked in the old days. The officers were the aristocrats, the upper class, whereas the soldiers were the serfs. The officers simply told the soldiers what to do, and the soldiers did all the work. The Iraqi military did not embrace the concept of hands-on leadership. The idea that any leader must be prepared to do anything he asked his troops to do was as foreign to the Iraqis as equal rights. While I had never doubted the warnings, seeing this aristocratic system in action was shocking.

I watched as Lieutenant Ahmed barked orders at some of the jundees. They responded to him by running off like scared children. When Ahmed caught my stare he smiled, thinking a fellow lieutenant would understand. I shook my head.

Major Ali, I concluded, was virtually clueless. Looking as though he were daydreaming, he stood in the middle as his whole company scattered around him on move-in day. Jundees scurried about, some carrying their bed rolls, others washing their hands and feet with the bottles of water that were supposed to be for drinking. Still another ran into the outside toilet. He too had the requisite water bottle with him. I cringed.

"Hello, Mister. Hello," said a random Iraqi as he walked by. The absurdity I encountered at Drifter Base was only beginning.

Making sure our position was as secure as it could possibly be turned into a full-time job in and of itself. While patrolling added a level of depth to our defense by extending our presence outside the wire and into the surrounding city streets, the way the Iraqis behaved inside the wire threatened that same defense.

For example, the house 2nd Company decided to make a home had one of the base's guard posts positioned on its roof. Thus 2nd Company was responsible for manning that post with two jundees at all times. I had to remind Major Ali on a daily basis to ensure that in fact two jundees were manning the machine-gun post. On occasions when I found two jundees at the post, the guards were usually not manning the machine gun but, rather, leaning over the edge of the roof, unarmed, jabbering on with their friends, who were washing themselves in the courtyard. On these occasions, I had to yell at them and act out what I wanted them to do.

"You," I said, pointing to one, "you sit here." I sat down inside the sandbagged post, facing out toward the city. "You look for wahhabi." I grabbed a hold of the machine gun and swiveled it back and forth, pretending to look for bad guys.

"Ah, Mister, wahhabi, wahhabi." This was all the Iraqi could say that made any sense. Otherwise, I could make out only garbled Arabic.

"Mister, madam? Baby?" His partner was more interested in my family makeup.

"Not now, you fucking idiot. God, what am I saying? You can't even understand me," I yelled out to no one in particular.

"Mister, fiki-fiki?" Was he asking me if I wanted to fuck? I stood there and exhaled. "Insha Allah," I said to the two Iraqis. I shrugged my shoulders and stormed off. I knew they would nod, give the "Yes, yes, Mister," and then go right back to gossiping after I left. My frustration was mounting.

One of the main reasons for this growing frustration was our proximity to the Iraqis. Staff Sergeant Sullivan and I lived in the new house with Major Ali and nearly one hundred jundees. We needed to be nearby to carry out our job: teaching the Iraqis how to organize and conduct combat operations properly and supervising them in the course of those same operations. If necessary, during the times when lives hung in the balance, I needed to be able to take the lead and control the Iraqis when they could not effectively employ themselves in a military manner.

To understand why the Iraqi guards behaved the way they did, one first has to understand the disposition of the forces involved. I will use 2nd Company's house as a microcosm of the situation.

Once Major Ali and the remainder of 2nd Company not staying with India Company of 3/5 had settled into their new house, Staff Sergeant Sullivan and I had to choose a room for ourselves. We chose a room right next to Major Ali's on the top floor of the two-story concrete house. This position would allow us to meet with Ali on a daily basis, map out our operational plans, hear any commotion that went on with the company leadership, and ultimately, keep our fingers on the pulse of the unit.

Our new room was interesting, to say the least. I stood in the doorway for a moment before I moved in, surveying the space. It had once been the room of two little girls. Pictures of them were all over the room and tons of dolls and small dresses were strewn about. They looked like twins, perhaps no older than four years old. They were cute. I imagined the life the room once had, with the two little girls playing dress up with their dolls, laughing, and smiling. I imagined a family in the house, living their lives, raising their children. I imagined a father tucking in his little girls at bedtime, and I imagined the love that was once in the room.

The room had been drastically altered in the last year. Proof of its transformation was everywhere. Bullet holes lined the walls. Most of the girls' clothes were shredded. The dolls had been left in dirty corners. One of the girls' pictures was smashed. In addition, the countless empty pill bottles and used syringes that littered the room provided evidence that the enemy must've used it at some point. The reports of enemy drug use were common, and this scene did nothing to dispel them. We found a teacup with a weird substance coagulated in the bottom of it and a syringe sticking out. The enemy fighters were probably trying to stay as high as possible as they fought. This way, when they were shot, they wouldn't feel anything.

To me, this evidence of drug use signaled that the insurgents were not waging a jihad against us, that the "jihad" was pure propaganda. Didn't drug use conflict with the tenants of their religion? How could they claim to be fighting in the name of Islam and yet be high as a kite as they went off into the afterlife? Would all those virgins care that they were stoned? How about Allah? Were these the kinds of martyrs He was looking for? The enemy seemed to have twisted his religion for their own political goals, not for a high-minded purpose.

Major Ali, however, had no idea what I thinking as he watched us move in next door. He seemed to be pleased with our moving next to him. He smiled, then nodded and grunted something in Arabic that I assumed was his sign of approval. Living with Major Ali was the only way to build the sense of trust and togetherness that would be needed to train and fight with these Iraqis. It was an integral part of the job, and while I already knew I needed to be there, it was reassuring to see that Ali felt the same way. At least, that's how I understood his expression. Of course, he could have been cursing me off, and I wouldn't have been able to tell. Insha Allah.

For the rest of the day, Staff Sergeant Sullivan and I set to packing sandbags into the gaping holes in the room's walls that used to be windows. The idea that a sniper's bullet or an RPG could slip into the room at any moment made us anxious to lodge the sandbags into their places as soon as possible. While we were busy securing our space, the Iraqis decided they had more pressing needs. Instead of hardening their own rooms, they concentrated on setting up television sets and satellite dishes they had stolen from the houses that still stood in the area. That they had left our friendly lines to scavenge did not exactly indicate the sense of professionalism we Americans were working toward. "This is a work in progress. This is a work in progress," I kept telling myself. But, when I saw Major Ali playing with the antenna of his own TV so that he could watch the Arabic version of MTV, I couldn't take it anymore and hid in my own room.

The good thing about our room was that it was on the top floor. It gave us some distance from the jundees who had crammed into the bottom floor. We could still hear their jabbering in the halls, but as long as we kept the door closed, we had relative peace.

The bad thing about our room was that it was on the top floor and thus right below the roof. On the roof was the guard post that was responsible for the security of our corner of Drifter Base. As were the other posts, this post was a wooden shelter reinforced with sandbags to protect the guards from getting shot. It contained the standard PKC medium machine gun and allowed an excellent view of the surrounding buildings. Again, it was supposed to have two Iraqis in it at all time, but we hadn't managed to get this point across yet.

Sullivan and I didn't know what we were in for that first night. We had gone to bed and were resting in our sleeping bags. The jundees had fallen asleep. A UAV droned overhead. All was quiet.

Rat-tat-tat-tat-tat! The guard post above us erupted in a long, loud burst of automatic fire. We both immediately jumped up and geared up. I had the process down to under three minutes, but the staff sergeant, being more experienced, was dressed, armed, and out the door before me. I threw on my flak jacket and Kevlar helmet and grabbed my rifle all in one motion and was out the door right behind him. The hallway was crowded with jundees moving all around in the darkness. A couple of them were startled when I stomped out of the room.

"Amreeki. Amreeki. Hello. Hello. Marine." I had learned to say out loud so that they would hear my English and be reassured I wasn't an enemy infiltrator and shoot me by mistake. We picked up such behaviors to keep ourselves alive among the Iraqis.

"Ah, Mister. Marine good." They kept moving past me. I could hear the click of the safety on one of their AKs. One of the jundees had his rifle pointed at me. I would have to talk to Ali about that in the morning.

Rat-tat-tat-tat-tat! I would have to deal with the continued firing first. Was this another attack? I was going through all the possibilities in my mind. Our house was close to another one that was behind us. Maybe the enemy was trying to sneak into our lines through that back alley. Maybe our guards saw them. Each post had been given a pair of imitation NVGs. They weren't as good as ours, but they worked. Could the Iraqis have seen suspicious activity and reacted appropriately?

I went up the stairs to the roof. It was a chilly night, but I couldn't feel the cold. My blood was pumping hot.

Rat-tat-tat-tat-tat! Another long burst. The muzzle flashes from the machine gun were interfering with my own night vision, sans goggles. Just when my eyes had adjusted, more shooting would temporarily blind me again. What were they shooting at?

Another burst sounded. I could see a couple of red tracers flying from the machine gun. They were like lasers in the night sky. They were traveling south.

Sullivan was standing by the roof's edge, looking for the enemy. He didn't seem to care that he was exposed. He thought he was invincible. I wasn't so sure.

"Staff Sergeant, what are they shooting at?" I yelled out to him above the shooting.

"I don't know, Sir!" he screamed back.

Soon the other guard posts, all of them, started opening up. They all faced different directions to provide all-around security for the camp. So, as a result, when they started shooting they were firing in all directions. Red laser-like flashes went off everywhere. We drifters later called this light show effect "the death blossom," a reference to an obscure B-movie called *The Last Starfighter*.

The whole neighborhood was lit up. Anyone in the immediate vicinity must've been dead by that point. But I still had questions racing through my mind. Were we under a massive attack from the muj? From all directions? Were we in danger of being overrun?

Rat-tat-tat-tat-tat! The guards on our roof, who had started this whole party, kept running through more ammunition. They were shooting south of our position. The bullets started ricocheting off a crumbled building right in front of the post. I could see the tracers going right into the wall, less than fifty meters from where we were standing. I could hear the ricochets whizzing in all directions around us.

"This is ridiculous," I said out loud. We were going to be killed standing up there looking stupid. I rushed into the post and grabbed hold of the crazy Iraqi shooter by the shoulder. "Why are you shooting?" I screamed at him. I couldn't see his face, but his eyes seemed to almost glow in the dark they were so wide and white with fear.

"Wahhabi! Ithnein [two] wahhabi! Mister. Wahhabi!" he repeated over and over again. So, we had two bad guys lurking around our position.

"Mister, Mister, Ithnein wahhabi!" the other guard said in agreement. Two insurgents were out there, and these fine soldiers of the New Iraqi Army were engaging them—I hoped.

"OK. OK. Where did you see them? Wayn wahhabi? Wayn?" I was trying to gather as much information about the threat as possible. Drifter Six, Major Lawson, was going to call me on the radio any minute now, and I would have to provide a detailed report.

"Staff Sergeant, they said they saw two bad guys. Do you see anything?" Sullivan was already scanning the streets. Luckily the moon was providing decent illumination. We should've been able to see anyone moving through the alleys and streets.

"I don't see anything, Sir," he responded.

"Wayn wahhabi?" I repeated to the Iraqi guards. The other posts in the camp were still shooting. The Iraqi jundee was pointing feverishly to a nearby alley. He was rambling on in frenzied Arabic. This was the ultimate in communications breakdown.

"Wait a minute. Wait a minute. Wayn? Wayn wahhabi?" I was confused.

"Wahhabi. Wahhabi. Mister. Ithnein wahhabi." He kept pointing in the same direction as before. There was one major problem: the Iraqi was pointing in a completely different direction from where he had been shooting. It made no sense.

"Why were you shooting to the south if you say the wahhabi were to the west?" In my frustration, I was speaking in English to the Iraqi who knew none. I screamed at him. He looked at me, smiling. I shook my head.

"Wahhabi," I pointed where he had pointed a second ago, west. "Over there. You," I pointed to him, grabbed hold of the machine gun, "Bang, bang, bang," and pretended to be firing the weapon. I was pointing south. "Leish?" The two Iraqis might have understood the word, but they had no idea what I was asking. Either that or, confronted with their own stupidity, they feigned ignorance. "Leish? If you saw the bad guys one way, then why are you shooting in the other direction? Why?"

I received no response. The other posts were dying down now. They must have had no idea what they were shooting at in the first place. Hearing their friends open up, they probably became scared and thought we were all under attack. It was as though they were playing follow the leader. Once one started, the rest had to join in, and when the initial post stopped firing, the rest followed suit again. The machine-gun fire soon ended completely. My anger was still going, however.

"Bad, Jundee. Jundee no good!" I growled at them. I grabbed hold of the machine gun, pulled open the feed cover, and ripped the ammo out. That gun was going to be out of commission for the rest of the night. "Bad, Jundee!" I repeated as if scolding two small children, like the girls whose room we were now sleeping in. I didn't notice the irony until I was back in bed.

I finally gave my report to Drifter Six, who laughed me off the radio. Then I scolded the Iraqis once more, for good measure, before going back to the girls' room to escape the madness. Was that where we were with these Iraqis? Were they our children? While I had no kids back home yet, it seemed as though I had adopted over one hundred in Iraq. Would we Americans have to stay until they had all grown up? I asked this one final question before drifting back off to sleep.

An hour later, the answer came in the form of another burst of machine-gun fire. Sullivan cursed under his breath, dressed in two minutes, and was out the door and on the roof, yelling his head off at the jundees. I was a little slower that second time. There was no need to rush.

The frequency of the Death Blossoms forced me to evaluate the Iraqi guards on the military level. What was the unit's failing that gave rise to random shootings from the Iraqis who sat on watch every night? The answers were the usual pair: a lack of effective leadership and a lack of military discipline at the basic jundee level. This conclusion gave rise to the next question: What could we do to rectify the situation? At first, we tried to address their problem on the local level. We made each adviser group responsible for the guard posts that their respective companies manned. So, when the post on the roof above Sullivan and I erupted, we were to focus on that post and that post alone. If, on another night, the 3rd Company's guards decided they were going to initiate a free-fire eruption, then the two advisers assigned to 3rd Company would have to go to their post and rein in the jundees. This approach worked only for the short-term. Not only did it leave us advisers exhausted from having to constantly address each new Death Blossom, but it also failed to put the responsibility where it should have been in the first place— on the Iraqi leaders.

A new approach was agreed upon soon after we realized this first approach would not do. We had the battalion assemble a battalion guard force. This guard force included soldiers from both 2nd and 3rd companies and even some soldiers from the underdeveloped H&S Company. Once assembled the guard force would be solely responsible for running continual shifts that manned all of the guard posts for Drifter Base. The jundees in the force would do nothing else but stand guard duty.

The plan made sense. If it worked, we would have better control over who was standing duty and the Iraqis would effectively be in charge of their own base's security. A junior Iraqi officer was designated the guard force officer, and he brought with him to the guard force several NCOs who would each supervise one of the three shifts. One unlucky adviser was given the guard force supervisory mission as a collateral duty. I was that adviser.

So, not only was I expected to work directly with Major Ali on anything pertaining to 2nd Company, such as logistics and the day-to-day patrolling of the sector, but I was also supposed to work in close concert with the Iraqi guard force officer. The fact that I had volunteered for the additional duties made me think I was going crazy.

I organized the guard force into three different eight-hour shifts. To facilitate better communication between the Iraqis and myself, I labeled the three shifts as different colors—green, yellow, and red. I used the colors associated with the traffic lights because I thought they were universal. The schedule was drawn up as a big checkerboard with red, yellow, and green rotating duty throughout the week. The plan seemed fairly easy to understand to me, and when I checked up on the guard posts during random times of the day and night, everything seemed to be working accordingly. But I failed again to take into account a second nonmilitary and more perplexing part of the Death Blossom equation: the Iraqis' psychological and cultural makeup.

The same mental devices that gave rise to Insha Allah, the polychronic mind-set, and all the problems of context and personal responsibility could explain why the Iraqis continued to shoot up the night's sky. Even though we had increased the NCO and officer supervision of the guard shifts, the individual jundees continued to exhibit poor fire discipline every time they heard a bump in the night or saw a shadow move. They continued to fire long bursts of automatic weapon fire, and their buddies next to them in the posts would still decide they too had to shoot along with their friend. I wondered if this was an extension of a systemic groupthink. The Iraqi soldiers never seemed to do anything or think anything as mere individuals, at least not in front of their brethren. It was as if they thought they would be left out if they didn't join in the collective actions. They were always actively trying to be part of the tribe, and their idea of a tribe that thought and acted as one. Their unfaltering excuse—"two wahhabi, two wahhabi"—was evidence of this. It was also two, never one, never three. And the same reason was given each and every time a guard fired. And when a guard was scolded for shooting at nothing, he consistently offered the usual excuse of "Insha Allah," thereby avoiding responsibility for his behavior.

I also considered the possibility that the Iraqis might be scared of the dark. While at first I thought this fear was simply the result of a lack of training, I ultimately decided it sprung from something more basic. Something about the evidence convinced me that the problem lay outside the training deficiencies. These shooting barrages never occurred during daylight hours. They happened only in the dead of night, especially on nights with little to no moonlight. The less the Iraqis could see, the more their imaginations created. The more they let their imaginations run wild, the more dangers they drew up. The more dangers they "saw," the more frightened they became. And, as I had already learned, when the Iraqi soldiers became frightened they seemed to respond in only one way: shoot first and ask questions later. The outlook for the guard force was bleak.

Another insult to our effort came when the Iraqi battalion staff, following our initial setup meeting, assigned one of the weakest officers in the battalion to act as the guard force officer. I had never seen the soldier before, but the deer-in-the-headlights-look in his eyes immediately revealed he was in way over his head. In a few weeks, he deserted, and the guard force almost disbanded on the spot.

Following that incident, none other than Lieutenant Ahmed was assigned as the guard force officer. While Ahmed's dictatorial style kept the jundees from leaving, it also guaranteed constant conflicts between Ahmed and the jundees, and the Iraqi battalion staff knew this. Ahmed's difficulties with both the Marines of India Company and his own soldiers were well known.

When the battalion staff chose to replace the deserter with Ahmed, I had the distinct feeling that the Iraqis were not all that interested in seeing the guard force work. This seemed to be a symptom of the classic Iraqi leadership method of undercutting the plan even while nodding in agreement. It had taken some time to convince the staff of the worthiness of our guard force plan. When they saw that we advisers were going to continue to push it, the Iraqis nodded and then immediately set to pull the rug out from under us.

The final insult came when I was forced to decide whether

we should move all of the guard force soldiers into one building within the Drifter Base complex. The reason for doing
this was clear: the Iraqi problem with context. I realized that
the guard force soldiers would become confused if they continued to live with their old units, the soldiers of which had
different responsibilities. They would not understand the context. They would think that if they continued to live with 2nd
Company they were still part of 2nd Company. Thus, to get
them to work together as a unified guard force, they would
have to live together. Unfortunately, no Iraqi leader wanted
to give up one of his cushier buildings. The only building that
remained vacant was located right near Drifter Base's front
gate, its roof was partially collapsed, and the rest of the structure looked like it was going to follow the roof into ruin.

Lacking strong leadership and a suitable house to live in,
the Iraqis on the green, yellow, and red shifts soon strayed
from the plan. I started to find soldiers from one shift going
on duty with their friends on another shift. The entire plan
was doomed.

I learned a new meaning of Insha Allah from this episode.
At the end of my meeting with the battalion staff, when we
were trying to start up the guard force, all the officers nodded in agreement that the guard force was a good idea and a
good plan.

"This is good, no?" I said, looking for reassurance one last
time.

"Insha Allah," they all said in unison.

Given what seemed like a concerted effort to ruin the
guard force, I figured out that sometimes when an Iraqi
said "Insha Allah" he really meant something else: "Go fuck
yourself."

As a result, the Iraqis never stopped shooting at nothing,
and we, like the overwhelmed parents we were, never stopped
scolding them.

7

FORGING BONDS

Overwhelmed, I had already learned, was a state of mind. Whether by relying on training or becoming further infected with Insha Allah fatalism, our AST had learned to cope with the madness. Perhaps, it didn't matter that we were overwhelmed. We weren't going anywhere, and the Iraqis certainly weren't going anywhere either. We were sharing the same space, and we could not get away from them.

Time itself had a strange way of stretching within the confines of Drifter Base. We were living in the polychronic world of our hosts. "A long time" in Iraq was a relative phrase. An entire hour could be spent in one conversation with an Iraqi, and all the pointing and gesturing in the world still wouldn't make him understand that his helmet was on backwards. Just when I solved the problem of jundees washing their feet in streets where sewage water was pooling, I'd find an areef awal, equivalent to a staff NCO, smoking a cigarette while leaning against one of the fully loaded fuel trucks.

In such an environment, we didn't keep time by the ticktock of a watch. We measured it in tasks completed and tasks left undone. We had a never-ending to-do list. Every day was measured by the progress of a nation, one Iraqi at a time.

In this pursuit, I concentrated on further developing a personal relationship with as many Iraqis as possible. I did not spend a lot of time with every single jundee or areef or mulazem, but that didn't necessarily matter. Sharing the same space and fighting for the same cause, I learned, meant to the Iraqis that we were friends. At times, if I merely returned a smile to a random jundee, he would say, "You, Amreeki, my friend." I did not have to say anything to him, I had only to show simple courtesy or respect to forge a bond, at least in his mind. Through moments like this, I learned that, in Iraq, the word *friend* meant many things.

I soon realized friendship in its many forms held potential benefits. With strong enough bonds, with close enough friends, I hoped I would be welcomed into the extended family and become part of the tribe. I knew that once part of the tribe I could expect to be protected and, more important, I could exert greater influence throughout the company. From there, I could better motivate the Iraqi soldiers and prepare them to fight for their own country.

Understanding this equation motivated me even more to forge new bonds with the Iraqis. One important element that aided in this endeavor was the eventual arrival of our first official interpreter. Using the Iraqis who spoke broken English had become less reliable as our operational meetings became more complicated. In this regard, the young man I'll call Snoop was a godsend.

Snoop was handed his nickname as soon as we laid eyes on him. Though he was an Iraqi citizen, he could not only easily pass for an American but also bore an obvious resemblance to the rapper Snoop Dogg. Not to mention, our new interpreter carried himself with the same kind of stoner calm and swagger that the recording artist, known for his fondness for marijuana, did. He was a Sunni from Baghdad whose father was a wealthy civil engineer back in the capital city. He was in college when Operation Iraqi Freedom started and began working with the Americans for reasons still unknown to me. None of his friends knew what he was doing, and if the insurgents ever found out, he would have been killed on the spot.

Once Snoop arrived, the advisers continually fought over his services. Each of us had important tasks to attend to and each one of us made the case that we absolutely needed an interpreter to complete these tasks. Because of both the high demand for his translating skills and the obvious fear for his safety, Snoop slept with the battalion advisers. He was our most important resource, and Major Lawson was not going to let him out of his sight. Unfortunately for Major Lawson, Captain Yamamoto also lived with Snoop.

Captain Yamamoto was in a precarious position. The major was the officer in charge of the team and his main goal was to advise the Iraqi battalion commander and run the team of advisers. Because I was paired with 2nd Company, the captain was the lone officer left to advise the Iraqi battalion staff. The inefficiency of this scenario is obvious: one Marine captain was supposed to advise not only the Iraqi executive officer, but the battalion's operations, logistics, and intelligence officers as well. In short, Captain Yamamoto was expected to make sure the Iraqis could run their own battalion. His was not an enviable position. Thus, Captain Yamamoto was always trying to meet with one Iraqi staff member after another, and once Snoop was brought on board, the captain would unconsciously monopolize his services for his various meetings. Thus, the rest of us had to try to steal Snoop away whenever we could. Poor Snoop was caught in the middle. I'm not sure he ever slept.

"How are you doing today, Snoop?" I said, after I had pried him away from Yamamoto one day. I was intent on understanding the Iraqis better, and I needed him to do this.

"OK, Sir," he replied in a low, heavily accented voice as we walked toward 2nd Company's house. When Snoop walked he sauntered, nice and easy. He had a helmet and flak jacket on, and he even carried an AK for his own protection. But he carried it like he didn't have any intention of ever using it. He thought it looked cool. A cigarette hung on his lip at some impossible angle.

We arrived at the courtyard of 2nd Company's house at prayer time. As soon as civilians started reentering the city, the mosques resumed their daily calls to prayer. I was alarmed when I started to see jundees sitting on cardboard mats on the sidewalk outside the house. The more religious of the Iraqis prayed five times a day. That didn't give them much time to do anything else.

"Why don't they pray inside the courtyard, so they are not out in the open? I don't get it," I said to Snoop.

"Sir, because it is not their house," Snoop replied.

"I don't understand. What do you mean it's not their house? They live in it."

"No, no. It is not their house. The owner, whoever he is, must invite them into his home first. Then they pray inside. But not until invited."

"Oh, now I get it." It was against Islamic tradition to pray in another man's house without his permission. "But, the owner's not coming back. They're just going to keep doing it this way?"

"Yes, Sir."

"But they're going to get shot eventually."

"Insha Allah." There were those words again. They were inescapable.

I decided to put the praying thing on the back burner. I wasn't going to change over a thousand years of tradition in one day, if ever. Instead, I concentrated on new ways to bond with the Iraqis. A simple way, I deduced, to accomplish this goal was to share a meal with Major Ali and his staff.

"Ahmed, I was hoping to join Raaed Ali, you, and the rest of the company leadership for dinner tonight. Would that be alright?" I wasn't really asking Lieutenant Ahmed, but I phrased it that way for his benefit. We had an audience of several jundees watching our body language. I did not want to appear as if I was ordering around their lieutenant, even if that was exactly what I was doing. Diplomacy, I was learning, was all about helping the Iraqis appear strong in public.

"Yes, is OK. I will tell Major Ali that you and staff sergeant come to dinner. Yes?" Ahmed was serious when answering. I think he was honored and happy that the Americans were going to sit down and break bread with his boss and himself. I was definitely scoring points.

"Yes. Definitely. I look forward to it. Shukran." I left, and the jundees from the audience immediately besieged Ahmed with questions. I couldn't make out what they were saying. I just hoped my plan would have the desired effect. I wanted word of my meal with the major to trickle through the ranks of the enlisted and reinforce my standing in the eyes of the entire company.

Dinnertime came with a flurry of activity throughout the house. Iraqis seemed to be spilling out of the walls. A Nissan was backed up into the courtyard to dump supplies of water bottles.

In Fallujah's strangely shaped buildings, the kitchen was the first room one walked into from the front door. The first thing Staff Sergeant Sullivan and I encountered as we entered the house was a stove set up on the side of the wall. The Iraqis had rigged a small propane gas tank to the pipes. Mixing a pair of huge bags of rice and some mystery meat, they made a stew of some sort that bubbled in a giant vat ready to be served. A line snaked in and around the house. As expected, the feeding process was not exactly orderly. Some jundees tried to help their friends cut the line. The obligatory arguments ensued and chaos prevailed.

I could hear the jundees stop their shouting and start whispering to each other as we went by. I could make out "Mulazem Awal" and "Good Marines, zain, zain." I paid the comments no mind. I just wanted the jundees to know that I was going to eat with their company commander and that we were going to sit down as equals.

When we arrived at Major Ali's door, it was open. The room was small, maybe eight feet by six feet. Major Ali and Lieutenant Ahmed had placed two beds to the left against the walls. This was where they slept. To the right, in an apparent attempt at creating some semblance of a company office, the Iraqis had put a metal desk on which were a couple of stacks of paper. I was impressed. They were trying to get their act together. Of course, the papers could have been only a list of those Saddam collaborators in the area that still needed to be killed, but at least the officers were being diligent.

Major Ali was ready to receive us. He was flanked by Ahmed on one side and, surprisingly, Snoop on the other. Apparently, Snoop had beaten us up to the room in anticipation of the feast. Lieutenant Khalil and Lieutenant Jalal, the battalions' other officers who were living with India Company at the time, could not join us for dinner. The room's occupants were rounded out by two jundees named Saaid and Salah. They were a pair I was quickly getting to know by sight. Both were heavyset, overweight by any military standard, with obligatory thick black Saddam moustaches. They were jundees, but the way they walked around and carried themselves suggested they had been NCOs in the old army. None of the other jundees ever clashed with them.

Saaid was Major Ali's personal chauffer. He drove one of the Nissans around whenever Ali had to go somewhere. He was probably responsible for the Nissan in the courtyard. Hell, he was so fat he'd probably have driven from one end of Drifter Base to the other just to avoid any hint of exercise. He wore a black beret sideways across his head.

Salah performed most of the administrative duties for the company. I later saw him writing away at the metal desk, trying to keep accurate records of what was going on in the unit. He always had on a vest that looked like it came from a goat's hide.

Everyone was all smiles.

"Marhaba," I said to the entire gathering.

Each Iraqi in the room greeted us differently. "Hello, Nevarra. Hello Sergeant," said Saaid. Salah said "Hello, Sir" to both the staff sergeant and me. "Hey, that's staff sergeant to you, buddy." Marine staff sergeants were very particular about how people addressed them. Salah didn't understand. Ahmed said "Hello" like a shy boy. Ali smiled the whole time and nodded his head, until he could find the right words in English. "Good . . . morning."

"Ah, very good Inglise. Tisbah Alkhair [Good evening]," I said. I didn't try to correct Ali in front of his subordinates. It would've made him look bad.

"Ah, Tisbah Alnoor," Ali replied, as was customary in his language.

"Hey, Snoop, shlonek?" He laughed at me. He was amused by the interplay between the two peoples.

"Fine, Sir, how are you?" he responded. He was smoking a cigarette as usual.

"Well, I don't know about anyone else, but I'm hungry," Staff Sergeant Sullivan blurted out. He spoke for everyone. I could hear a couple of rumbling stomachs in the crowd. Life in Fallujah had a way of burning off calories at a rapid rate.

A small coffee table stood in the center of the room with plastic plates and utensils on it for everyone. Another jundee, a young one, was in the room, and he seemed to have been assigned the role of man servant for the meal. He filled each plate with food he scooped from the kind of plastic cooler that normally would have kept beer cold back in America.

Everyone sat down. Staff Sergeant Sullivan and I on one of the beds, and Snoop, Ali, and Ahmed on the other. Salah sat at his desk, and Saaid walked around making sure everyone had at least one can of soda and a couple of cucumbers for a snack. I, the highest-ranking guest, was given the first plate. The man servant handed me a plate with a pile of food on it and two big pieces of flat bread that resembled pita. Later, I learned the bread was served with practically every meal. The soda can had the Arabic writing on its side, so I had to look at the pictures of small red strawberries to figure out what flavor it was.

"Shukran," I said to both of the servers. I waited patiently while everyone else was served. Then, I looked at the plate to see what was for dinner. The fact that I was going to eat whatever was on my plate was a given. I was not about to offend Ali and the rest of the company staff. Despite the meager surroundings, this was to be a meal of some international significance. I was not about to make the wrong face or refuse my meal or do anything else that would jeopardize the relationships we drifters were working so hard to develop.

Having said all of that, when I took that first look at what was being served, I seriously considered my options. The plate had a base of sticky, half-cooked white rice. A red, soupy sauce with beans in it had been poured all over the rice. On top of that mound was a big piece of boiled chicken that was colored green.

"Mmmm, looks good. Don't you think, Staff Sergeant?" I was trying to think of a way to excuse myself from the meal. Could I feign sickness? Would they believe it? How could I still make friends without eating the slop that was coagulating around my fork? I turned to Staff Sergeant Sullivan to see how he was handling it.

"Come on, Sir, this is good eats." He was already digging in. I exhaled and took my first bite of the green chicken breast. I could see the Iraqis watching me, looking for my reaction. They were not testing me. They were just concerned about their guest. I bit in and almost puked immediately. Below the strangely colored skin, the meat was cold and almost completely uncooked. With eyes all over me, I kept chewing until the meat was a pulp, and then, taking a deep breath, I finally swallowed. It felt like a giant piece of cold phlegm was sliding down into my stomach. When it hit down there, my stomach almost immediately rebelled. A loud gurgle escaped.

Ahmed smiled, "Good food, yes?" He was chowing down.

"Yes, it is good. Snoop, tell Major Ali that the staff sergeant and I want to thank him for having us for dinner. We appreciate this food and spending time with him." I was putting on a brave face. My insides were tumbling even as I complimented the meal.

Once Snoop finished translating, Ali smiled and nodded in a sign of respect. Every other Iraqi in the room also nodded to themselves. This was not a private conversation, in the least. Every word I spoke was going to be examined, and I was holding my own.

Then, I noticed Major Ali kept looking away from me. Snoop would translate something, Ali would turn to me and respond, then immediately turn to his other side. Ahmed was looking off in the same direction. I followed their eyes and realized a TV was sitting against the wall opposite our semicircle. Although the sound was turned down, the Iraqis in the room were captivated. They were watching Arabic MTV.

"Now, Sir, Major Ali wants to know what we gonna do with the soldiers who are still with the Marines? When are they coming back? How can we give them food and water?" Snoop translated for Ali. The major was referring to Mohammed and the rest of the Iraqis who were living with India Company 3/5.

"Well, tell him that the Marines are feeding and taking care of his men and that they are going stay with them for a couple of weeks. When they are ready, we are going to switch more jundees out with them. We are going to rotate soldiers, so that, eventually, all of 2nd Company will have patrolled with the Marines." I waited for Snoop to translate before I went on. I was happy that Ali seemed concerned about the welfare of his men. I concentrated on eating the flat bread. I was hungry, but my stomach wasn't going to take much more of the uncooked chicken and the red rice soup.

"Major Ali, in the meantime, we have to train and patrol with the soldiers who are still here. We are going to patrol right around our area here." I kept trying to use hand gestures to reinforce my words. I made a big all encompassing circle with both hands to signal that I was talking about Drifter Base. They kept nodding, but I was not sure if they understood or didn't want to hurt my feelings. Snoop kept translating, and I took a sip of the Arabic soda, turning to see what Arabic MTV was all about. It was identical to the American version. There were plenty of scantily clad, young, nubile women shaking their asses to a beat. The sound was low, but I could make out a mixture of belly-dancing tunes and pop beats. It sounded like an updated, electronic form of the sitar and bongo drums.

Snoop finished translating, and I looked to Ali for a reaction. I wanted us to be on the same page. Major Ali, in his typically deferent manner, smiled, nodded, and said, "OK." That was it. Then his eyes turned back to the TV and the shaking booty. I decided not to fight against the tide. The whole room—Iraqis, Americans, and one interpreter—was preoccupied with stuffing their faces and watching half-naked women. I was not going to compete with my business talk. Besides, the main purpose of this meal was to bond on a personal level.

"Snoop, can you ask Major Ali where he's from?" He translated.

"Basra. Basra." Ali answered for himself.

"And is that where your family is?" I had been told never to ask an Iraqi man about his wife or daughters directly. This was not polite in Arabic society. I could only ask about his family in general. If he wanted to talk about his wife or female offspring, he had to bring them up first.

"Madame Basra, baby Basra," Ali said after Snoop finished

his translation. He continued to say something to Snoop, who kept nodding and eating his food.

"Now, Sir, Major Ali, he said he had a son, but he does not know where he is." Snoop said in between bites of flat bread and sips of soda.

"What does he mean? Where is he?" Snoop looked at me, then back to Ali, before he finally uttered the one word, a name, that always seemed to hover around Iraq.

"Saddam," Snoop shrugged and kept eating.

"Saddam," Ali repeated.

"Saddam no good, Nevarra," Saaid shouted out.

"No good," Salah echoed.

I couldn't tell if they were saying that for our benefit or if they actually meant it. I wanted to believe these men were, indeed, happy that Saddam was gone. I wanted to believe they were sitting with me, working with me, for the very reason I was sitting with them—to build up their country. But in too many instances they proved either incapable or unwilling to do just that. Too many jundees just sat around. There was too much focus on TV or batteries or duct tape. Perhaps it was because most of these men had been deprived of so much that they always seemed to want things and they always expected the all-powerful Americans to give those things to them. They didn't seem to understand that we had come here, not with the promise of happiness itself, but with the promise of the right to pursue happiness. It was up to them to do the pursuing. We would only show them the way.

Of course, I didn't say any of this to the men eating dinner with me. I was not going to figure out and change the nature of this entire country and its people all in one meal. We were all going to be there for the long haul.

I tried to eat as much of my meal as possible. I inspected my chicken and looked for the most thoroughly cooked sections; this proved difficult. I picked through the bones and then hid the rest underneath some of the rice. I filled myself up on bread.

The whole room was still watching the music videos. They couldn't take their eyes away from the Arabic women. I had to admit they were pretty. They moved in a very sexual manner. I wondered how the more religious Muslims felt about such displays. I wanted to ask these particular Muslims how the displays of flesh fit into their strict customs dictating the behavior of women. Was this programming a result of Muslims being exposed to Western culture? Was this what had the wahhabis so riled up? I remembered my setting and thought better of bringing up religion and politics with mere acquaintances. Besides, the TV show didn't seem to bother Ahmed.

"Hey, Lieutenant Ahmed, do you have a family back home?" I asked.

"No," he said, a little sadly.

"No madame? No babies?"

"Not yet, no. But soon I go in the home and make a marriage." Snoop was translating this into Arabic for the others. Saaid belted out a hearty laugh from his big belly and said something to Ahmed to which Snoop chuckled.

"What'd he say, Snoop?"

"He said, Sir, that Ahmed is looking for his bride on the television." We all laughed in response.

"I can't blame you, Ahmed, those chicks are looking good to me right about now," said Staff Sergeant Sullivan, smiling through his wrinkled face.

"Yes, this one here, she good," said Ahmed, shyly smiling.

Watching Arabic MTV, I had to hand it to them, the videos all had the same production values, the special effects, the backup dancers, and a marketable, sexy singing star lip-synching for the camera, just as Britney Spears would back home.

"She definitely looks good. Her lips especially." I was trying to get him to open up some more. The more comfortable he felt with us, the better we could work together, obviously.

"Oh, yeah, she looks like she wants to get fucked!" Sullivan said, throwing all diplomatic decorum out the window. I winced. Sex was a tricky subject with the Muslims. Ahmed and Snoop, the only Iraqis who understood what the staff sergeant had said, started to laugh. This only made the other Iraqis more curious. Snoop translated, and the room erupted in more laughter. Apparently, I was wrong about their attitude toward sex.

"Ah, Nevarra, fiki-fiki?" Saaid said, while simulating sexual hip thrusts into the empty air. He looked like a horny cartoon character on speed. His eyes bulged out of their sockets and his tongue wagged almost past his chin. Everyone kept laughing. While we weren't going by the State Department's book on international relations, we were connecting on a basic personal level with our new Iraqi friends, thanks to the staff sergeant. And, in his typical fashion, Sullivan couldn't help but keep going.

"Would you look at those lips, Sir. She looks like she loves the cock, doesn't she?" I was sipping my Arab strawberry soda when he said it and nearly sprayed it all back out into the room. Snoop couldn't contain himself he was laughing so hard.

Ahmed was silent for one long moment. His face turned serious. He was watching the singer intently. I was afraid we had offended him. I was worried we might've lost our first and only chance to establish a personal rapport with the Iraqis. But then the lieutenant opened his mouth.

"All women . . . love . . . the . . . cock!" He said in his thick Iraqi accent.

Amid the raucous laughter that ensued, I sat back to watch the interaction. We had finally broken through. From then on, we could talk to the Iraqi officers as friends. We could work together to build up this company. We would fight together and build up this country one Iraqi at a time. All it took was one Iraqi to show that he was just like any other man—horny.

"We might actually succeed," I said to myself and took another bite of my uncooked chicken. I discreetly spit it into my hand a second later.

PLAK-A-BO, CHI, TOBACCO, AND PORN

I lived in the city of Fallujah for two and a half months. It is important to understand that the events already documented occurred one on top of the other. Patrols were conducted, the guard force was assembled, meals were shared, and cultural miscommunications all happened during the same period. The city welcomed back more and more citizens each day. The Marines of 3/5 continued to conduct combat operations. The Iraqis of the 9th Battalion continued to try to get their act together, and our team of drifters continued to put ourselves on the line day in and day out to help them become a more effective fighting force. As a result, our reality constantly evolved, and ever-present was the threat of danger and mission failure—not to mention the possibility that all of us advisers might go insane.

Our reality kept shifting from day to day, moment to moment. We were living in an alien world, and it is instructive to examine this setting, which embodied the surreal qualities of our experience, and the effects it had on all of us.

Some of the strangeness was, of course, simple cultural difference. For example, no matter how many times I explained that it was not safe, more Iraqis prayed in the streets every day. When they prayed, they did not wear their helmets or flak jackets. They stood on rectangular pieces of cardboard with their feet bare, their eyes closed, and their palms flat, open, and held out and up. All of the men faced the same direction, south or southwest, toward Mecca, Saudi Arabia, the holiest of cities for Muslims. In unison, they kneeled, spoke words under their breath and to themselves, and then bowed. When praying in this manner, the men were easy targets for any snipers hiding in the neighborhood and they didn't care. If they were shot, so be it, they would say. It would only happen if God willed it. Insha Allah. The philosophy invaded all their lives, even matters of life and death.

While the praying could be explained by culture, other occurrences could not. One day I was standing in the center of Drifter Base. The street that ran north to south through the base was also the main avenue to get in and out of the base. That day the street had been turned into a makeshift soccer field. Fifteen jundees were kicking a soccer ball around. They were not wearing their helmets or flak jackets. They did not have their weapons with them. They were playing out in the open. When I yelled out to them to stop, they looked at me like hurt children. When I took the ball away, some of them looked as if they wanted to kill me. My right index finger was straight and off the trigger of my weapon during this entire episode. My thumb was waiting to flick downward and take the weapon off safe.

Danger was present in Fallujah at all times and came from both outside the wire of Drifter Base and within that same perimeter. We were surrounded—but by whom exactly? We continued to wonder who these men we were living with were. Were the Iraqis serious people? Were they aware of their own situation? Were they dangerous by design? I didn't think so, and this led me to an even more disconcerting conclusion: they simply didn't know any better. Too many occurrences reinforced this idea.

I remember seeing two jundees riding bicycles around the camp one day. One of them was ringing a little bell on his bike's handlebars. He didn't seem to care that he was riding a purple bike with daisies on it.

"Mister, no danger, no wahhabi," he said to me with a big grin. He was the areef who had the negligent discharge during our first patrol with the Marines. He was so worthless to the Marines of India Company that they sent him back to us.

"No, mu zain [no good]," I said in my best scolding tone, but both the areef and his companion continued to ride. The riding lasted until Drifter Six, Major Lawson, personally grabbed the bikes, punctured the tires with his K-bar knife, and threw them into one of the pools of raw sewage. The Iraqis almost cried.

Another time, I saw an Iraqi standing in the courtyard with his buddy, practicing bayonet thrusts with his AK rifle. This would have been encouraging, except he was practicing his thrusts with his fellow jundee as the target. The jundee who almost had his chest sliced open smiled the whole time. When I saw the tip of the blade come within only a few inches from the other's chest, I went over to stop the shenanigans. As I started to scold the jundee, I noticed a cigarette sticking out of the AK's muzzle. The two Iraqis were laughing. It was all a big joke to them.

On another occasion, I heard a random shot ring out from inside the 2nd Company's house. A second later, I saw two jundees carrying a third Iraqi out of the house. His foot had a big, bloody hole in it. One of his toes was missing. They explained that the jundee had been cleaning his rifle, while it was still loaded. He had pulled the trigger and shot himself.

"Better not take him to your doctor," I told Ahmed. The Iraqis had their own doctor, Diktor Moussa, who was worthless. He had studied anesthesiology in Jordan, and somehow that training had made him qualified to be the 9th Battalion's doctor.

"Plak-A-Bo is not going to take care of that wound either," I said out loud.

Ahmed laughed. He didn't know what I was talking about. "Jundee mu zain," he said.

"No shit," I thought but didn't say.

Plak-A-Bo was something I was introduced to after a few new Americans joined us to support our team of advisers. They were three young Marines whom Captain Yamamoto secretly grabbed from a nearby unit. A Navy corpsman assigned to the AST advising the 9th Battalion's higher headquarters also thought we could use them. Doc Simpson, the corpsman, was old and portly and had a whisker moustache that made him look like a catfish. His life's ambition was to become a professional bass fisherman.

One night two jundees approached Doc and started rambling. Snoop translated: "Sir, he said this soldier hurt his foot. He said he needs your special cream?"

"What special cream?" we asked. Doc smiled and giggled to himself. He walked over to his medical bag and started rummaging through all the different supplies.

"A-ha. Here it is." He pulled out a nondescript white plastic bottle with white medical tape wrapped around it so that we couldn't read the label.

"I call it Plak-A-Bo." Doc turned the bottle around, and sure enough, there was the word spelled out in black magic marker.

"Plak-A-Bo? I don't get it," said a lance corporal, one of the new Marines, stumped.

"Oh no, you're not serious," I said. I had a feeling I knew what was going on.

Doc walked over to the Iraqi and started applying the mystery cream to his "injured" foot.

"Plak-A-Bo. Otherwise known as placebo," I said to the room. Everyone instantly understood and erupted in laughter. Even Snoop was chuckling. The Iraqi soldiers had no idea what was going on. The one was just happy Doc was giving him the powerful medical cream. The Iraqi smiled and was already putting pressure back on his "injured" foot as if the Plak-A-Bo was having an immediate effect. It was magical.

"What kind of cream is it actually?" I asked.

"Sunscreen," Doc, the great medicine man of Fallujah, said matter-of-factly. He had single-handedly set medical science back a few hundred years. "You laugh, Sir, but these Iraqis thank me all the time. It's either the cream or pills. Any kind of pills. They don't care what kind. They figure it's coming from an American it must be advanced. Hell, just last month an Iraqi came by complaining of a headache. I gave him two laxatives and told him to call me in the morning."

While more laughter ensued, we understood that such jokes, made at the expense of the Iraqis, were the means for us Americans to cope with this alien world. We were being bombarded by strange scenarios, and the only way to deal with some of the harder to explain phenomena was through sarcastic humor.

Certain scenes, however, would prove humorous only upon later reflection. One situation that seemed funny only after it happened was dealing with a particular, seriously injured Iraqi. According to the reports, a sandbag had fallen on the Iraqi's head while he was watching TV. He had a concussion and possible brain damage. Let me repeat this: a sandbag fell on his head. This was not a usual combat casualty.

Someone had to evacuate the jundee to the medical facilities at Camp Fallujah immediately. Since I was the only drifter who had deployed with night-vision goggles, I volunteered to drive, but I was a bit concerned. I had never driven a Humvee with NVGs on. And that was not my only fear. The battalion commander of 3/5 had issued standing orders that all convoys in the city have at least two up-armored vehicles involved in each movement. Unfortunately, we drifters were so few and so spread out we had to ride in one lone Humvee.

Barreling down the roads in the city, I tried to ignore the facts that I was driving with no night training and that we were riding through the center of Fallujah by ourselves. Not to mention, an Iraqi soldier was puking his guts out in the backseat. Add to the scene a soundtrack, courtesy of a CD player someone had hooked up in the back of the vehicle, and the absurd picture becomes more complete. "Like a drifter, I was born . . . " Whitesnake blared out. The layers of strangeness fell one on top of the other.

We dropped the jundee off at Bravo Surgical in Camp Fallujah, and the Americans flew him out to Baghdad by helicopter the same night. We never learned what happened to him. It was as if Baghdad's bureaucracy swallowed him up whole. Weeks later the Iraqis were still asking us about the guy with the sandbag on his head, and we were still shrugging our shoulders and shaking our heads. We had no clue.

Something else we had limited knowledge of was how the city, and our mission, would change as more and more of Fallujah's original inhabitants were let back in. The civilians were trickling into the city, returning to their homes to pick up the pieces. Many of their houses had been looted, some by our soldiers. The TVs that kept popping up in the rooms in Drifter Base were evidence of this.

At one point the civilians came to the gates of Drifter Base looking for help, and our jundees, in response, started giving away their own food. One day, I caught the guards handing a whole box of water bottles to some strangers on the other side of the concertina wire. I yelled at them, but they didn't understand that we couldn't start a soup kitchen at the entrance to Drifter Base. They said, "OK, Mister, OK," waited for me to leave, and then turned around to start giving away more of our supplies.

On another day, an old Iraqi man arrived at the front gate. Second Company was living in his old house. He knew he could not have it back, but he wanted to get some of his belongings, so we let him in. When he looked around, he could see the house was looted of most of the valuables. Much of the furniture was gone. Jundees were sleeping all about. I didn't need an interpreter to tell me his heart was breaking. Even the Iraqis couldn't meet the old man's pleading eyes.

The old man grabbed a radio and some old family pictures, and then we escorted him out of the base. He walked slowly down the street. When he got to the intersection, he turned around and looked back at us one final time. He didn't say anything. His eyes told the whole story of a life interrupted. At least he still had a life, I thought to myself. The danger to the civilians was still real, despite the Marines' control of the city. Sometimes, the danger didn't even come from the insurgents.

When nighttime guard duty brought another episode of all-out shooting to Drifter Base, a representative for the community came to the base's front gate the next day. He came to plead his neighborhood's case. "Please, Mister, can you make the soldiers stop shooting us?" he asked me through Snoop's translation. He stood with his little daughter holding onto his leg, pleading with his eyes. I didn't have any answers for him. I wanted to point to the Iraqi soldiers and then to him to indicate they'd be better off talking directly but thought better of it. Instead we all tried to convey the neighborhood's message to the Iraqi leadership. The thinking was that perhaps, if the Iraqis knew the danger their uncontrolled shooting posed to their fellow Iraqis now living in the area, they would be more careful about what they did when they were on watch at night.

In response to our plea for greater vigilance, we received only more absurdity. One night I was on the roof of Major Lawson's house, checking out a report of gunfire in the nearby streets. I looked all around Drifter Base. Nothing was in our immediate vicinity. Then I noticed a glow emanating from the roof of 2nd Company's house.

"Drifter Two Alpha, this is Drifter Two," I used my handheld radio to call Staff Sergeant Sullivan, who was in our room in the house in question.

"This is Drifter Two Alpha, send it."

"Roger. There is a glow coming from your roof there. Can you check it out?"

"Wait one."

A minute went by, and I kept my gaze on the roof. The glow was made of soft white light that occasionally flickered. There was a guard post on that roof responsible for security in that corner of the base, and the glow was giving away the post's location.

"Drifter Two, this is Two Alpha."

"This is Two. Send it."

"Roger. The guards have set up a satellite dish and are watching TV."

"I copy. Please kindly inform them that they are idiots."

"Roger."

The glow disappeared and was replaced by yelling and cursing, in English.

Finally, on another night, Captain Yamamoto reached his quota of insanity. During a usual Iraqi nighttime gunfire erup-tion, he ran up to the roof and shot off a red star cluster flare into the air above the center of Drifter Base. Every Iraqi dropped whatever they were doing and simply stared up into the sky at the pretty red lights.

"Wow, Mister," were the only words I heard them say. They stared as though they were children who had never before seen fireworks.

Speaking of fireworks, New Year's Eve was a blast, of sorts. Explosions erupted across the city at midnight. White star parachute flares burst into the night's sky. We all went to the roof to watch the fireworks, and eventually both the enemy and our Iraqi friends decided they had to get in on the festivities. Red tracers crisscrossed in the air like lasers.

Later that night, Colonel Klink, Major Lawson's boss, ordered the major to report down the road to the colonel's position to discuss an urgent matter. First Sergeant Smith and Gunny Babineaux joined the major for the short trip. Hours passed before they returned to Drifter Base. Something was up. All three of them were deathly quiet. The first sergeant was walking with a slight limp. Gunny Babineaux was the quietist he had ever been. He sat down and looked straight ahead, like a statue.

Gunny had been the driver. Apparently, he was not as good a driver as he said he was. He was spooked by a burst of red tracers in the air and lost sight of the road. He plowed right into a concrete divider and flipped the Humvee clear over. The first sergeant was in the turret at the time and was thrown fifty feet from the vehicle. The Humvee landed on its back, right outside Colonel Klink's position. Miraculously, no one was seriously hurt. The first sergeant was going to be bruised for a while, however.

"Not to make light of this, but what did Colonel Klink want in the first place?" I asked, after the major finished telling the story.

"Oh, yeah, that's the best part." The major paused for effect. "He wanted to discuss the leave policy for the Iraqis."

The major did not have to add another word. Klink had put peoples' lives at risk so that he could talk about how we were going to let the Iraqis go on vacation.

"Common sense is an uncommon virtue," I muttered. The first sergeant snorted. It was an old Marine saying, and it had never been more appropriate. Apparently, the Iraqis hadn't cornered the market on stupidity just yet.

At some point, Marine engineers built wooden outhouses, called Turkish shitters, for the Iraqis at Drifter Base. The shitters were wooden shelters with holes in the floor placed over a hole dug into the ground. After a few weeks we had to dig new holes and move the wooden shelter. While this seemed a good setup at first, I quickly realized the Turkish shitters were placed too far away from 2nd Company's house for them to be used by our soldiers. In addition, the one toilet in 2nd Company's house, a porcelain hole in the ground, did not flush. Of course, that didn't stop the entire Iraqi company from using it. As a result, a pile of human feces continued to grow by the day to well over two feet high. The flies were so bloated and obese from their fecal feast, they could hardly move through the air. A pile of dirty water bottles, from the water the Iraqis used to clean their asses, rose next to the toilet. It amazed me that someone could actually walk in, see the giant pile, and then decide, "Yep, this looks like a good place to go." The stench overpowered the entire courtyard.

We Americans were only slightly better on the sanitation front. Engineers dug a trench for us to urinate in, a three-by-eight-foot hole in the ground that was supposed to be filled with gravel to soak up copious amounts of urine. We never managed to fill in the gravel, so it soon became a giant pool of yellow.

For whatever reason, the engineers dug the latrine right behind the house the battalion AST members lived in. It was centrally located, yes, but it was right out in the open. The entire neighborhood could see us pissing each day. Aside from the embarrassment, there was also an element of danger. We were completely exposed to sniper fire. At night, the scary situation was even worse. I remember standing there one night when it was pitch-black. I couldn't see anything. I knew I was hitting my mark only because I could hear my stream splashing in the pool. It occurred to me that I could be kidnapped at any moment. I was all alone. From that night forward the trench became know as "the Scary Pisser." Urinate at your own risk.

Such conditions were definitely taking a toll on our sanity. The two 3rd Company advisers decided that our Drifter Base collection of houses resembled a group of college fraternity houses. It was Fallujah's version of frat row. The advisers had come up with names for the three houses that the Americans lived in. Second Company's house was dubbed Tri-Lam, or Lamda Lamda Lamda, from *Revenge of the Nerds*. The house with Major Lawson and the rest of the battalion AST members was called Delta Muj, a play on the sorority Delta Mu. Third Company's house became known as Kappa Omega Kappa, KOK for short.

Such high jinks proved the isolation was getting to us all. But nothing was going to change. Our operations only intensified. More patrols were conducted on a daily basis. We were working the Iraqis hard. With more civilians on the streets, there came more threats. Occasionally a car came down the road near the base, and children continually stopped by, asking for candy. Were they lookouts for the insurgents returning to the city? We never knew.

"Mister, Mister, chocolat, chocolat," they said, smiling until we ran out of candy. Then they stomped off angry and unsatisfied. We were forced to mix with the civilians more and more, to spread word of the coming elections, to hand out propaganda, and to look for information about potential enemy targets.

While we were out on one particular patrol, a car came speeding down the road. The driver didn't see us right away. Or maybe he did. We thought it might be a car bomb. I raised my rifle. The car continued its approach. I placed my finger on the trigger and took my weapon off safe. I focused the red-dot scope on the driver.

Bang! Bang! Bang! An Iraqi shot a three-round burst. This time it was the right thing to do. He shot into the ground in front of the car, bringing the vehicle to a screeching halt. It was as if the driver had just noticed us. My sight never left the driver's heart. We looked at the car's other occupants. They were the man's entire family, a wife and three kids. Lieutenant Jalal, back from India Company and acting patrol leader, was on top of things. He screamed at the man in Arabic. I didn't need to understand the words. I knew he was telling him he almost got his whole family killed.

Such incidents kept teasing me. Not all of our Iraqis were crazy or incompetent, obviously. Certain individuals were downright excellent military men. I visited the Iraqis who were living with India Company 3/5 to check on one of those all-stars in particular: Mohammed. When I arrived, I could tell that the Iraqis were in good spirits and had bonded with the Marines. Mohammed, of course, was the star of the show. Everyone, both American and Iraqi, liked him. He went out on patrol and controlled his Iraqis easily. The Marines already trusted him.

When Mohammed saw me, he smiled broadly and looked at me like I was his long lost father. He gave me a standard Iraqi salute. I was flattered by the show of respect.

"Hello, Sir."

"Well, hello to you too, Mohammed. Shlonek?"

"Is good."

"Are they feeding you? Taking care of you?"

"Oh, yes. Is good." We started walking together.

"And how 'bout the patrols? How are they going?"

"Very good. I go on patrol and look for the wahhabis. I want to find wahhabi. I want to kill wahhabi."

"Ha. Me too, Mohammed. Me too."

"Is there anything I can bring you? Do you have enough chi? Food?" I asked.

"Chi is good. Food, plenty of food." Nothing in the world seemed to bother him.

Just then, out of nowhere, a yellow brick came raining down from the blue sky and hit Mohammed smack dab on the top of his head. Thud.

"Oh, is OK, is OK." Mohammed tried to play it off. He had a smile on his face, but his eyes were wincing in obvious pain. I looked up to see where the brick projectile had come from. Two Marines were throwing more bricks off the top of the roof. I had no idea why. Mohammed sat down. It was a few seconds before the blood started to pour out from a huge gash in Mohammed's scalp and down his face.

"Mohammed, are you OK?" I asked, genuinely concerned. Plus, I couldn't have my best jundee lost to such a stupid accident.

"No, no. Never you mind. Never you mind." He tried to play it off again. "Never you mind. Never you mind," Mohammed repeated himself. It was as if he felt guilty for getting hit and bleeding, like it was his fault for making a mess and being rude and disrupting everyone's day. He looked ashamed. The Iraqis were such strange, interesting, and often endearing people, I thought. Subsequent dealings with them did not change my mind.

The strange nature of our interactions with the Iraqis extended to daily language exchanges. For example, one morning, an alarm clock went off in one of the Iraqi rooms next door to mine. This was the third morning in a row that my sleep had been cut short by the booming of "Allah Akbar [God is great]." I stormed into the room. Everyone in it was sleeping through the alarm. I grabbed hold of the clock, which was a small white plastic version of a mosque, and shook it in front of a jundee's face until he woke up.

"Mu zain! No more Allah Akbar!"

"OK, Mister, OK." He took the clock from me and turned it off.

"OK. Sabbah Alkhair." I waved and quickly left.

"Hello, Mister," the Iraqi replied, nonsensically.

Five times a day, calls to prayer washed over the entire city. "Allah Akbar. Allah Akbar." Over and over again. The tones were hypnotic. I wondered if they were part of a mass brainwashing effort, which in turn coaxed me to consider the similar hypnotic tactics of other organized religions. But I didn't have time to tackle such heady issues. Instead, I focused on trying to make sense of the miscommunications that were becoming too commonplace between the Iraqis and us drifters.

"Mister, Mister, chi? Chi?" asked a jundee, holding out a small teacup on one particular morning. He was sitting in the courtyard with a few of his buddies, and I didn't want to offend them. So, I took the cup, which was more like a shot glass, and chugged the heavily sugared tea. They smiled then poured another cup before I could refuse.

"To the new Iraq," I made a toast. They didn't understand a word but went along with it anyway. We all chugged our cups of chi.

"Ah, Mister, good chi, good," three of them said at once and over top of one another. Before I knew it, my chi cup was refilled yet again. They all watched and waited for me to drink.

"Good chi, good," they chorused again. It was probably the only English these particular jundees knew.

"Shukran. Sabbah Alkhair," I said and left before I could be forced to drink anymore. The chi was already working on me.

"Hello, Mister, hello," they replied.

Did they just say "hello"? I wasn't sure I'd heard them correctly. I was already feeling warm and fuzzy all over. My heart was pounding against my ribs. I was sweating profusely. My thoughts were rapid and confused.

"Good-bye, Jundees," I said.

"Hello." They waved and turned away from me.

On a later occasion, when I was walking around at night, I passed a jundee.

"Good morning, Mister," he said in his best English. It was pitch black out.

I felt like I was living in the twilight zone. Black was white; up was down. The effect of such exchanges reinforced the sense of otherworldliness we drifters felt. Even though our basic exchanges with the Iraqis were merely cultural misunderstandings, they contributed to the advisers' life, which was now well outside the normal combat configuration. "See the enemy, shoot the enemy" scenarios did not exist in our world. There was only social confusion and cultural isolation.

The confusion and anger was not felt only by the advisers. While most of the Iraqis had prior experience in Saddam's military, the New Iraqi Army, the IFF, was a completely different animal. All of the Iraqi soldiers were still trying to learn how to even get along with one another on a daily basis. We Americans were not the only ones struggling to define the rules of the new Iraq.

During one exchange, I learned that Salah, the administrative force within 2nd Company, was not getting along with Lieutenant Ahmed. In fact, he hated Ahmed. Using Snoop to translate during an informal conversation with Salah and several other jundees, I found out that Salah felt so strongly about the lieutenant that he was plotting to kill him. I understood the roots of the hatred. Ahmed was a tyrant. He didn't lead. He simply barked orders. He sat around and told others what to do. Salah, in contrast, was a hard worker. He kept the records for the company and provided its only semblance of administrative organization. During the course of our talk, he threatened to quit the New Iraqi Army altogether, which would have been a disaster organization-wise. I tried to talk him out of it.

While struggling to convince Salah that sticking it out with 2nd Company and the rest of 9th Battalion was worth it, I noticed the Iraqis had a hookah pipe sitting in the center of the room. They were smoking the flavored tobacco, which was popular throughout the Middle East. Deciding to be social, I approached the pipe to suck down some smoke. None of the Iraqis warned me about how concentrated the tobacco was. It was flavored orange, but that didn't prevent it from searing my lungs. My eyes teared up, and I coughed all the smoke out in gulps. Although Salah was busy trying to state his case for assassinating an officer, I couldn't pay him any attention. I was too busy turning green. I felt like I was going to die. The insurgents weren't going to kill me; the Iraqi soldiers were. At least that's how I felt as I staggered from that smoke-filled room.

My time in Fallujah continued on like that. A blend of menace and humor lingered in the air at all times. I never knew which side of the coin would turn up. Even during serious meetings, the Iraqis' absurdities revealed themselves. At one of the battalion staff meetings, I noticed that one particular jundee always served as a servant. He was fat and old and had only two cracked, yellow teeth in his entire mouth. His name was Hussein, and his job seemed to entail serving only the Iraqi battalion commander, Lieutenant Colonel Mehgid.

Hussein was always snooping around the American areas. He had a thick moustache that twitched as if he was sniffing for something.

"What do you want there, Hussein?" asked the first sergeant, who had bonded with the fat old guy. Each time Hussein came by the first sergeant gave him some batteries or some candy, anything to make him go away. But Hussein kept coming back for more.

"Uhhhh . . . fiki-fiki?" Hussein asked, wearing his big toothless grin. He pretended like he was flipping the pages of a book.

"Oh, I see. You want a magazine." The first sergeant went over to a pile, picked out an issue of *Maxim*, and put it into Hussein's hands. To the Iraqis *Maxim* and *FHM* were akin to hardcore porn.

Beginning with those initial trade-offs, porn became a good negotiating tool. Some of us used it to get the jundees to do work: clean your room and I'll give you this issue of *FHM*. The Iraqis looked at the pictures of the women and went crazy. They sat there in groups with giant smiles stuck onto their faces. Sex was a universal need. This concept made sense to us Americans to some degree. Was it possible that through porn we were starting to understand the way the Iraqis thought and behaved? Were we making sense of this insane world? Maybe we were simply trying to find some common ground, a common humanity with the Iraqis.

Either way, the elections were approaching and so too was word of the Iraqi leave policy. We knew the challenges would keep coming, though there were some signs of progress. Our Iraqis were getting better at planning and preparing for the patrols. They were gathering intelligence from the locals and putting an Iraqi face on our operations. Most of them even started to use the Turkish shitters regularly. Was life in Fallujah getting any better? None of us knew for sure. I just knew that if all else failed, we would still have plenty of chi, tobacco, and porn. And, sometimes, that was enough.

9

THE MAIN EFFORT

Life in Fallujah reached its logical conclusion when democratic elections arrived. It was time for our main effort. By the time discussion of the main effort began, I was keenly aware of the differences between the two cultures and the ramifications these differences would have for our mission. The idea of two different worlds—one Iraqi and one American—was reinforced everyday, whether through the way the two groups acted in a military unit or how they viewed the wider world around them. The contrasts were startling. As an adviser, I knew, I was adrift in between the two worlds. I was an observer. I watched what happened on the yin side and then what other, completely opposite things, happened on the yang side. The dichotomy was real. The two words, "Insha Allah," were just one initial example. This example was soon joined by "main effort" and "leave policy."

Democratic elections, the first of their kind in Iraq since the fall of Saddam, were approaching. Since the desired end state of Operation Iraqi Freedom was a free, sovereign, and democratic Iraq, the main effort was any operation that would help the Iraqis ultimately govern themselves. The words applied not only to the elections but also to our adviser mission. Once a democratic Iraqi government was in place, it would need to provide security for the country. That was where the New Iraqi Army would come into play. On a personal level, given these considerations, I could surmise only that my AST, the drifters, was at the forefront of the main effort for the entire war.

"As they stand up, we will stand down" was the common refrain of policymakers back in Washington, D.C. President George W. Bush and Secretary of State Donald Rumsfeld said as much in speeches given right before we deployed to Fallujah.

Forget for a moment all the events, such as the unarmored Nissan pickup ride, that have already been examined that undercut the notion that we advisers were the main effort. Instead let's focus on the one aspect that no one took into account during this entire mission: the Iraqis. What did the Iraqis consider their main effort?

The answer to this question came during one of our drifter meetings in the form of two simple words: leave policy. While those two words, along with Insha Allah, quickly became a running joke among us drifters, the events that transpired as a result of this effort were anything but funny.

The new policy could be summed up as follows: We were occupying a battle position in the center of Fallujah. We were trying to turn a ragtag group of Iraqis into a professional military capable of combating and defeating an insurgency that threatened their entire country. Incredibly, in the middle of all of this, someone from our higher headquarters decided we should let the Iraqi soldiers go on vacation.

"Sir, who the hell came up with this plan?" I was probably a little out of line when I asked this, but judging from the looks from the rest of the team assembled for the meeting, I was asking the one question everyone wanted answered.

"Colonel Mehgid has been talking about it for a few days now. Then he got word from his boss, the brigade general—I don't know his name—and he told him they were going to leave in a day or two. So, that's where we're at." Major Lawson didn't like the answers himself.

"Yes, but, who was it that decided to let them go out on leave in the first place. I think that is the question we all should be asking. Who was that person?" Gunny Babineaux asked. He had a nervous tick that became exaggerated the more agitated he was. The leave policy simply didn't compute for him.

He blinked twenty-five times in between sentences. It was unnerving.

"Well, I think the order came down from the Ministry of Defense," Captain Yamamoto answered.

"But, who is advising that guy?" Babineaux replied. He couldn't let go.

"What do you mean?" Major Lawson asked, getting annoyed.

"I mean, there has to be an American advising that guy in the Ministry of Defense. How come he isn't advising him not to send his units out on leave? That's the crux of this matter. That's who we have to get a hold of." If Babineaux thought we had a direct line to President Bush, he would have called up to complain.

"Listen, I don't know who that guy is, and I don't really care. We really don't have any say in this anyway. This is an Iraqi deal." The major didn't need to discuss the matter any further. We were following orders, and that was that.

"So, I guess we are not actually in charge of them, are we?" It took the first sergeant, and his twenty-plus years of experience, to put it out there point-blank.

"Right. We are here as advisers. We are not actually in command of the Iraqis," Yamamoto said. "Now, that's not to say that we don't use our influence and force of will to allow the Iraqis to think we are in charge. But, really, all we're doing is trying to use the Jedi mind trick to shape them from within."

"What you're really saying is that the inmates are running the asylum," I said, cutting through all the chatter. "The only difference is they don't realize it yet. Right? So, what happens when they start picking up on that fact? Where does that leave us?" Everyone in the room fell silent. The answer was too obvious to be stated.

During that uncomfortable silence, I had another revelation. The AST was not just a small group of military advisers but a microcosm of the overall American war effort in Iraq. We advisers had good intentions, we worked hard to accomplish our mission, and we were good at what we did. However, we did not have enough troops for our task. We were told we had a critical job—training the Iraqi military—but we had almost no support from the other American units. Whoever came up with the brilliant idea of training Iraq's indigenous forces so that we could eventually hand the country over, seriously miscalculated the amount of time and number of resources that the task would require. Finally, and most important, no one bothered to take into consideration the nature or motivations of the Iraqi people themselves. No one had asked them if they could build a successful military or even if they wanted to do this in the first place.

Now that the Iraqis' main focus was turning away from finding and killing the enemy and toward going on vacation, I sensed they had their own ideas about the direction of their country and these ideas had nothing to do with establishing a free and sovereign government.

"OK. Now that it's settled that we're fucked, how is this leave thing going to go down?" Staff Sergeant Sullivan often remained quiet during the drifter group meetings, but at this point even he was tiring of the back and forth. The circus was going on the road regardless, and he wanted to know where it was headed.

"I still have to sit down with Colonel Mehgid and hammer out the details. But, we can assume they're going to go back down to Numeniya. They're mostly from the south, and that will probably be their rally point. From there, your guess is as good as mine." The major finished just as the Iraqi Leland trucks roared to life outside in Drifter Base's main parking area.

When we arrived outside, the Iraqis were on autopilot. I had never seen them so motivated. They were moving with a purpose that I had never seen in them, even when we had been shot at.

"Maybe we should promise leave more often?" I cracked.

"I'm just wondering how many are going to come back," Lawson replied. I hadn't even thought about the possibility of desertion. Rumors were rampant that most of our jundees were there only for the paycheck. This made sense given the state of Iraq's economy. There were few other ways to make a living, except for selling bootleg movies.

"That's the one aspect about this that I understand," Yamamoto continued.

An Iraqi soldier, or Jundee, prays on the sidewalk in Fallujah.

First moments in Fallujah.

A squad of Iraqis with its embedded American advisers exits the "friendly" lines of Camp Habbaniyah to begin a security patrol in the surrounding areas.

Notice the rather relaxed posture . . . two Iraqi soldiers are supposed to be conducting a vehicle checkpoint.

The commandant of the Marine Corps, Gen. Michael Hagee, pays a personal visit to the Iraqi battalion and the Marine advisers.

Lieutenant Colonel Meghid addresses his troops, his American partners, and the press.

Two Iraqi Jundees pose for the camera.

The Jundee Mohammed is seen here with the author (right). Mohammed is easily the best soldier in the entire battalion.

Efforts of cultural communication.

Two Jundees (not pictured) try to cook the overly caffeinated and heavily sugared tea called chi, but instead start a forest fire on base.

Finding enemy caches by the side of the road.

Iraqi and U.S. soldiers search a house.

A young Iraqi Jundee passes a group of Iraqi civilians during a patrol in Fallujah.

The author on a cordon and search mission.

During the January 2005 elections in Fallujah violence is kept to a minimum and people wait in long lines to cast their votes for a new government.

In an attempt to win the hearts and minds of the local populace, an Iraqi sergeant, or areef, *hands out candy to a young girl while members of her family watch.*

"What's that?"

"Well, you see, there is no banking system here and the jundees are paid in cash. So there's no other way to get the money back to their families." I had to admit this was a good point. Still, there had to be a better way of transferring money to the soldiers' families than losing a good portion of our combat forces to a paid vacation.

"How many are going on leave at a time?" I asked.

"I'm sure the major will talk to Colonel Mehgid and try and keep the numbers down. But it's going to be at least a quarter of the battalion. Then, you've got to think, what happens when the next rotation goes out and the first one hasn't come back yet? Then what?" Yamamoto was making too much sense. It was bothering me.

"Then, Sir, we're going to be down under 50 percent of our combat power. That's what." The first sergeant had been standing within earshot, smoking a cigarette. He didn't have to say how he felt. The disgust was on his face, plain for all the world to see.

A Leland truck with over forty jundees packed into it, rocked up and down through the potholes and passed by us.

"Mister, Mister, we go famly. Good, Mister, good," one of the Iraqis called out.

"Hello, hello, Mister. We go see famly," an Iraqi from the next Leland truck in line shouted out. When one talked, another always had to join in. Bang! Bang! Bang! The Iraqi pointed his AK up into the air, pulled the trigger, and let loose a burst that flew off in the sky. Where the bullets went I had no idea.

Bang! Another one joined in. The tribe mentality was kicking in.

"Stop!" Yamamoto shouted. "Stop!" Another six gunshots greeted his pleas. He turned to me and asked, "What's the Arabic word for stop?"

"Awgif," I answered.

"Awgif!" He tried to scream above the gunfire, which was still spreading from jundee to jundee.

"Ah, Mister, awgif, awgif," replied a jundee, before squeezing off a few more rounds. Soon, the shooting was out of control. It was not like the nighttime shooting. That shooting came out of fear of the dark and the unknown. This shooting came out of a sense of celebration. The Iraqis were all so happy to be going on vacation, they couldn't contain their excitement.

"It's like a hundred premature ejaculations!" I shouted to Captain Yamamoto over the shots. He wasn't finding any humor in the situation. As an artillery officer, he had a keen understanding of trajectory and the effect of gravity on a projectile. He knew the bullets going up were, of course, eventually going to come down. The Iraqis apparently had not learned about Newton and the apple falling off the tree.

Captain Yamamoto stomped toward the nearest Iraqi truck.

"Hello, hello, Mister, Mister." None of the Iraqis were taking him seriously.

"La! La! La! La! [No! No! No! No!]" he shouted. I taught him that word too.

The jundees kept smiling. A couple of shots rang out from the back of a Nissan that was next in the line. Captain Yamamoto brought his rifle to his cheek and pointed it at the Iraqi who had fired the shots.

"No, Mister, no," the Iraqi's arms quickly came off his weapon. Now they were listening to him. It took a good twenty minutes for the rest of us to give the evil eyes to the remainder of the Iraqis and end the pointless celebratory firing.

The convoy, which was more than ten vehicles long, lined up on the main road through Drifter Base. An American Humvee was in the lead. A couple of us drifters were ordered to escort the Iraqis back to EFIC. From there the convoy would link up with the other Iraqis from the rest of the brigade. Colonel Klink would be at EFIC to coordinate this. Once all the Iraqis were gathered up, a new, bigger convoy would set out from EFIC and travel to Numeniya. There, all the Iraqis' weapons and uniforms would be put in storage. Each Iraqi would take a set of civilian clothes with them, change into them at Numeniya, then simply walk off the base, and somehow make his way to whatever town he called home.

This was the sophisticated plan drawn up by the Iraqis and their American advisers. The Iraqis were going to walk off an American base, in civilian clothes, unarmed, and go right into town, where they hoped to meet their friends or family, instead of the enemy.

As I watched the Iraqi trucks lurch through the front gate and out of sight, it became obvious that the Iraqis had found their own version of the main effort—the mission they deemed the most important, the mission they put the most energy into planning and seeing through to completion. The emphasis placed on the leave policy signaled, in my mind, the end of any illusions I still had about what I was doing in Fallujah. I was pissing into the wind.

Two hours after the leave convoy left, we received word of an incident.

"The convoy was hit by an IED," Major Lawson told us.

"How are our boys?" the first sergeant asked, referring to the drifters who had been sent with the Iraqis. The Americans were, understandably, his first priority.

"They're fine. Apparently, Colonel Mehgid's vehicle was the one that was hit. He has at least a shattered arm. Two jundees were killed and a lieutenant might have lost a leg. Reports are coming in sketchy. But, that's the latest," the major said. No one knew what else to say. Until, that is, my sarcasm got the better of me.

"Sir, does this mean they might be ready to rethink their leave policy?" Despite the seriousness of the situation, no one could contain a laugh.

The Iraqis continued on to Numeniya and then to the freedom of leave. Colonel Mehgid had to have surgery on his arm and was going to be on medical leave for at least a month. We were down one Iraqi battalion commander and his replacement definitely didn't seem up to the task. Thus we were left scratching our heads. The leave policy had come and thrown the entire battalion off course. True to our call signs, we were all drifting.

"Why did they have to go home now?" I asked out loud.

Snoop offered a new explanation: "Now, Sir, it is very important for Muslim men to be with their families."

"I understand that, but do you think we Americans don't want to be with our families? Hell, I'd love to go home every month." The Ministry of Defense had issued an official policy that each jundee was entitled to seven days of leave for every month they were in the army. So, every month they were supposed to get a week off. How were we going to run an army if the soldiers kept leaving?

"Sir, I know what you mean, but in Islam, a man has to be with his wife within a certain number of days. Otherwise he is bad husband in the eyes of Allah," Snoop continued, in explanation.

"So, you're saying, according to Islam, a guy has to, I mean, he absolutely has to, fuck his wife every so often. Otherwise he is a sinner?" I asked.

"Yes, Sir. It is so," Snoop answered.

"Hell, where can I sign up? Is it too late to convert?" I joked.

Unfortunately, the joke was on us. Before the first convoy had returned a whole new batch of leave-thirsty Iraqis were pulling together another convoy. Before we knew it, all six Americans remained on the base with fewer than half the Iraqis in the entire battalion. Combat operations came to a halt. Whatever progress we had made through constant patrolling and interacting with the civilians in the city was wiped away in a few days.

Finally, two days later than expected, the first group returned to Drifter Base. And gunfire erupted again when the Iraqis who made it back in one piece became so happy to see their friends again that they squeezed their triggers in excitement.

"We need to put an end to this, for God's sake," Captain Yamamoto said.

"Insha Allah, Sir," I replied. I was in danger of going native at that point.

We spent a lot of time attempting to explain the physics involved when bullets are shot into the air before the celebratory shooting was brought under control. Staff Sergeant Sullivan and I even tried calling a 2nd Company formation to drill it into the Iraqis' heads that what went up eventually came down—possibly right on top of someone's head. Sullivan would throw a handful of rocks up into the air above the formation, just to watch the Iraqi's reactions when those same rocks came down. While they didn't like getting hit in the heads, Staff Sergeant was able to make his point. To punctuate the lesson, Lieutenant Ahmed approached the formation a second after Sullivan finished with a jundee draped over his shoulder. The jundee had a dark red gash across the side of his head with blood pouring out. He wobbled and groaned and needed help standing.

"Don't tell me this jundee got shot in the head during the celebrating gunfire!" I shouted.

Ahmed grudgingly nodded, "Yes."

"I told you so!" Sullivan's wrinkled face was creased with lines of continued frustration, and he threw more rocks in the air for good measure.

While the celebratory gunfire eventually came under control, the effect of the Iraqi main effort, the leave policy, was far-reaching for our mission. Shortly after the initial leave convoy returned to Drifter Base, we tallied the returning soldiers. Out of nearly one hundred and twenty Iraqis that went out, only seventy came back. The numbers didn't lie. The Iraqi main effort was crippling our best efforts to get the battalion up to a solid level of competency. When I considered the fast approach of the election, I knew we had a serious problem on our hands.

The January 2005 elections were to be the first truly democratic elections in the history of the country. We planned to use the Iraqi units as the lead forces on missions we conducted during the run-up to the day of voting. We were going to "put an Iraqi face on it" and thereby take advantage of the Iraqi forces' ability to speak to the people, to spread the word about the coming election, and to inspire confidence in the new government that was going to be formed based on the election results. Further, if violence increased as election day approached, like we expected, we wanted the insurgents to attack their fellow Iraqis so they couldn't say they were simply fighting the infidel American occupiers.

Unfortunately, by the time the entire battalion rotated through leave time, we lost one-quarter of the unit. Those who deserted were either sick of being told what to do as a member of the military, had legitimate family concerns they had to tend to, or were threatened with death by the insurgents for working with the Americans. Our combat strength was drastically depleted at the worst possible time for such a reduction in power—election time. Every day we were supposed to move the Iraqis one step closer to being ready to take the lead. Every day was supposed to build on the last. Instead, the days became a series of steps backward.

What kind of place was Iraq? I asked myself. How far backward could one country go? How long would this go on? How in the world did we think this place was ready for democracy?

I sat down with Major Ali to go over all the details and preparations for the elections. We were going to increase our patrols and have the jundees hand out fliers and pamphlets that explained how the election would work. In addition, the Iraqis would provide security for the polling places.

As Snoop translated my meeting with Major Ali, I noticed that the major kept looking over his shoulder. He was not paying attention to me at all. Instead, he was focused on a toy, a small robot bird that sat on a perch hanging from the ceiling. When a door slammed in the adjacent hallway, the bird suddenly sprung into motion: Tweet-tweet-tweet! The bird proceeded to make electronic noises that sounded to me like a nursery rhyme. Ali's face was aglow. He was fascinated. The thought of elections was the farthest thing from his mind.

"Oh, yeah, you guys are definitely ready for democracy," I quipped.

Regardless of whether the Iraqis were ready for democracy, they were going to get it. The U.S. president was making the elections the centerpiece of his strategic picture in Iraq. Those of us on the ground were tasked with making this strategic vision a reality, and doing so was going to be easier said than done. The president could make all the speeches he wanted about the Iraqis' innate thirst for freedom, but living among them, I had trouble seeing this thirst. Most of the jundees didn't know there was going to be a vote in the coming days. Even when we told them that they could vote, most refused. Maybe they thought Election Day was some kind of trick, or perhaps they feared the unknown just as they feared the dark. Regardless, we used the jundees as a barometer for the Fallujan population as a whole. If our own soldiers weren't sure what was going on, how could we expect a solid turnout?

To rectify this, we embarked on a big public relations offensive. We conducted numerous propaganda patrols right up to the day before the elections. Lieutenant Jalal was the patrol leader for the final patrol. By this point, I had already been on close to thirty foot patrols and we regularly conducted patrols with only two Americans and at least ten Iraqis. The Iraqi fatalism was actually of some use to us when coping with the threat of snipers and IEDs on the patrols. I could walk through Fallujah, waiting to get shot at, and think if I was hit, I could do nothing about it. If the enemy missed, then we would find him and kill him. In the meantime, I just walked.

"Bad boys, bad boys, whacha gonna do? Whacha gonna do when they come for you? Bad boys," I started singing out loud during that final patrol. We were like cops on the beat. Too bad the combination of improper American planning and the desertions from the Iraqi main effort had robbed us of the number of cops we needed to finish the job. Still, in spite of the numerical limitations, we were showing our presence to the people, trying to make them feel safe. Our beat was getting busier by the day, too. All the civilians were back in their neighborhoods. The goal was to have the whole city reopened in time for the elections, and that goal was met. But there were some problems: the people didn't have much to come back to, and supplies—food, water, fuel for the generators, gas for their vehicles, etc.—were scarce.

"Mister, Mister, chocolat, chocolat." A group of at least twenty little Iraqi children approached our patrol. By now, we came prepared for such occurrences. Jalal had designated one of his jundees as the "candy-giver-outer." The jundee, I think his name was Motham, walked around with his pockets bulging out. He stuffed hundreds of pieces of hard candy and chocolate into them. As soon as he pulled a couple of pieces out, the horde of children rushed over to surround him. Dozens of short arms reached up as Motham dangled the candy tantalizingly out of reach.

"Chocolat, chocolat." They kept repeating the chant. They were like rabid scavengers, driven crazy by the scent of sugar in the air. I exchanged a smile with Jalal and he ordered Motham to relent and give in to the horde's demands. Motham started throwing some of the candy, and the kids chased it down, scooped it up, and returned for more. They were insatiable.

I turned my attention to the children's parents. The grown-ups congregated outside their houses or on street corners. Sometimes they grabbed plastic chairs, sat down, and sipped chi for hours. They were our real targets.

"Salaam Alaikum," I said and waved to them. I made sure I used my right hand, not the shit hand, and waved to them.

"Asalaam Alaikum," they responded and waved back, some of them more halfheartedly than others. I looked to Jalal, and he nodded, understanding. Our mission was not only to show our faces and our presence in the community, it was to spread word of the vote that was going to take place the next day.

Jalal walked over to a group of four men on one corner and handed them the pamphlets that 3/5 had issued to us. The pamphlets were designed to educate the Iraqis on the nuts and bolts of the election process: how they would vote, what forms of identification were required, where the polling places were, etc. I watched the exchange between Jalal and the Iraqi civilians. Although I couldn't understand what they were saying, I had become a master at reading body language. Jalal was doing his best to put on a good face for the election. He told me before, through Snoop, that he had no intention of actually voting.

"Why not?" I asked him.

He shrugged and gave the usual answer, "Insha Allah."

But now, he was encouraging the civilians to vote, or at least, I hoped he was. Jalal handed out more pamphlets as more Iraqi men came over to see what all the commotion was. All Iraqis seemed to love congregating. Judging by the faces of many of the Iraqi men, they were unsure about the whole democratic process. They had questioning eyes and kept reading and rereading the pieces of paper in their hands. The idea of democracy didn't seem to translate between the two worlds. How do you explain to someone who has never tasted freedom that they can actually choose their new leaders?

I was reminded of the dichotomy between the Iraqi and the American ways. Could the two ever come together in a meaningful way? The process of bringing democracy to a country previously ruled by a despot was definitely messy, and once again, I was in the middle watching it all unfold. As an observer, I took a digital camera from my cargo pocket and focused the lens in on one of the jundees handing out candy to a little girl. I snapped a quick picture. It was a positive image for the new Iraq: the new Iraqi Army giving back to the Iraqi people.

I hoped we would have more positive images to capture as we continued on through the city, which was bustling with a new life. Fruit stands were popping up at the intersections and cars were filling the main avenues. Large groups of people gathered at every main intersection. Women, dressed in black burkas, carried food on the tops of their heads. A young boy rode by on a small carriage pulled by a tired-looking donkey.

We, ten Iraqi soldiers and two Marines, strode through the masses. We were symbols of Iraq's new reality. We were a curiosity. The civilians stopped and watched us move by them. I couldn't read their thoughts, but I wanted to make sure I controlled what they saw. The civilians needed to see the jundees acting diligently in their duties.

The soldiers were talking to each group of civilians we came across, passing out the information and discussing the election. They posted signs on the walls announcing the election. They were doing a good job of spreading the word and even had a list of the couple hundred candidates people could vote for.

An older gentleman approached our formation. Jalal started talking to him. He handed Jalal and some of the other jundees a few cards that looked like business cards. Jalal smiled and said "Shukran" to the man. Jalal then walked over to me and handed over the card. There was a picture of another man on it. "Election . . . bacher" was all Jalal could say. He didn't speak any English. I knew *bacher* meant "tomorrow." Jalal kept pointing to the man in the picture on the card. I finally figured it out. The man on the card was one of the candidates in the election tomorrow. The man who was handing out the cards was a political volunteer working to get the other guy elected. Amazing. It was just like back home in the United States.

"Maybe these people are going to get the hang of this election thing after all," I said aloud. Staff Sergeant Sullivan snorted. He remained unconvinced.

Our patrol wound through Fallujah's labyrinthine streets. Everywhere we went, crowds of hungry children and curious groups of adults greeted us. Anticipation hung in the air. Maybe I was imagining it, but I thought I felt a sense of hope too. Iraq had a way of teasing and tormenting, of always holding promise just out of reach. One day, like the day the Iraqis went home on leave, the frustration of working with them would boil over and all would seem lost. The next day, some sign of progress would restore my belief in the overall effort. Election Day was one of those times of progress.

Despite the Iraqis' focus on vacation, and the resulting desertions, once the elections arrived, the soldiers seemed genuinely engaged in the process. I wasn't sure whether this enthusiasm was out of simple curiosity or whether they were beginning to understand our American idea of the main effort. Did they finally realize that we were there to help them govern and protect themselves? Did they understand the strategic sequence that was about to unfold?

We Americans were trying to put in place an elected government so that we could disband the Coalition Provisional Authority and turn over sovereignty to the new Iraqi government. We hoped that this momentous event would act as a turning point for our anti-insurgency campaign. We also hoped that if the Iraqi people saw that Americans were not in Iraq to occupy but rather to liberate, then the enemy's resolve would weaken and the silent majority, which had so far sat on the sidelines, would strengthen. While this plan made sense to me, I was never sure that the soldiers of the Iraqi 9th Battalion understood. Were their political leaders in Baghdad communicating the significance of Election Day to them?

On Election Day, the symbolic or strategic significance mattered less than the nuts and bolts. Jolan Park was the main polling place in our sector. It was normally a site for humanitarian assistance but was turned into a heavily fortified voting center. It had to be heavily fortified because of the nature of the main threat for that day: a car bomb at the polling place. When large groups of people gather at a specific place and at a specifc time, the potential for a catastrophic attack is obviously huge. The enemy could deter more civilians from voting if they could render a significant number of casualties. If too few people voted the election's results would be called into question, and the entire process would be invalidated.

I went to the Jolan Park to supervise the way our Iraqis were used on the day of voting. I felt like the soldiers were our children who were trying to walk out on their own for the first time. Standing on the roof of a building in the center of the complex, I surveyed the whole operation. All the voters had to pass through one main gate. Our Iraqi jundees were primarily being employed at this gate. They were in charge of searching everyone who came into the complex. They used metal-detecting wands, standard personnel search techniques, and their common language ability to make sure none of the Iraqis civilians who were let in were of the suspicious sort.

The Marines of India Company remained in charge of the entire operation, but they kept out of sight as much as possible. They were on the roof with thermal sights, sniper rifles pointed at the main gate, and binoculars pointing in every other direction. I borrowed a set of binos and looked at the main gate. I could make out one Iraqi soldier who seemed to be directing the rest. It came as no surprise when I finally recognized his face.

"It's Mohammed!" I said, handing the binos over to Captain Yamamoto.

"Yeah, Mohammed's the shit. We just let him do his thing and take care of the others," a Marine lieutenant said.

"Yep, that's him, the finest soldier in the Iraqi Army," Captain Yamamoto said.

I beamed like a proud parent. I watched Mohammed make sure the other jundees searched everyone properly. Once done with the search, the civilians moved one by one through a clearing until they reached the end of a long line. The line, the voting line, snaked its way through aisles of concertina wire and fences. The Iraqi civilians waited, some of them for hours, to cross through the main gate, only to wait still more time to finally enter the polling place. The polling area itself was nothing but a small, one-story concrete square. I was told the actual polls were stalls with thin cardboard squares for walls. Once the Iraqi civilians made it into the polling area, they provided proper documentation, dipped their thumbs in purple ink, and stamped their votes into the history books.

I watched the line of voters ebb and flow. An Iraqi came out of the polling place, looked up at us Marines and made eye contact with me.

"Mister, Good Bush, Good Bush. Shukran. Shukran," he shouted.

Was democracy actually being born right in front of our eyes? It was too soon to tell, but the early returns were positive. The actual returns came in two weeks after the election. Each polling place's votes were taken by armed guard and someone from the Ministry of the Interior, who supervised the actual voting, on a cross-country trip to, I presumed, Baghdad for counting.

After I returned to Drifter Base from the polling place on Election Day, I sat in a room with many of 2nd Company's jundees who were watching coverage of the election on an Iraqi TV network. The similarities of the Iraqi election coverage to the U.S. election coverage, back in November 2004, were startling. I didn't understand a word of what the Iraqis on TV were saying, and I didn't have to. We watched a studio show with a male and a female anchor. They showed early exit polling results with graphs and charts detailing the different percentages tallied for each candidate. Then they cut to a reporter who was live on the scene of one of the polling places, giving a report of what the election was like on the ground. The entire production seemed directly lifted from CBS, NBC, or ABC.

The news programs were reporting scattered violence throughout the country. But, despite the reports, the Iraqis were still venturing out to vote. The news showed a smoldering car and, right alongside of it, a line of people waiting to vote. The people looked at the wreckage but paid it no mind. It was not going to stop them from exercising their new rights. Even in the face of the enemy's fire, out from the ashes, they were going to rise.

Was it the rebirth of a nation? I wasn't sure. I wanted to believe in what I saw, but I couldn't help but wonder, would our jundees remember this day the next time they went out on leave?

A QUESTION OF LEADERSHIP

Despite the good feelings engendered by the election results, Iraq's reconstruction was clearly still in its infancy. The development of the New Iraqi Army, in particular, remained a work in progress. As in all works in progress, we advisers were forced to reevaluate the nature of our relationship with our Iraqi counterparts during each stage of the deployment. We had to figure out what worked and what didn't work. At one point, Major Lawson asked us for feedback about how we could improve the effectiveness of our interactions with the Iraqi IIF battalion. The intent of his request was clear: if we could improve our communication with and oversight of the Iraqi battalion leadership, we could likely improve the battalion's overall operational effectiveness.

Our experiences up to this point had supported this calculation. For example, the rocket attack on 2nd Company's position in the mosque and the ensuing Iraqi reaction during our first few hours in Fallujah exposed two critical deficiencies. First, the Iraqi jundees were not prepared for combat, likely because of improper initial training. Second, and more damning, the Iraqi leadership failed to act in a manner befitting their placement as leaders within the battalion. Almost to a man, the Iraqi staff NCOs and officers demonstrated a complete inability to control their men and provide sound judgment and leadership during a crisis. This deficiency reared its head time and time again.

More evidence of the Iraqi leadership's deficiencies came that same day, after the rocket attack, when I suggested to Major Ali a course of action I thought might be prudent.

"Major Ali, Raed Ali, we need to make sure no wahhabis are in the area around our position," I said. I was using Ahmed to translate, and he was staring blankly at me. He didn't want to admit he didn't understand. He was waiting for me to repeat myself.

"We have to check for bad guys in the buildings around us," I said. I used a lot of hand gestures to make my points, and I thought this was working. Major Ali and the others were nodding and talking to each other. They were excited. It looked like they were making plans. Ahmed turned away from the frenzied Iraqi conversation to tell us Americans what they had come up with: "We will patrol the buildings." He gestured to the area around us.

"Good. Tell Raed Ali that I think this is a good plan," I responded. Then I sat back and watched as Ali, Ahmed, and the rest of the company leadership stirred up the jundees. The courtyard erupted into chaos as the entire company seemed to mobilize all at once. Jundees were running around trying to put on their gear. A few forgot their weapons and had to go back for them. Some reported to the formation wearing full battle gear but with flip-flop sandals on their feet. Others wore bandannas instead of helmets. Still others ran around with loaded RPGs on their shoulders. I cringed at the sight.

Major Ali and the other officers were yelling and shouting and pointing in all directions. They somehow kicked and cajoled the jundees into a formation that took up the whole courtyard. Then, all of a sudden, the Iraqis were on the move. Before I knew what was going on, Major Ali was leading his company out the front gates. The *entire* company was leaving. Almost all one hundred men were haphazardly marching out of the gate and into the dangerous city streets. Save for a few guards manning the machine-gun posts, Staff Sergeants Tewilliger and Turner and I were the only men left in our mosque battle position. I quickly realized that this was what Ali and Ahmed meant when they said a patrol of the area. I made a mental note to talk to them about their definition of patrol.

The problems that resulted from the core leadership deficiencies continued in the weeks following that first full day in Fallujah. We were faced with countless scenarios that required a steady and strong Iraqi leader to step up and take charge. Too few times did that actually happen.

The reasons for this deficiency were varied. Of course the Iraqis' lack of proper training was a contributing factor. The Iraqis' psychology and cultural beliefs were another major factor. The main question for our group of advisers was, what could we do to change the way the Iraqis provided leadership?

To answer this fundamental question, as posed by Major Lawson, I first examined the evidence I had gathered during my time in Fallujah. It was damning. The Iraqis did not follow sound military doctrine. Their officers and senior NCOs did not exhibit the expected qualities of true leaders, which in turn hurt troop morale and degraded the unit's overall effectiveness. This lack of effectiveness seeped right down to the individual basic jundees, who did not act in a professional military manner.

Additionally, the only time that the Iraqis tried to act professionally was when one or more of us American advisers was in their presence. If we stood and watched them as they conducted an accountability formation, the Iraqi officers would notice and take special care to try to get an accurate count. If an American wasn't present, they would allow their soldiers to mill about in a gaggle and make up a number. When the Iraqis were on guard duty and they saw us Americans watching, they exhibited perfect behavior. They sat in their posts, alert, with helmets and flaks on and weapons at the ready. If we disappeared out of sight for a while, by the time we returned to check on them they would have their helmets and flaks off and their weapons leaning against the post and they'd be lounging in lawn chairs. As if they were children who had been caught by their disapproving parents, the Iraqis would jump up and put their gear back on as soon as we approached. This pattern repeated over and over again.

The Iraqis' childlike behavior extended all the way up the chain of command. For example, when the battalion executive officer didn't show up at a battalion staff meeting one day, we went looking for him. We found him sitting in his private room watching TV off a satellite dish he had had his men steal from one of the abandoned houses next to our firm base. This sort of dereliction of duty required our constant vigilance and, in the process, exposed one of the major weaknesses of our team dynamic: lack of American manpower.

The ten-man AST was simply too small to engage all of the appropriate Iraqi leaders at the same time. Thus, we were forced to wear multiple hats and quickly found ourselves spread way too thin. For example, in our original disposition we had only two advisers for the three line companies. Major Lawson advised the Iraqi battalion commander, and First Sergeant Smith advised his enlisted counterpart, an Iraqi sergeant major who didn't seem like he wanted to be there. That left one captain and one staff sergeant to work with the entire battalion staff. So, Captain Yamamoto was left trying to advise the operations officer, the intelligence officer, and the logistics officer. All of them! And, remember, Captain Yamamoto was an artilleryman by trade, and his understanding of the inner functions of an infantry battalion, which is what the 9th was supposed to be, was limited.

Even our setup with two advisers per company was fraught with problems of manpower. The two advisers could start to develop a relationship with the company commander and his senior enlisted, but who was going to develop the individual platoons? Who was supervising them? Who was advising the individual Iraqi platoon commanders? No one. All of this responsibility fell on the shoulders of the same two advisers who were busy trying to get the company commander to act professionally. So, each adviser was forced to take on the task of developing every level of leadership throughout the unit.

Consider the Iraqis the soft parts of a human body: the skin, the muscles, and the organs. Now consider the American advisers the more rigid part: the bones. As the bones, we were there to support the rest of the body. With the number of advisers originally deployed, the body was missing too many bones and was falling in on itself as a result. We needed more bones. It was that simple.

In retrospect I see three possible courses of action (COAs) that could have achieved this more rigid structure:

COA #1: Simply add more Marine advisers to each AST attached to the Iraqi battalions.

COA #2: Have the adjacent American military unit provide the advisers instead of creating ASTs sourced through individual augments. The advisers from the adjacent unit would attach to the leadership of the Iraqi battalion and help facilitate a tight partnership between the two.

COA #3: Eliminate the advisers altogether. Have two units—one American, one Iraqi—completely marry up so that all soldiers live and work side by side in everything they do.

Obviously, each approach has pros and cons. First, let's eliminate COA #3 as being too much too soon. The American forces would never have completely embraced such an approach, especially so soon after the second Battle of Fallujah. The Iraqis probably wouldn't have wanted to go that route either. While eliminating the middle men had a certain logic, the cultural differences between the two units would have been simply too great to facilitate efficient cooperation. Also, because security vetting of the individual Iraqi jundees was limited, the potential for insurgent infiltration was great. This would pose a serious security problem for the American forces. For example, would the Iraqis be allowed near the American Ammunition Supply Point? Probably not.

The two remaining courses of action are more practical. They both recognize the need for an increase in the number of advisers. With more advisers, an AST would have a bigger footprint in an Iraqi battalion and, thus, more influence over the Iraqis. The added benefit of increasing the number of advisers would be increased personal security of the AST members; any imbedded force greater than ten would have been preferable because it would have had a more adequate number of weapons and watchful eyes for protection.

To further explain the manpower additions I have recommended, let's breakdown the requirements, as I saw them, of a standard Iraqi infantry battalion. The battalion would include the three line companies, an H&S company, and the battalion staff. (At the time we didn't have enough heavy weapons to consider an Iraqi weapons company.) So, how far down the hierarchy would you push the advisers? At a bare minimum, advisers have to go down to the platoon level. Thus, each platoon commander, or platoon leader as the Iraqis called them, would be assigned a single U.S. adviser. This would be in addition to the advisers assigned to each company commander. Furthermore, the battalion staff needed to be covered. The administration, intelligence, operations, logistics, and communications staffs each had to have at least one U.S. adviser to turn to for counsel. Plus there was the medical shop: the doctor assigned to the battalion would probably require a U.S. Navy corpsman to advise him on the soldiers' medical care. Finally, the Iraqi battalion commander and the Iraqi sergeant major should both have dedicated advisers. While I was in Iraq, Major Lawson directly advised Lieutenant Colonel Meghid, and First Sergeant Smith directly advised the Iraqi sergeant major Haider. In my scenario, the American officer would advise the Iraqi officer, and the American staff NCO would advise the Iraqi senior enlisted man.

Adding up all of these advisers for three platoons per company and four companies per battalion, we see the total number of advisers required for a standard Iraqi battalion was twenty-four. If we considered standing up a weapons company, then the total would be twenty-eight. Without a weapons company, the number of advisers necessary was more than double the number of advisers assigned, and with a weapons company, the number of advisers necessary was almost triple the original AST number of ten.

These numbers brought new concerns into the equation. How would we be able to source the necessary manpower requirement? Would we pull in more individual augmentees, like ourselves, from the operating forces back in the United States? What effect would this practice have on the operational readiness of the affected U.S. forces? Or, as in COA #2, should the entire adviser team be sourced from the American unit directly adjacent to the Iraqi battalion? Remember, the Iraqis were not supposed to operate on their own within the battle space. They were supposed to be working alongside an American battalion.

At the time, when we were still in Fallujah and in the early stages of our time with the Iraqis, I was under the impression that the adjacent American unit was better suited for the mission. Later experiences tempered that assessment, but my initial impression could be correct under certain conditions.

The most important aspect of teaming up an American unit with a similar-size Iraqi unit was the level of commitment on both sides to making the partnership work. The Iraqis had to be willing to work with the Americans. They had to be willing to learn from the Americans as well. The Americans, for their part, had to believe that what they were doing was in the best interest of accomplishing the mission. The Americans had to be willing to give up some of their men to advise the Iraqis directly, and they also had to take the time to meet with the Iraqi leadership throughout all phases of training, planning, and operating.

This willingness to help the Iraqis was critical for the success of COA #2. Whereas our AST was formed for the express purpose of embedding ourselves within an Iraqi battalion and going to war with them to protect their country from insurgents, the soldiers or Marines of adjacent American units believed that many of the Iraqi soldiers *were* the insurgents. This difference in mind-sets gave me pause before recommending COA #2 over COA #1. The only way for COA #2 to work was to convince the adjacent American units in the field that it was vital to our mission in Iraq for them to partner up with Iraqi units in the New Iraqi Army. If we couldn't convince the Americans to work seriously with the Iraqis, the Iraqis would no longer benefit from the training and assistance we could provide them.

Through greater coverage, discipline and professionalism could be instilled, especially in the Iraqi leaders. Only with discipline, professionalism, and commitment could the Iraqis prepare to provide security for their country.

Unfortunately, the concept of Insha Allah continued to hinder our pursuit of Iraqi professionalism. How could an Iraqi become more professional if he believed that the way to do so was not through hard work but through prayer? And how could we, as Westerners who didn't speak the language or fully understand the culture, break through and instill the required work ethic? As infidels who didn't believe in Allah, how could we tell them how to run their military? The only way to provide adequate training for the Iraqis was to keep at it with perseverance, patience, and, of course, more advisers.

STRATEGIC PARENTS

It was obvious to everyone on the AST that we needed more advisers to accomplish our mission in Iraq. In fact, it was probably true that we needed more troops to succeed in the whole effort of the occupation following the fall of Saddam Hussein. The more troops, the better. It was that simple.

However, more advisers would not have effectively dealt with the main problem underlying the New Iraqi Army as I saw it following my time in Fallujah: the cultural anomalies of Iraq. The Iraqi soldiers' behavior—namely, their lack of professionalism and discipline—could not simply have been the result of a failure of training and poor leadership. These factors no doubt played an enormously important role in the continuing difficulties, but they did not explain them to their core. In fact, I came to believe that the explanation was much more devastating for our overall ambitions in the country. I felt I had to further explore the Iraqi culture to better understand what we were dealing with. The Insha Allah concept—the Iraqi fatalism—was, again, a factor. How had this fatalism affected the Iraqi psyche? Were the Iraqi children taught at an early age that nothing they did mattered? If so, could this explain why most of them seemed to not take any of their own actions seriously, no matter how irresponsible they were?

And what of the effect of Saddam Hussein's reign? He was, in many respects, the ultimate father figure for the Iraqis. He ruled with an iron fist. His government controlled almost every aspect of the Iraqi peoples' lives. The people were given money and power based on Hussein's political machinations. Could this have fostered a welfare state in which all of its occupants became wholly dependent on the government? Almost no personal freedom was allowed under Saddam's tight control. The effect of this would almost certainly have been the loss of any sense of personal responsibility.

All of these questions, and their uneasy answers, painted a bleak picture. Having deposed the Iraqis' ultimate father figure, the United States had effectively assumed the role of "strategic parent" to what it could only hope was a fledgling democracy. The citizens of this would-be democracy had been raised in a world in which a succession of dictators had denied them the right of self-governance, and thus they were forced to learn this art from scratch. When put into the child-parent context, it was as if the Iraqis had been prevented from growing up by their dictatorial leaders and, also, to some extent, by their belief in God's will.

As military advisers, we drifters were there to parent the Iraqi soldiers to the point at which they could operate on their own and police and protect their own country. One of our roles as advisers to the 9th Battalion was to make sure they were taken care of logistically. We were their lifeline to adjacent American units and to the rear of our position, a lifeline they would need to call in for reinforcements and re-supply. In short, we were fulfilling the traditional motherly role. Also, in an even more obvious a comparison, we were there to help bring a sense of order and discipline to the group. In this sense we were fulfilling the traditional fatherly role. And our parenting skills were going to have a direct effect on the Iraq reconstruction as a whole. Only with a capable military in place could Iraq's new sovereign government become more viable and eventually flourish. Once the country was back on its feet, the entire region of the Middle East would be affected. With Iraq in its current instability, the region has been destabilized. Iran is using this instability to make a power grab. Syria is not far behind. Turkey is concerned about the Kurds up north. And Saudi Arabia is worried about the Shiite Iranians gaining too much power. Also, if there was an actual democracy in the heart of the Middle East the surrounding nations would have to explain to their people why they too don't have democratic rights.

When viewed in the light of those first democratic elections, this analysis stood up to scrutiny. In this case, the Americans taught the Iraqis how to run an election. The Americans hung back, behind the scenes the whole time, as our Iraqi children took their first unsure steps out into the world of democracy. This metaphor also extended to the tactical level, as I tried to teach the Iraqis how to conduct a foot patrol and hold a weapon properly.

When I shared my parent-child thesis with my fellow drifters many of them recoiled. This was as expected because even I had tried to avoid coming to such a conclusion. We felt aversion to this politically incorrect idea because we, as Americans, wanted to believe that all men were created equal. We were not prepared to accept that the problem with our Iraqi counterparts was any deeper than a lack of training. We wanted to believe that all it would take to prepare the Iraqis for democracy was hard work from a small group of Marines. This idea, in part, of course, was based on our egocentric desires to believe that we could accomplish our mission and have a lasting effect on the 9th Battalion.

Going into this mission, I tried to pay particular attention to my preconceived notions about the Iraqis. I understood that they had been oppressed for over thirty years and that, as a result, I was bound to experience difficulties, but I also wanted to keep an open mind as much as possible. I definitely wanted to believe that with the right amount of time and effort the Iraqis could do the job. However, after just the first couple of months in Fallujah, there was far too much evidence piling up that our problems were much more fundamental than military training regimens.

Once I accepted my own conclusion, other questions needed to be answered. The answers to these questions had a direct impact on the adviser mission and on recommendations I made to my higher commanders. First, if the Iraqis were the children and we Americans were the parents, then why weren't the American advisers officially in charge? This was more of a rhetorical question. I already knew the answer—because someone had fucked up. We should have governed in a more forceful manner from the very beginning of our occupation. Instead we begged the Iraqis to help us. Once we invaded the country, we, the United States, controlled the country. We should have controlled the Iraqi military. Whoever started the program to reconstitute the Iraqi Army should have established this command relationship from the beginning.

Here we were, ten Americans assigned to train and take into battle an entire Iraqi infantry battalion, and we could never officially order the soldiers to do anything. We could only *ask* them to do things. We had to *persuade* them that what we were telling them was the best course of action. Even when we knew that they were acting inappropriately, we could change their behavior only with Jedi mind tricks; we had to almost fool them into being professional. Plus, if they didn't want to do what we told them, all they needed to say was one simple word: La.

Does this setup seem like sound military doctrine? How could we bring a unit up and running without having any authority over those we were trying to train? These Iraqis needed training on the most basic level. They needed to learn personal discipline, the ability to work as a team, and immediate obedience to orders given by sound leaders. Is nuance or persuasion required for such training? Absolutely not. This situation called for strong leaders with established, clear lines of authority. It required a drill sergeant-type leader, not a hands-off leader. More important, the mission required such a leader on each level of the unit. Advisers should have been placed in a supervisory role all the way down to, at least, the platoon level, if not down to the individual squads. The advisers should have been placed in charge and demanded, not asked, the Iraqis to conduct themselves in a military manner. Only over time, through regimented training and operational experience driven by the ASTs, could the entire Iraqi unit improve in combat effectiveness.

My idea was simple: we could have had a much greater impact on the battalion if we could tell them what to do and have the means to ensure that they listened to our orders. But, by what means could we ensure that the Iraqis listened to orders? The answer to this question only highlighted the problems with the entire adviser program.

When a child doesn't listen to his parents, what happens? The child is punished. Of course it may take many instances of punishment for a child to learn the lesson, but eventually he or she will learn. The drifters with the 9th Battalion could not punish their soldiers. If one of the Iraqi soldiers shot his fellow jundee in the head during celebratory gunfire, we drifters could only yell at the culprit and send him back to work. If a soldier didn't return with the convoy after leave but instead decided to take a few extra days off and return on the next convoy, he was not punished. He was welcomed back with open arms. If an Iraqi soldier fell asleep during guard duty, if he walked down the streets of Fallujah wearing pink flip flops and without a helmet, if he defecated in his own room, still he would receive no punishment.

We drifters were essentially powerless, and as a consequence, the battalion barely learned, and when they did learn, they learned at a slow rate. We could use our powers of persuasion only to keep up the illusion that we had some power and control. Only by the force of our wills and our constant presence could we make the Iraqis do what we asked them to do.

How, by what mechanisms, could we reverse our impotence? Once again, I considered the child-parent dynamic. Parents reward their children for good behavior, either with positive reinforcement or with gifts and material things. When children behave poorly, their parents admonish them and also take privileges away. If we applied positive reinforcement and punishment to the Iraqis, their behavior and professionalism would improve. The next time an Iraqi jundee fell asleep on guard duty or shot his buddy by accident, we had to take away one of his privileges. Perhaps we would take his free time by giving him extra guard duty. Perhaps we would charge him a day's pay. We could, in addition, punish the jundee's leader. For example, if we gave the jundee an extra guard duty shift, we could have the NCO or officer in charge of him stand that shift with him. This would force the leadership to take responsibility for the actions of their own soldiers.

Further, we could institute a promotion system to reward the jundees who were doing a good job. Thus, a soldier such as Mohammed, who was taking charge of operations and leading the Iraqis around him, would be promoted to an NCO rank for his hard work. The other Iraqis would see how Mohammed's hard work had brought him greater success and authority, and maybe they would be inspired to work harder for their own success. These were just a few of the methods for teaching the Iraqis that could have been employed had we been given authority.

A few months into the deployment, we tried to convince the Iraqis' leadership to use these methods. Unfortunately, the leadership was limited in terms of the rewards it could give for good behavior. For example, if Colonel Mehgid asked his boss, the brigade commander, whether he could promote some of his men, a political firestorm that reached up to the Ministry of Defense would ensue. Apparently, no one in the Iraqi chain of command had even considered allowing a colonel to promote his soldiers.

The question all of this raised was, why weren't we empowered with the proper level of authority? The answer: our powerlessness was a direct reflection of the strategic picture and further illuminated our predicament as mere advisers. As previously mentioned, the United States had invaded Iraq, toppled the government, and thereby assumed the role of the "strategic parent" of Iraq. Just as parents would, we should have remained in charge until we knew our "children" were ready to stand, walk, and eventually live on their own. Instead of being responsible parents, however, we sought to get rid of our responsibility as soon as possible. We let the Iraqis go out into the world without ensuring they had the tools to survive. Whether we did this because we feared appearing as an imperial power in politically correct times or because we desired to leave the country as soon as possible, the fact remained that we abdicated our authority at the earliest possible moment. This was clearly a mistake. Apparently no one in charge of the American strategy in Iraq thought to make sure the Iraqis were ready to take charge of their own lives.

We drifters should not only have been placed in charge of the 9th Battalion from our first day on the job, but we should also never have allowed the Iraqis to do anything on their own until we thought they were ready for this responsibility. If in charge, we could have immediately exerted greater control over the entire unit. We could have eliminated many of the negligent discharges. We could have discharged soldiers who caused serious problems by, for example, fighting with their fellow jundees or stealing from the civilians in the Fallujah neighborhood we lived in. We could have completely abolished the leave policy. In short, we could have brought a military unit into existence. Once the Iraqis were deemed ready, they could then have begun conducting combat operations on their own, and eventually, they would have reached a level where they could police, protect, and govern their own country. Wasn't that the objective of our mission?

I had to believe that if this recommendation was coupled with the course of action proposed in the previous chapter—increasing the numbers of Americans assigned to each Iraqi unit—many of the problems we encountered in Fallujah would have been dealt with swiftly. We would have had increased coverage of the Iraqi unit, and we would have also had sufficient authority to effectively manage the unit. With such increased supervision and management—with such increased "parenting," if you will—the Iraqis would have learned faster. They would eventually have been able to stand up on their own, and in turn, as the saying went, we could stand down.

Unfortunately, both recommendations did not seem realistic for the drifter mission on that first day after the elections. The number of advisers and the nature of our command relationship with our Iraqi counterparts were both established prior to our arrival. We advisers were powerless to change the course of our deployment. Our interactions with the Iraqis would remain as they were; we were advisers, not commanders.

While Major Lawson and the others were constantly trying to improve our performance, my two main recommendations seemed out of reach, or so I thought at the time. In fact, events immediately after the elections forced me and the rest of the drifters to leave Fallujah. What followed provided ample evidence that many people had already been working on the next iterations of the adviser mission. Many of their new ideas made an immediate impact on my team of drifters. Were those new ideas as fatally flawed as the original methods? Insha Allah.

NEW MISSION: HABBANIYAH

A disturbing trend among the so-called parents of the American-Iraqi relationship was surfacing. The Americans were proving that they were not above misunderstanding, lack of situational awareness, or out-and-out mismanagement. The next version of the ASTs, the new iteration of the adviser mission referenced in the previous chapter, was a clear example of this. What transpired following the successful democratic elections in Fallujah proved to me that the adviser operation was fatally flawed—even before one took the behavior and mind-set of the Iraqis into account. I did not reach this conclusion right away. It took almost five months, and it began with word of a new mission.

This new mission was spelled out in a brief conversation I had with Major Lawson only a short time after the elections were over.

"Right. Well, the battalion's going to be moving. I'm not sure when this is all going to happen. But, in the meantime, I'm going to need you to go out to the new base and make sure it's set up for the move," Major Lawson said.

"Where am I going?"

"I think it's called Habbaniyah. I know it's an Army base. Other than that, I don't have many details right now. That's really where you come in. You're going to have to get a lay of the land and make sure the basics, like life support, are in place."

"Do we know what kind of force protection there is at this new base?"

"Nope."

"Am I going alone?"

"Yep."

"So, I'm going to die."

"Possibly." This last comment was a joke, of course, and it provided only a small degree of comfort.

To repeat, the 9th Battalion was going to move from Fallujah to an Army base in a town called Habbaniyah. My new mission was to ensure the base could support the force of nearly four hundred men, the reduced number we were now working with because of desertions resulting from the Iraqi leave policy.

To put this new mission into perspective, let us first think about the parameters of my assignment. I was given no information about the area to which I was headed. I was given no information about the type of facilities I was going to find there. No one knew whom I was going to be working with to get the base up and running. Finally, and most unbelievable, no one knew for sure who was ordering this operation. In short, no one knew anything, and there was no one in charge to whom I could direct important questions. Did this sound like a well-thought-out, properly sourced, professional military operation? Clearly, no. And this type of disorganization had been plaguing me from the moment I was ordered to report for this mission, from limited predeployment training to the lack of operational planning behind the linkup with our Iraqi counterparts, to our relative lack of logistical support once in Fallujah.

The brunt of the responsibility, at least on the tactical level on the ground, fell on my shoulders for one specific reason: I was an engineer officer by trade. I had been trained, albeit to a limited degree, in the field of firm base construction. The fact that not all engineer officers were alike and that my particular field of expertise was explosives and obstacles didn't seem to matter to the powers that be.

Those powers, whoever they were, were set to gather at the new base in Habbaniyah for a planning conference, and I needed to be at their meeting. So, I packed up my gear in short order and informed Major Ali and the rest of 2nd Company's leadership that I was being sent to a place called Habbaniyah. They, of course, knew where the town was and indicated it lay about midway between Fallujah and Ramadi, the capital of the Al Anbar Province and an extremely dangerous city. This was the first bit of concrete intelligence I received about where I was going, and the irony that the Iraqis, not my American commanders, provided the information was not lost on me.

I said my good-byes and tried to ignore the sad looks on the Iraqis' faces. The Iraqis' strong sense of family and tribal connections made for an uncomfortable departure. We had all bonded during our brief time in Fallujah. We had survived the same attacks, lived in the same Spartan conditions, and shared many of the same meals. I had been welcomed into the 2nd Company tribe, and now I was leaving. But what of my own feelings? Did I feel sadness that I was leaving? Did I care about these men I was serving with? Were Iraq and its people actually beginning to seem worth all the effort?

These questions and their answers lay in the back of my mind when I arrived in my new home. They remained in the background, however, because one very apparent question consumed my first few moments in Habbaniyah and stayed with me for the rest of my deployment in Iraq: "What were they thinking?" I asked out loud to no one in particular.

I was standing near the eastern edge of the new base, facing due east. I was in full battle gear in the center of a concrete courtyard that had five one-story buildings on three of its sides. One rectangular building stood directly in front of me, two buildings stood to my right, and two more buildings stood to my left. The fourth side of the courtyard was left open to provide access to a road on which vehicles could drive in and out of the area. In this small grouping of five buildings the Americans planned to house the entire Iraqi 9th Battalion.

"What were they thinking?" escaped my lips once again.

They had not even planned to use the lone building on the eastern-most side as housing. That left four buildings to hold over four hundred Iraqis (the force had dropped in number from over five hundred since the Iraqis had starting taking regular leave). My brain immediately started calculating. The 9th Battalion had four companies, so each of the companies would take one building. Each building contained about eight rooms, and the rooms varied between two and three hundred square feet of space, the size of a walk-in closet. Since each company was made up of, on average, about one hundred men, one hundred men would have to live in one building and more than twelve men would sleep in each room. This calculation did not even take into consideration the Iraqi military caste system. The Iraqi officers would not share rooms with the jundees. The Iraqi battalion commander, Lieutenant Colonel Mehgid, would definitely want a room for himself, and this would limit the number of rooms provided to the jundees. Finally, there was the question of where we drifters would sleep. Since we would not be living with our Iraqi counterparts, we would take even more rooms away from the jundees. Thus, some rooms would have to be crammed with over twenty jundees.

I thought about all of them, stacked one on top of the other. Then I remembered the ethnic tensions between Shiite and Sunni, the Iraqis' general lack of hygiene, and the homosexual activity that everyone refused to acknowledge. The picture was getting so grotesque, I forced it from my mind. Unfortunately, I couldn't keep one final question from popping up. I had been with the Iraqis for so long by then that the question came naturally to me. Where were they all going to shit? I imagined four hundred Iraqis clumped together in one corner of the base without a place to relieve themselves. My mind screamed out in horror.

Next to force protection, waste management was going to be the most important logistical consideration of the entire base refurbishment effort. Judging by the layout of the remainder of the base, both issues were going to be difficult.

The grouping of five buildings, those designated to be our next home, sat on the eastern-most side of the base. Just a little farther east was the outer perimeter wall that separated the base from the neighboring towns. The wall was nothing more than a row of HESCO cubes filled with some dirt. In some sections there weren't even cubes, just a mound of dirt pushed up to form a crude barrier. One could look over the wall and into the buildings of the town right next to the base. I could see Iraqi civilians walking around with their children in plain view.

The base itself was huge. It started life as a base for the British back when they were in charge of the country. They imported tall Eucalyptus trees from Australia to line many of the service roads connecting the different parts of the base. There were buildings of all sizes and shapes that at one time housed hundreds of British troops. There was even a cemetery right next to our position. Rumor had it that a group of British citizens went around the world maintaining all the old cemeteries of their empire. To support such gossip, the headstones still stood upright in the day's sun.

Once the British left and Saddam gained power, Iraqi forces took over the base. The number of buildings led me to estimate that an entire Iraqi division probably once called the base home. Whether through Saddam's misrule or through UN sanctions, the base fell into ruin. The facilities were now rundown and had no power grid, no bathroom facilities, and only empty concrete barracks in disrepair.

In addition, the U.S. Army unit that was calling the base home had carved the base into two pieces. The U.S. soldiers resided on the western side, a side that extended all the way to a series of runways and hangars that formerly housed Saddam's air force. The U.S. Army's expanse was huge. The side of the base designated for the Iraqis, in contrast, was totally unprepared for human inhabitants. Nothing had been touched in years, and as previously mentioned, it lay right next to the outer perimeter and two towns on the edge of the base. Looking at this setup reminded me of waiting for our Iraqis to arrive at Camp Fallujah. The American Marines lived on one side of the camp, and they had reserved space for the Iraqi Army unit way out to the east, in a separate part of the complex. The segregation was indicative of how the frontline American units viewed a relationship with any and all Iraqi forces. This also reinforced my concerns about how the two militaries would work together.

Given the state of the facilities and the base layout, the situation began to seem more dire as my initial days went on. It seemed impossible for me to finish preparing the base for the Iraqis before the 9th Battalion was set to arrive. Regardless of these impossibilities, Camp Habbaniyah was going to be our new home. That was the sentiment I gathered as I spoke with the people involved in devising the plan. The plan, as far as I could tell, was for the 9th Battalion to move from Fallujah to Habbaniyah and make the base its permanent home. Once on the base, the Iraqis would endure more regimented training. They would be partnered up with the U.S. Army unit running the base and conduct operations throughout the area of operations. Eventually, the 9th Battalion would become the first Iraqi unit to operate independently in this area. Follow-on forces of Iraqis would then continue to pour into the base until an entire division of Iraqis would take over the base and be placed in charge—permanently.

The plan, more than a little ambitious, was in line with the strategic vision of the president and the other policymakers back in the United States. Unfortunately, it was not grounded in reality. The Iraqis were barely able to conduct independent squad-size patrols, let alone battalion-size operations. And the American resources that were being devoted to supporting the Iraqis were nowhere near what would be required to make this vision a reality. Further, the plan was not communicated in an effective manner. For example, an Army battalion that had been sent over from Korea, called the 1st of the 506th, was currently running the base. When I met the battalion commander, a man who looked like J. R. Ewing from the TV show *Dallas* named Colonel Jones, I promptly informed him that he could expect over four hundred Iraqi soldiers on his base in a few short weeks. It was clear not only that he was against the idea on its face but also that he had heard practically nothing about the plan. Incredibly, no one from the 1st of the 506th even knew the 9th Battalion was coming.

Whether the colonel was prepared or not, even he had to take orders from someone. Our move had been sanctioned from all the way up the chain of command. And it had high visibility because the 9th Battalion was supposed to be the first Iraqi unit to have a permanent base in the Al Anbar Province. After the elections and the subsequent handing over of sovereignty to the new Iraqi government, this move was of certain strategic importance.

The fact that I, a lieutenant on his first deployment, was supervising the initial efforts was not only disconcerting from a personal standpoint but from an operational one as well. Why weren't generals and other senior officers heading up this effort? The senior officers were present—that much was true. I rode out to Habbaniyah in a convoy that contained an admiral, a brigadier general, and a couple of colonels. But they were present only to listen to briefing points. A Marine major from the 1st Division gave a PowerPoint presentation about the base refurbishment plan indicating that the move had been in the works for a while. Why were the advisers assigned to the Iraqi units that were moving not briefed earlier? Why was the unit in charge of the base not informed of our impending arrival earlier? Who had come up with this plan? Were we just pawns on the game board for the generals to move around? The questions continued to pile up.

"What were they thinking?" I said, again out loud. This time my question was answered.

"What was who thinking?" a Marine captain asked me in return. The fact that I knew this captain from our predeployment training at SKETCHY made the moment all that more bizarre. I'm going to call him Captain Courageous because he looked like a cross between Captain America and Buzz Lightyear. I kept waiting for him to suddenly cry out, "To infinity and beyond!" But he never did. He was there to oversee the development of the base project. Since the Iraqis of 9th Battalion were eventually not going to be the only tenants at the Army base, the phantom organization called the Coalition Military Assistance Training Team (CMATT) had sent Captain Courageous to Habbaniyah to act as camp commandant. CMATT was the group that was in charge of the adviser mission. In effect, CMATT was our boss. Exactly who worked for CMATT and what they actually did, I never really knew. I understood only that it was an organization comprised of individual augmentees from the U.S. Navy, Marines, Army, and Air Force and that it seemed to have almost no authority within the actual battle space. For example, Captain Courageous arrived at the base proclaiming he was the camp commandant, but no one outside of myself knew who he was, who he worked for, or what he could offer. He arrived with no supplies and two junior Seabees who had never worked on a base refurbishment. He was just another piece of a puzzle that was getting more confusing by the day.

"Us, the Americans. What were we thinking? This base isn't ready to receive anyone," I answered him plainly, meaning I spoke my mind. This was a dangerous thing to do when discussing this particular mission. "There's nothing here. We still need the beds to arrive. And the water tanks to get set up. Supplies need to be delivered. And forget about the force protection. The muj could lob a grenade over that fence in the southeast corner without leaving their houses. Not to mention the Port-O-Jon situation. This is not good," I said. I immediately thought better of continuing.

In truth, I didn't need to go any further. Captain Courageous was not stupid. He could see the situation. However, it is worth reviewing that initial setup. The base was divided into two separate sides. The American side of Camp Habbaniyah had a chow hall, a mini-mart with American food, and a gym. The Iraqi side had nothing. In between the two sides was a guard post, manned by American soldiers. They were there to make sure no Iraqis ventured across the unofficial border. The post was a Checkpoint Charlie, much like the demilitarized zone (DMZ) that the 1st of the 506th was familiar with from its earlier experience in Korea.

The Iraqi side was abandoned. The buildings were completely empty, many of them in damaged condition. In some sections, only a short fence, maybe five feet tall, kept people from the neighboring towns out. Those towns were literally right next door. In fact, Iraqi civilians were living in houses less than a hundred feet from our corner of the base. If they wanted to, the Iraqi civilians could get up from the kitchen table, go to their window, and launch an RPG in our direction.

We could do nothing to stop them. We had a few guard towers with machine guns, but by the time the guards had the training and discipline necessary to shoot the enemy, the captain and I would be long gone.

Not that the enemy had much of value to target. Our billeting buildings were being renovated, even as we watched, but the project was way behind schedule mostly because the workers were Iraqi civilians. Not only did they use substandard construction practices, but they showed up to work only when they felt like it. The boss of the crew had been accused of stealing his workers' pay. The workers were suspected of collaborating with the insurgency. I even saw a ten-year-old child pushing a wheelbarrow around the job site one day. (Child labor laws did not exist in Iraq.) On another day an Iraqi worker electrocuted himself as he was repairing a generator. The workers carried his lifeless body out the front gate and were back to work in less than twenty minutes.

The American who was in charge of the renovation project prior to our arrival was a little man, a lieutenant commander in the Seabees. One day I intimidated him to the point that he actually called me "Sir." This was the caliber of officer that had been assigned to this supposedly strategically important job.

The Camp Habbaniyah project was, like the rest of my mission, a complete mess. The scenery had changed, but the theme of the drifters' time in Iraq remained the same.

"Well, when a general says 'this is going to happen,' it's going to happen," said Captain Courageous. It was the only thing he could muster in response to my negative assessment. And he was right. Generals were the lords over the military serfdom. Whenever they moved, they had four or five attendants, following them, hanging on their every word. Whenever they issued orders, their guidance cascaded down the ranks like rushing water over the falls. The brunt of the resulting torrents always came crashing down on the little guys at the bottom of the hill, in this case, the drifters.

Over the next couple of weeks, Gunny Babineaux and another Marine lieutenant joined me at Camp Habbaniyah. Gunny Babineaux brought twenty Iraqi jundees with him as a working party to help set up the barracks for the battalion's arrival. The Marine lieutenant brought only himself. He was a representative of the 1st Marine Division sent to make sure the base was ready for the Iraqis. To recap, we had representatives from the Marine higher command, the advisers to the Iraqis, a group called CMATT, the U.S. Navy's Seabees, and the U.S. Army's 1st of the 506th Infantry Battalion, as well as Iraqi civilian workers who came from the towns next to the base. Everyone brought their own agenda, chain of command, and limited resources to the mission. Our efforts could not have been more convoluted.

The efforts included but were not limited to the following: First, we had to build a new, higher HESCO wall that at least protected the barracks from direct rocket attacks. The engineers from the 1st of the 506th claimed they were too busy going out on missions to be bothered with this task, so I had to convince a group of U.S. Army soldiers with a bulldozer to come to the dark side of the base and fill some HESCOs with dirt.

Second, I begged the 1st of the 506th's logistics officer to give us conex boxes of bottled water and *halal* meals. Halal means permissible according to Islamic law, and these meals were prepackaged specifically for Muslims. The meals were made in Israel, but this information was never passed on to the Iraqis.

Third, we had to put pressure on the Iraqi civilian workers to finish the buildings in short order. New doors and windows had to be put in place, all the rooms needed to be repainted, and any defects in the walls needed to be repaired. Plus, lights and electric climate-control units needed to be installed as well. This led to an even more complicated dilemma: acquiring electricity.

The base did not have a reliable electrical grid. Even the U.S. Army was forced to use huge generators to fulfill its massive power requirements. Thus, we had to find a generator big enough to support the whole Iraqi battalion. To highlight the disjointedness that plagued the effort, the Seabee commander informed me that five generators of various sizes were sitting in a clearing in the southeastern corner of the base. No one knew who had sent them or who they were for.

Needless to say, I didn't wait to find out and simply assumed they now belonged to the Iraqi Army. I had to beg, borrow, and steal from another neighboring unit to find a big enough crane to lift one of the generators and carry it over to the billeting site. Once it was in place, we had to find a qualified electrician to hook up the generator to the wires connecting the four billeting buildings. As it happened, a few Navy SEALs were on the base, for a reason unbeknownst to me, and their chief was an expert in the electrical field. He was kind enough to loan us his services for this project.

The process of moving a generator and hooking it up to a building's grid was repeated several times. The refurbishment plan required not only that the four billeting buildings be ready for the Iraqis' arrival but also that the command post and chow hall be up and running. The two buildings were a quarter of a mile down the service road from our living quarters, toward the center of the Iraqi side of camp. The Iraqi civilian workers were still busy painting them, and it didn't look like we would have windows in place for the 9th Battalion's arrival. Insha Allah.

In addition to the power problem, we had the problem of waste management. This took precedence over all other components as far as I was concerned.

"Where are they all going to shit?" I repeatedly asked everyone involved. Eventually the 1st of the 506th realized it would be a problem if more than four hundred Iraqis were placed on its base and allowed to defecate all around the area. This problem had to be resolved before the Iraqis arrived.

One solution was to construct the now-famous Turkish shitters. As mentioned previously, these "toilets" were nothing more than glorified holes in the ground, and this fact raised the question, what would happen when the holes filled up? Given that the Iraqis were planning to make this base their permanent home, simply digging more holes was out of the question: pretty soon the entire base would start to resemble one giant latrine. Thus, instead of building Turkish shitters, we decided to import twenty Port-O-Jons and place them in a row by the road on the open side of our billeting area. It wasn't the perfect solution, but it worked for our expedition-ary purposes.

With time running out before the Iraqis arrived, the final pieces were thrown together. Hundreds of beds were shipped in, and they arrived only a day or two before the Iraqis. Gunny Babineaux led the Iraqi working party on a frantic stretch to put all the beds together and move them into the rooms in time. In addition, furniture needed to be in place in the com-mand post and the chow hall. The furniture didn't arrive until the last night, so we had to build the desks by the light of four Humvees pulled up by the side of the buildings. Finally, we made arrangements for the delivery of chow. The 1st of the 506th agreed to deliver portions of their own food, which was plenty, to the Iraqi side. Actually, Captain Courageous and his two Seabees agreed to pick up the chow every morning, afternoon, and evening and drive it over to the Iraqi side of the camp. The 1st of the 506th refused to personally deliver the food.

Once all of the last-minute preparations were put together, we waited for the coming storm. Because of the high profile of Camp Habbaniyah and its place in the plan to stand up the Iraqi military, the arrival of the 9th Battalion was hailed as an achievement worthy of the attention of generals and even some press. The hubbub started the day the battalion arrived. Senior officers of all ranks and services were on deck, and all, especially the generals, were patting themselves on the back. The soundness of the refurbishment plan was a moot point, as was whether this effort would make any difference in the Iraqi Army's training. It was startling to witness such willful blindness.

The 9th Battalion and the drifters arrived in a long snake of a convoy of Nissan pickups and Ashook Leland trucks. Upon arrival, the Iraqis set up shop in their new home like a plague of locusts. They flooded the rooms and unloaded their be-longings. It was chaos.

After the drifters' arrival, we gave the American generals a formal tour of all of the facilities. We even sat down in the new Iraqi chow hall and ate a symbolic first meal. I ate lunch sitting next to the two highest-ranking generals in the room.

One was the division commander, and the other was his boss, the Marine Expeditionary Force commander. We sat together and ate greasy beef patties and soggy carrots.

"So, Sir, what do you think of the place?" I asked the three-star, trying to act normally. He looked around at the shabbily built concrete rectangle we were sitting in. A coat of fresh paint had been brushed onto the walls to make it look presentable. Wooden boards were covering the spaces that would at some point be windows. The actual windows hadn't arrived yet. Squeaky ceiling fans were twirling above us. As he looked around, still examining, the fluorescent lights above us started to blink in and out. We could hear the generator cutting off and back on every three seconds. The lights continued to flicker on and off the whole meal. The three-star looked at the lights then back down at me.

"Lieutenant, you guys' have done a hell of a job, son." He scooped up some more carrots. The moment spoke volumes about the generals' approach to this mission. They cared less about the details than about checking an item off their checklist. The Iraqis needed only to have a base, not necessarily suitable living conditions.

The same three-star stood before the Iraqi battalion minutes later during an official ceremony to turn over that part of the base to the 9th Battalion. The Iraqis, all four hundred of them, stood in a giant formation while the three-star spoke from a podium with a microphone. An Iraqi flag was raised during the speech. That's right: we spent two weeks searching for a suitable metal pole and someone to dig a hole, stick the pole in the hole, and fill the hole with concrete. But I digress.

Speeches were then given by all the American officers. The Iraqis saluted them as they were introduced, one by one. The three-star delivered his best inspirational speech without noticing that his backdrop was a row of Port-O-Jons. "This base is a symbol of the new Iraq. And it is up to you, the soldiers of this battalion, to live up to these high standards. Now that elections have occurred and you and your people have voted for your own government, it will be up to the Iraqis, you, to fight for your own country. I have no doubt that you will succeed."

I couldn't listen to the remaining, hollow words. The image of the American general telling the Iraqi Army to fight for its country, with the row of twenty Port-O-Jons accenting his every word, was more than I could bear.

As the ceremony ended, Staff Sergeant Collier, one of the drifters I had been reunited with at Habbaniyah, approached the rest of us drifters, gave us a look, and then broke out in grunting laughter.

"What's so funny?" Gunny Babineaux asked. He had worked with Collier in advising 3rd Company back in Fallujah, and he always had to know what the staff sergeant was doing.

"I just caught a jundee . . . " Collier began. He couldn't finish he was laughing too hard.

"Come on. Finish." I said.

"I just caught a jundee taking a shit *behind* the row of Port-O-Jons!"

"What?" All of us asked in unison.

I looked across from our new buildings, where I had positioned the whole row of shitters. Not only were there twenty Port-O-Jons, but we had built a few Turkish shitters just in case, holes be damned. I thought this would cover any number of Iraqis, Americans, and others who needed to go. It now looked like I hadn't thought of all the possibilities.

"Staff Sergeant, what do you mean?" Captain Yamamoto had trouble wrapping his head around Collier's comment.

"Here, I'll show you," he said and urged us to follow him toward the row of Port-O-Jons. "I was trying to round any stragglers up for the formation." We followed him around the end of the row. "Then I get right here," he points to the area behind the toilets, "and I see a jundee popping a squat right here out in the open."

"I don't believe it." The words escaped my lips before I realized it. The comment was ridiculous. Of course I believed it.

"Take a look," said Collier, pointing a finger toward the ground.

Right there, not two feet from the back of a Port-O-Jon, sat a pile of human shit.

"Come on. You've got to be kidding me!" one of the others blurted out.

"These people have got to be crazy or some shit," someone else said.

"That's just wrong," said the first sergeant, a germaphobe, cringing.

Major Lawson shook his head.

I stood there, staring, even as the others dispersed. A man had walked past a row of toilets and decided to relieve himself out in the open. This event had a larger significance, I thought. This was evidence of the underlying problem with this mission. No one—not the generals, the policymakers, the 1st of the 506th, CMATT, Captain Courageous, the 1st Marine Division, or even myself—had factored the Iraqis into the equation. We had expended so much time and effort getting the 9th Battalion to its new home, and despite severe logistical constraints, we succeeded in moving the Iraqis to Habbaniyah. But all we really did was move the problem. This new mission was the same as the last. Nothing had changed except the scenery and the name of the town.

"They are barbarians," I said to the air in disgust. No one was around. I went back to the barracks, back to training the New Iraqi Army, with nothing on my mind but the fact that an Iraqi soldier took a shit *behind* a row of Port-O-Jons.

Unity of Command

The sight of the turd sitting behind the Port-O-Jons remained on my mind the entire first month we were in our new home. It sat there, figuratively, underneath the surface of all the events of those early days in Habbaniyah, acting as a reminder of what we were up against. Every time an American talked about grandiose plans to develop the Iraqis into a serviceable fighting force, every time a general came by to reassure us of our mission's vital importance, and every time I heard an Iraqi success story, I made sure I had a mental picture of that fecal matter. For me, it sliced through all of the rhetoric and crystallized our plight: the outcome of our mission was out of our hands. Insha Allah had never made as much sense as it did after that moment.

Not that this realization stopped the rest of the drifters and me from flying in the face of reality. In fact, Camp Habbaniyah represented an even greater American effort to turn the tide from unprofessional chaos to some semblance of military order. The problem was that our new efforts only provided a better illustration of the fundamental flaws in our plans. These plans included not only the refurbishment of the facilities at Camp Habbaniyah but also the plans for the training and operations of the Iraqis once they arrived.

Sometime before the 9th Battalion arrived at Habbaniyah, I attended a high-level planning conference. This conference was attended by all sorts of officers from various organizations. It was meant to discuss and set in motion the plans for the Iraqis' training once they became permanent residents of the base. Every single Marine, U.S. soldier, and U.S. sailor in the room was either a senior captain, major, lieutenant colonel, lieutenant commander, warrant officer, or senior enlisted. I was the lone lieutenant in the room. I was also the lone representative for the advisers working with the 9th Battalion.

The men in the room represented the following organizations, in no particular order: the 1st of the 506th Army Battalion, the 1st Marine Division, the 1st Marine Expeditionary Force, the Army regiment in charge of the 1st of the 506th, the 2nd Marine Division, the Seabees, the Navy SEALs, CMATT, the Iraqi Security Forces (ISF)—the ISF representatives were actually Marines—and a couple of AST members who were assigned to the 2nd Brigade, the 9th Battalion's higher command. There was also a Marine gunner who seemed to represent himself, to what purpose I learned only later. Throw in Captain Courageous—still no one understood what he was doing in Habbaniyah—and that left me, the lone AST lieutenant.

During the meeting the men presented slide shows about the different training the Iraqis would receive once on base. The dates and details presented indicated someone had been hard at work for a while putting together this plan. People talked about the necessity of focusing on certain military skills. Marksmanship and basic weapons handling were the focus of the Marine gunner. Development of better NCOs was the point of emphasis for a couple of U.S. Army sergeants major. The SEALs talked about some kind of reconnaissance platoon. Everyone took turns pushing their own agendas and tried to shift the focus of the conversation to training points that aligned with their respective plans.

I tried speaking up only once. When I attempted to throw some sanity into the mix by relating some of the events I had witnessed, an Army major who already had a plan in place and did not want to hear any dissenting voices quickly rebuked my points. For the remainder of the meeting, I stood against the wall and simply watched. The events of Fallujah were fresh in my mind as these men plotted to build the New Iraqi Army in the small conference room. The scene was instructive if only because it was absolutely absurd.

The problems with the approach as laid out in this conference were obvious to me. No one involved in the development of the plan had ever consulted with men on the ground. No one talked to the advisers, that is, to us drifters. How could there be a plan in place to train the Iraqis if the observations of the men with the most intimate knowledge of the Iraqis had not been asked for? How did these men know what would or wouldn't work without our observations?

Furthermore, who were these men and their organizations? Each one of them had a different agenda, and it seems no one had asked whether all of these different parts could fit together into a coherent, comprehensive plan. No one had asked if they *should* fit together. For example, what were the SEALs doing there? Since when were they fluent in advising foreign troops? Also, who came up with the idea to develop a reconnaissance platoon from the 9th Battalion in the first place? The Iraqi soldiers couldn't even go to the bathroom in the right places. How were they going to conduct highly skilled recon missions? And why should they conduct such missions at all? Iraq needed functional standard infantry battalions first and foremost. The soldiers needed to be able to secure their own country on the most basic level. This mission had no place for commando-like raids. But that didn't stop some high-ranking admiral from sending his SEALs to Habbaniyah to take some of the 9th Battalion's soldiers and start training them for a recon platoon.

The effect of such ancillary agendas was immediately evident. Since the SEALs needed Iraqis who could perform many different demanding missions, they obviously wanted only the best Iraqi recruits for their recon platoon. Thus, the 9th Battalion would lose about thirty to forty of its best men. As soon as I heard this I knew who would be their number one recon Iraqi: Mohammed. Not one week after the 9th arrived did I see Mohammed leading the rest of the recon Iraqis on a long physical fitness run. I shook my head at the sight.

So, not only did we lose Iraqis as a result of the continuing Iraqi leave policy, but now other American organizations were picking and pulling soldiers from our ranks. Did this make any sense? If the Iraqi battalion kept losing men, how could it be expected to stand on its own? The SEALs were not the only Americans to take Iraqi soldiers, either. The NCO Academy did as well.

Apparently, someone noticed the lack of strong NCO leadership throughout the Iraqi Army units and decided we Americans would have to fix it. While the conclusion was correct, the method these planners decided on was as far off the mark as any other effort we saw for the remainder of the deployment. It was decided—by whom, I do not know—that a set of buildings in the center of the Iraqi section of Camp Habbaniyah would be used for an NCO academy. Five to six U.S. Army drill sergeants were on deck to take the 9th Battalion's NCOs and put them through a rigorous boot camp-style training regimen. So, not only had the SEALs taken many of our best soldiers for a recon mission that was superfluous at best, but now a group of U.S. Army soldiers wanted to take our small unit leaders. Again, did this make any sense? How was the 9th Battalion expected to survive? Additionally, how did these drill sergeants expect to put Iraqi NCOs through boot camp? Most of these men had already served in the military for many years. Now the drill sergeants were going to start yelling and screaming in their faces and making them do push-ups? Did anyone consider the cultural difficulties involved in having Americans screaming and yelling at Iraqis?

Had any of the American officers considered the Iraqis when drawing up their plans? Obviously not, but still, the plans continued to flow. The Marine gunner, a man who had been in the military for nearly thirty years and often called generals by their first names, was not about to miss out on the advising mission. He had planned to set up a weapons training school for the Iraqis. Picture this for a moment: the Americans wanted to start a school that would teach the Iraqis how to use the Russian-made AK-47, a weapon the Iraqis had been using for decades, the most popular weapon in the Arab world. The fact that the Iraqis actually needed such training was even more ironic. But how many Iraqis would go through the training at a time? Would any be left for Colonel Mehgid to actually command? What did the Iraqi chain of command think about these plans? Did anyone even consult the Iraqis on any of this?

The questions were piling up fast as I watched the powers that be spawn even more plans. Had these people ever heard the phrase *unity of effort?* Weren't we all supposed to be focused on one common goal? How could this mission be accomplished if each organization had a different idea about what that mission was? Who was in charge of this effort anyway? Wasn't it a tenant of the 1st Marine Division to require unity of command?

Unity of command would have required clear lines of command all the way up the chain and a clear understanding of who was actually in command by everyone involved. From my vantage point in the corner of the conference room, I could see no clarity at all. For this mission, no one knew who was in charge of what. And the roles of some organizations, particularly CMATT and ISF, were never clarified for anyone. I knew we drifters were working for CMATT, but even we had no idea what the organization did for us. Any support we received came from begging and borrowing from adjacent units. CMATT was nowhere to be found. A general somewhere, presumably in Baghdad, called himself our boss, but we never saw him.

The chain of command for this mission was, if not broken, bent and twisted beyond any reasonable comprehension. Different people were pursuing different ways to achieve what they each believed was the intent behind the adviser mission. This violated every conceivable interpretation of the unity of command tenant and had real consequences on the ground.

One of those consequences was the drastic changing of the composition of our adviser team upon the 9th Battalion's arrival. This subject became the most important segment of the planning and made an immediate impact on the drifters and on my role on the team. It seemed someone was coming up with many of the same ideas I was regarding the sourcing of the adviser mission. The ASTs were finally going to get help. Approximately sixteen members of the 1st of the 506th were reassigned as advisers to the 9th Battalion.

The results of this reassignment complicated our effort in a way I had anticipated when I first made the recommendation. First, most of the soldiers, if not all, came from the line companies and had spent the months prior to our arrival conducting combat operations against the insurgents in the area. Thus they had the same attitude toward the Iraqis as many of the frontline Marine units back in Fallujah had. They were used to shooting and killing the enemy, not training men that looked much like that same enemy.

Second, they had only just been ordered to take part in this mission. They were frontline soldiers one week and advisers to a foreign military the next. Though we drifters received only limited predeployment training, at least we always knew we were going to Iraq to act as advisers. The adviser mind-set was totally different from the frontline soldier mind-set, and these soldiers were being asked to make the mental transition almost immediately.

Third, the battalion commander of the 1st of the 506th gave the strong impression that he, his leadership, and his soldiers wanted nothing to do with the Iraqis. This became more evident as time went on, and I will examine examples closely in later chapters, but the fact that these undercurrents existed supported my own previous theories. The partnership program would succeed only if the adjacent American unit bought into the mission 100 percent. The advisers had to work together with the Iraqis and ensure that their focus was the Iraqis' development, not direct combat operations against the insurgents. With the addition of the soldiers from a less than hospitable 1st of the 506th, this focus was more difficult to achieve.

These new advisers were not going to live with us drifters and the Iraqis, and the mission was limited in part by this arrangement. We didn't have enough suitable rooms for the additional advisers in our four billeting buildings, but I knew that the main reason they had rejected living quarters on our side was because they didn't trust the Iraqis. Their leadership never came over to the Iraqi side without being fully armed and escorted by a gun truck. They looked at the ten drifters walking around among the Iraqis as though we were complete lunatics.

The new advisers were breaking one of the mission's most important rules: one had to live in close proximity to the men one was advising. Close quarters were the only means to form the requisite sense of trust and camaraderie needed to effectively advise. The Iraqis instantly took note of how the new advisers drove off after a day's work while the drifters stayed back, lived with, and ate meals with them. This dichotomy definitely limited our ability to act as a cohesive unit.

And cohesion was the primary problem with the newly established advising team of ten Marines and sixteen U.S. Army soldiers. The soldiers included three lieutenants, a couple of sergeants first class, several staff sergeants, and a few sergeants and corporals. All were professional military men who would do their best to accomplish the new mission they had been assigned.

Major Lawson remained the officer in charge of the entire team. Captain Yamamoto, the next senior man, was entrenched in an executive officer-type role. That left me, the lieutenant with the most experience with the 9th Battalion, as the next senior adviser. As third in the chain, I was no longer attached to 2nd Company. I joined the group of advisers with the battalion group and worked with the Iraqi battalion's leadership. This left the three U.S. Army lieutenants to be assigned to each one of the three Iraqi line companies.

This setup was flawed from its inception. What it created was an environment in which the Marine officers were in charge of the team, and the Army soldiers acted according to the plans and directions coming from those Marines. Given interservice rivalries, differences in tactical and training doctrines, and a lack of shared experiences with the Iraqis, tension was an inevitable result of such a command relationship.

In hindsight, I realize that every adviser assigned to the Iraqi battalion should have been part of one service and one team. So, in this case, either the Marines AST members should have received reinforcements from CMATT, which was supposed to be sourcing us, or the 1st of the 506th should have provided all of the advisers to the 9th Battalion, allowing the Marines to move off of the Iraqi unit altogether. This would have aided the cohesion of the team and allowed it to begin its training and operations with a clear direction.

The patchwork approach we ended up with only highlights the lack of clear planning involved in the entire effort. Again, different organizations were pursuing the same mission through different means, and no one was able to clarify and unify the different elements. The president dictated that we would stand up a New Iraqi Army, the secretary of defense then told his generals to put a plan into action, and then the generals put together many different plans based on each of their own interpretations of the new mission. And because each general had command of a different Iraqi organization, each had the ability to pursue what he thought was the right course of action separate from his fellow flag officers' pursuits. So, the commander of CMATT decided individual augments should be sent in as ten-man adviser teams, whereas the commander of the 1st Marine Division decided to form a group called ISF. Still another general decided the ASTs needed help and pulled soldiers from adjacent American combat units to be advisers. The end result was what I saw on the ground in Habbaniyah: a laboratory experiment run amok.

Thus, we had people reporting to a wide array of commands. Even within our own newly comprised adviser team, we wondered who we belonged to and who the soldiers from the 1st of the 506th belonged to. We gathered that the ten Marines still reported to the brigade advisers. In the past the brigade adviser was Lieutenant Colonel Klink, but he was now out of the picture. A new sheriff, a big burly man from Texas named Lieutenant Colonel Welker, was in town. He had a new Marine AST with him to advise the Iraqi 2nd Brigade, which was supposed to be in charge of the 9th Battalion. What the Iraqi brigade did besides set up the leave convoys I never knew.

On the other side of the equation, the U.S. Army soldiers from the 1st of the 506th while technically working for Major Lawson still administratively belonged to the 1st of the 506th. They then reported to their own company commanders and, ultimately, to their colonel. This setup created a clear conflict of interest. Who would the adviser soldiers listen to? What would happen if Major Lawson wanted us to do one thing and their colonel wanted them to do another? What about the Iraqis? What was going to happen in regard to their command relationship? Who was in charge of them? How would they be employed in this new area of operations? Who would employ them?

Despite the complete lack of unity of command that they had created by failing to get together to form one clear operational plan, the generals continued to visit Camp Habbaniyah to admire their handiwork. During the first month in our new home, generals of all ranks, services, and positions visited us in a seemingly never-ending series of ceremonies, formations, and speeches. Each time we gathered up and came to attention as the general of the moment approached. We saluted and waited to be put at ease to listen to his speech, which was always the same:

"Gentlemen, I am telling you, you have one of the most important jobs in our entire effort here in Iraq. Yours is the strategic main effort. The president, the secretary of defense, General Abizaid—everyone has now said our main goal is to get these Iraqi forces stood up and taking over areas of operations for themselves as soon as possible. It's not about killing the enemy anymore. It's about getting the Iraqis to kill the enemy. I can't thank you enough for all your hard work."

Though every time we were told ours was the most important job, as soon as the generals left, things returned to their natural imbalance. Supplies were hard to come by. The enemy kept pinging us with sniper shots and mortar rounds. And the base's renovation continued on a slow, Iraqi timetable. The American Army stayed on one side of the camp, the Iraqis on the other. We drifters were as always in the middle.

I couldn't help but think the base, in its disorder, was a microcosm for the entire country. The higher-ups swung by for the usual pomp and circumstance; they would deliver flowery speeches that failed to accurately describe the realities on the ground. All the while we had to deal with the results of their ill-conceived grandiose plans.

"You guys," the general, a short, grouchy guy, began—then stopped and in an aside to his aide said, "What are we calling them now? Right, you guys are the MATTs. Your job is the most important."

The name of our team, once supplemented by the U.S. Army soldiers, had been changed. We were now the Military Assistance Training Team (MATT), not the Adviser Support Team. But the name made no difference to us. The dysfunction was still present. By the time the final general came to visit, it was rumored our name had changed again.

"Hey, Sir, what are we called this day?" Gunny Gonzalez asked Captain Yamamoto with unhidden sarcasm. Major Lawson was right there but pretended not to hear. He had the hardest job of all: trying to keep us all from going berserk.

"Well, Gunny, I believe it is now going to be MiTT," Yamamoto answered.

"Mitt?" Gonzalez replied, unconvinced.

"Yes. Big M, little I, big T, big T. Stands for Military Training Team."

"What happened to MATT?" I asked.

"Apparently, someone in the Ministry of Defense had a problem with it. They were offended by the word *assistance*. They didn't think they needed any assistance." When Yamamoto finished, no one could even muster a joke. Of course the Iraqis didn't need assistance. We all shook our heads and got in formation for the next general.

The high-level visits reached a climax when the commandant of the Marine Corps arrived. His four stars seemed to blind even the most hardened of service members, American or Iraqi. Colonel Jones from the 1st of the 506th could barely speak to the general without flubbing his words. Colonel Mehgid kept staring at the four stars as if they were priceless diamonds.

The commandant, attended by majors, colonels, and other lesser generals, approached our formation and started in on the same speech. We were the main effort, getting the Iraqis up to speed was the most important thing, and so on. I kept thinking about the Iraqi who squatted behind the Port-O-Jons. I wondered if the commandant heard about that informative encounter.

In the middle of my formation daydreaming, the commandant did something out of the ordinary, something that threw us all for a loop. He asked for comments. "Alright, now you've heard what I've got to say, but you are the ones on the ground. I want to hear from you all. What do you think of this mission? What about the Iraqis? What would you do differently? Please, someone, tell me."

It was incredible. Here was a chance to voice our frustrations about all the madness. I wanted to scream out, but I was too nervous. So was everyone else. It was stone-cold silent. He could not actually want to hear what we had to say, could he? Another long minute went by without anyone uttering a word. The four-star stood there, sizing up his audience. He started to scan the formation, looking for a suitable target. The general's eyes stopped scanning. They fixed on their target and that target was me.

"Lieutenant, how 'bout it?" he boomed.

My shoulders slumped visibly. I had been in the very back of the formation, and as I walked up toward the front of the formation I thought about what I should say.

"Sir, to be honest," I began. My brain was screaming inside. I wanted to shout out all of my frustrations.

"Hey, General. First, we were sent into battle with these guys without having even met them. And we didn't have any interpreters. Or enough armed vehicles. And did you know that they shit everywhere. Hell, we caught one of them the other day taking a shit *behind* a row of Port-O-Jons. What's up with that? And did you know they all go on vacation at least a week out of every month. They get seven days of leave plus travel days. Plus they don't work on Fridays because it's their day of prayer. So, if you add that up they work fewer than half the days of every month. Did your aides tell you that? What about the fact that there's no system for promotions? So, even if we have one or two soldiers who actually get it and work hard, they have no incentive because they can't even be recognized. And the Americans involved in this thing are just as bad. They barely want to support the mission. They don't see the long-term ramifications. They don't care. And my team and I have been hung out to dry I don't know how many times. Has anyone told you that yet? Is that what you want to hear from me? Huh?"

This is what I wanted to say, but something about discretion being the better part of valor kept me in check. "Sir, to be honest, the Iraqis are . . . a work in progress." I copped out. I made the understatement of the century.

"Well . . . obviously . . . what else do you have for me?" he pressed.

I remember stumbling through something about the need for improved Iraqi leadership. While it wasn't the best of answers, it seemed to get the ball rolling. Eventually others offered some constructive recommendations, including creating a promotion system for the Iraqis. The general actually cared enough about that recommendation to call a two-star general over and order him to take notes. The ripples from those notes were felt about a month after the commandant's visit, when a system was put in place at the Iraqi Ministry of Defense. But rather than being encouraged by such responsiveness to our insights, I became even more despondent. The responsiveness fostered still more rapid-fire questions.

Why did it take a personal order from the commandant of the Marine Corps to make a much-needed change to this mission? What did that say about the chain of command between the commandant and the drifters? Was anyone listening? Did anyone care? Were they so focused on their own designs that they ignored all other advice and input?

Was there one person in command? Who was it? Where was he? Could I talk to him? Could I share a couple of stories with him? Did he know about "the Death Blossom"? Did anyone tell him about the Iraqi leave policy? How about the one where an Iraqi squatted behind a row of Port-O-Jons? And one last question: Had he ever heard the phrase *Insha Allah*?

THE STAFF AND THE PLAN

Most of my questions, I knew, would go unanswered. In fact, while asking these questions fulfilled some masochistic need to delve deeper into our illogical plight, it really served no useful purpose in terms of my responsibilities on the ground. I remained at the lowest end of the totem pole and would have to adapt and overcome any obstacles the powers that be threw at me whether I liked it or not.

This matter-of-fact approach to the drifter mission was starting to sound uncomfortably familiar. Because people other than us drifters continued to change our mission's parameters and because we had no control over those changes' results, we were essentially being forced to buy into the Iraqi idea that everything was up to God. Could it be that the Iraqis' fatalism was a natural coping mechanism people employed when surrounded by forces outside their control?

This question seemed to have an actual answer, but I wasn't prepared to accept it just yet. I couldn't accept that the Iraqis were correct in their worldview. Instead, I acknowledged that Insha Allah had a place in our vocabulary to explain the unexplainable, but for me, hard work and personal responsibility could still manage to shape the outcome of our mission. With this in mind, I recognized some of the positive aspects of the new MiTT approach and set to apply those new advantages to better our prospects for success.

One of the advantages was the increase of men assigned to advise the 9th Battalion. With the additional manpower, we could assign more people to each company. Also, we now could assign a U.S. Army lieutenant to the Iraqi company commander and a staff NCO from the Americans to the Iraqi company first sergeant or senior-most enlisted man in the company. The remaining advisers assigned to each company, the sergeants and corporals, could be pushed down to the Iraqi platoon level. In Fallujah, we had only two advisers per company, and now we would have approximately six per company. This was going to make a big difference.

Even more important, the increased coverage of the line companies enabled us to address the Iraqi Battalion Staff with more advisers. We could also assign specific advisers to specific sections of the Iraqi Battalion Staff. This area of need had been identified at the beginning of the mission. Up until the MiTT was formed, Major Lawson, the first sergeant, and Captain Yamamoto were the only AST members who worked directly with the Iraqi battalion commander, his sergeant major, and his Battalion Staff. With such minimal coverage, the 9th Battalion's staff could not function in any meaningful way while we were in Fallujah.

Once in Habbaniyah and once the MiTT was put together, several of the AST members were pulled back from the line companies and assigned to specific staff sections. Gunny Gonzalez, a logistics chief by trade, was assigned to the Iraqi S-4 (Logistics) shop. One of the other AST members, a staff sergeant with a communications background, was assigned to work with the Iraqi S-6 (Communications) to get radios up and running. His special focus was the command post communications. The first sergeant remained in his role of advising the Iraqi sergeant major in all things enlisted, plus he worked with the S-1 (Administration) to teach them about the administrative side of running an infantry battalion. Captain Yamamoto, the senior adviser in the battalion group outside of Major Lawson, stayed with the Iraqi executive officer. He was also kept as adviser to the Iraqi S-3 (Operations). Finally, as previously stated, I was reassigned to advise the S-3A and the Iraqi S-2 (Intelligence). Thus, I would not only be working with the Iraqi intelligence officer but also with Captain Yamamoto in advising the Operations group from the 9th Battalion. Of course "advising" was an ever-evolving concept. Were we there to merely suggest courses of action? Or were we there to dictate those same actions? It was a balancing act that required communication skills and tact.

After being assigned the new positions, I first had to say good-bye to Major Ali, Lieutenant Ahmed, and the rest of the 2nd Company leadership. When I walked into Major Ali's new room in one of the four billeting buildings, I used Snoop to break the news. I introduced the new U.S. Army members of our team, who would be replacing me.

"Raed Ali, this is Lieutenant Grissom. He'll be working with you from now on," I said, pointing to the U.S. Army officer. Grissom looked unsure of himself. I didn't know yet if his uncertainty was the product of a lack of familiarity with Iraqi soldiers or his natural makeup, but he was definitely nervous. I wondered if I had looked like him when I first met the Iraqis. I hoped I wasn't looking at my past self. The beads of sweat on his forehead made me worry that Grissom was going to faint.

Major Ali gave Lieutenant Grissom a halfhearted smile once Snoop finished translating. Then he looked back at me. He was sad. His eyes were those I imagined children had when their parents left them. The look was almost unbearable. Snoop reminded me that the Iraqis became attached quickly. Once you have broken bread with them, lived with them, fought with them, been welcomed into the tribe, you were like family. I shook Ali's hand, then we both pressed our hands to our hearts in a sign of respect.

"Ani mutassef [I am sorry]," I said, and then I walked out of the room. Once outside the room, I exhaled one long breath. My own reaction to the separation surprised me. Did I actually have feelings for these Iraqis? I had to admit, many of them had grown on me.

One Iraqi who endeared himself to me almost immediately was one of my new counterparts, Lieutenant Hamza. He was the battalion intelligence officer, a big, thick man with a dark black Saddam moustache. He always greeted me with a huge grin.

"Ah, Nevarra, hello! Salaam Alaikum!" he would say. He would come over shake my hand heartily and then give me a big bear hug. He tried to kiss me on the cheek one time, but I managed to pull away.

"No, no, you Iraqi, me Amreeki," I said, by way of explaining to him the difference between the two cultures. Even though he didn't understand the words, he grasped the point. From then on he gave me only a shake and a manly hug.

Hamza was eager to learn and willing to do almost anything I asked. These were his good traits. However, he was not without some of the limitations I had grown to expect from many of the Iraqis. Captain Yamamoto, who had worked with him in Fallujah, relayed a revealing story. Yamamoto told me how he had given Hamza a list of some of the key informants and high-value targets in the Fallujah area. Giving Hamza such sensitive information was a sign of trust. Yamamoto told Hamza he needed to protect the list at all costs. Hamza said he would rather die than give up the list. Satisfied with this pledge, Captain Yamamoto adjourned the meeting. As they both headed to the door, the captain looked back at the table. Wouldn't you know it, the list was still sitting right there. Hamza continued out the door. He had forgotten the top-secret memo. This was not exactly confidence inspiring.

Having received my assignment, I immediately began to train Hamza and the small crew of jundees assigned to his Intelligence shop. I was not trained as an intelligence officer myself, but that did not deter me. I focused on the types of tasks I knew could be of benefit to the battalion's operations. Working with the Iraqis on intelligence matters had its advantages. The Iraqis had working knowledge of the towns we were going to be operating in, even if they were not from those exact towns. They could speak the language of the locals and could gather intelligence about insurgent activity in the neighborhood more easily than we Americans could. They could also help spread positive information, aka propaganda, about the arrival of the New Iraqi Army throughout the towns neighboring Camp Habbaniyah. And, during detainee interrogations, Iraqis were better able to decipher whether a prisoner was an insurgent or not. The downside to working with

Iraqis on intelligence was prisoner treatment. Hamza and his men tended not to understand the nuances of the Geneva Convention.

Given the missions we would conduct, I began by organizing the Intelligence shop to concentrate on three specific areas: developing informants and keeping records of every meeting with informants, creating informational fliers that spread the word of the New Iraqi Army, and developing interrogation practices for the detainees plus keeping accurate records of those prisoners who were sent off to Abu Gharaib. The Iraqis loved to keep written records, and having information down on paper allowed me to ensure they were actually organizing.

I had difficulty evaluating the Iraqis' progress, however, because I did not have an interpreter at my disposal. With the increase in the number of advisers came a proportional increase in the demand for interpreters. As was the case in Fallujah, the factor that most limited the MiTT's dealings with the Iraqis was our small pool of interpreters. Word trickled down to us that many of the combat commanders still fighting on the front lines against the insurgency were scooping up most of the qualified translators. The question had to be asked: who needed the interpreters more?

Since Hamza could not speak a word of English, my interactions with him past the hello stage definitely required an interpreter. Snoop was stretched so thin and our need was so great that we were eventually able to secure a few more terps, but the newbies just caused more headaches. The first three were all Jordanian, and each had different degrees of skills. One was decent all around. Another was much better at writing than he was at translating oral conversations. The third was not good at either. All three also had wildly different personalities that had to be managed constantly. One was thin as a rail and looked like a heroin addict. Another was well built but carried himself effeminately. The final one took the prize as the strangest: he told everyone he idolized Adolf Hitler and even started to draw swastikas on his arms as fake tattoos. When one of the black staff sergeants from our original AST saw the tattoos, he threatened to either slice the skin from the terp's arm or burn the symbol off. Needless to say, the swastika was removed shortly thereafter.

My other new partner spoke some English. His name was Captain Omar, and he was the 9th Battalion's S-3A, or assistant battalion operations officer. While his English was not great, it allowed the two of us to converse on a daily basis. He was a smallish man with a huge nose, the obligatory black moustache, and an aristocratic air about him. He had a pregnant wife at home, somewhere near Basra, who was about to give birth to their first child. He talked about wanting a son all the time. He didn't have to explain why, given the way women were treated in his culture.

Our job was to assist both Omar's boss, Major Mohammed, and mine, Captain Yamamoto, as far as planning and overseeing training and, eventually, the 9th Battalion's operations in Habbaniyah. The American advisers, as Major Lawson explained it, would devise a training plan to present to the Iraqis as an option. We would explain to them the way the plan should work and the reasons for all the different aspects of the plan. We hoped our presentation would not offend the Iraqis and would instead bring them on board.

So, we MiTT advisers first put together our own plan. Major Lawson indicated that he wanted to focus at first on the three line companies, exclude Headquarters and Service Company, and involve the Battalion Staff as much as possible with all the planning. Lawson also indicated that additional force requirements would be placed on the Iraqis, including guard force duty and eventually patrolling the areas surrounding the camp. Given this direction, it was obvious that we would have to rotate the companies through training, guard duty, and patrols and operations. Not so obvious was what the training component would include.

Captain Yamamoto called a meeting to determine the breadth and scope of the training plan. The meeting involved me, the captain, the three U.S. Army lieutenants who were now assigned to the three Iraqi line companies, and the three senior enlisted advisers who were assigned under each of those lieutenants: a U.S. Army sergeant first-class, a U.S. Army staff sergeant, and Gunnery Sergeant Babineaux. Gunny

Babineaux, who had spent his days in Fallujah advising 3rd Company and its commander, Captain Akeel, was now acting as the adviser to the 3rd Company's first sergeant. I didn't know whether he saw the new position as a demotion, he was still bitter about not having an interpreter to use back in Fallujah, or he simply had personality quirks, but he carried a great deal of baggage into the meeting with Captain Yamamoto. Babineaux's idiosyncrasies coupled with the original AST's disconnect from the new advisers from the 1st of the 506th set the meeting up for failure almost from its inception.

What transpired was a lesson in how to get off on the wrong foot in a new relationship. The meeting also illustrated a fundamental flaw in suddenly slapping together military personnel from different services and with different experiences to form one team. Finally, the results of the meeting highlight the important aspect of what to focus on during the training of a foreign military force.

The basic format for the training plan was easily agreed upon. Each of the companies would rotate. One would take part in training, one would stand watch on the guard posts on the Iraqi side of Camp Habbaniyah, and one company would start patrolling the area and also remain on-call to work with 1st of the 506th on joint operations. The training component of this rotation would further be divided into blocks. The first block would concentrate on squad-level skills and operations. The next would move up to platoon-level operations, and from there we would ambitiously attempt to conduct company-level training. Each block of training would take many weeks because we could not move to the next level of training until all three companies rotated through all three parts of the process: training, guard force, patrolling/operations. Thus, we would train the battalion up to company-level operations just before the end of our tour with the Iraqis. This goal was laudable, but as usual, it did not take into consideration the realities on the ground. How were the Iraqis going to react to such a goal? Would they learn fast enough? How would the U.S. Army interact with their new neighbors? What would joint operations look like? These questions could only be answered as training progressed.

During the meeting we had other more pressing questions. What would the training blocks focus on? We started
with squad-level operations. This block would include the
obvious classes such as basic weapons handling, marksmanship, formations, and movement. These classes would focus
on the individual jundees and their actions. We all agreed that
this block should also focus on developing the squad leader
in order to develop the Iraqis' small unit leadership. Thus, we
would train and test the squad leaders' ability to control their
men, organize them, and direct them in a tactical situation.
The culminating exercise for this block would involve each
squad leader leading his squad in an attack on a designated
objective.

The problems that arose from this plan were twofold. First,
we all disagreed on the types of missions we should train the
Iraqis for. Captain Yamamoto and I both agreed that we should
train the Iraqis in the fundamentals of military actions. The
new members of the MiTT from the U.S. Army saw the issue
differently. They believed we should train the Iraqis in missions that were specific to the Habbaniyah area of operations.
If Habbaniyah was going to be the 9th Battalion's permanent
home, why not train them to fight in this specific area? And,
since the 1st of the 506th had been in this area for many
months now, they thought they could best decide how to
train the Iraqis. Needless to say, these two points of view
caused immediate friction.

Not only had the U.S. soldiers never been advisers before,
but they had obviously forgotten their own basic training.
Even American forces had to first learn the basics of soldier-
ing before they learned area-specific missions. In addition,
anyone who had spent any time with these Iraqis knew that
they needed retraining in every aspect of military life. They
may have been soldiers in Saddam's Army for years, but most
of them barely knew how to carry a weapon. Furthermore,
any of the drifters could tell the American soldiers that nothing about this adviser mission was ever set in stone. Just because a few generals said the Iraqis would have a permanent
home in Habbaniyah today, didn't mean that would remain
the case tomorrow. In fact, the mission's parameters were

guaranteed to change in the near future. That had been the nature of our entire deployment. As a result, the situation cried out for a reteaching of the fundamentals. Once trained in the fundamentals, the Iraqis could apply basic lessons to any future missions they were assigned.

The tension between us Marines and the soldiers escalated as we continued to disagree on what specific classes should be taught. Captain Yamamoto did not help the situation by being passive in the face of resistance from his subordinates. He should have nipped the dissension in the bud immediately. He could have listened to everyone's points, thanked them for their input, and then dictated what we were going to do. Instead, he allowed the dissension to fester and grow, thereby spoiling the cohesiveness of the new MiTT and undermining the training plan. The meeting spoke volumes of the challenges that resulted from the lack of unity of command in our adviser setup.

However, the greatest single contributor to the friction was one man: Gunny Babineaux. Single-handedly, he worked to undermine Captain Yamamoto and the comprehensive training plan we attempted to create by openly scoffing at the captain. Babineaux repeatedly snorted in derision at the captain's ideas and mumbled under his breath to the other MiTT members, highlighting his displeasure with the plan and the entire process.

I had never witnessed anything like this before. Here was a gunnery sergeant, a man who had been in the Marine Corps for over twenty years, openly undermining a captain in front of other officers. My anger swelled as the meeting dragged on. What was supposed to be a short one-hour gathering turned into a nearly three-hour-long negotiation. I stopped listening to the pros and cons from each side of the debate. Instead, I fixed my rage on one man. To me, Gunny Babineaux's actions constituted a complete lack of professionalism and threatened the entire training plan, not to mention his fellow MiTT members' view of Captain Yamamoto and the mission. This pessimistic attitude had been threatening the adviser mission from the moment we had landed in Iraq. Everyone had their own opinions, and everyone thought they were right.

As a consequence, no single cohesive plan was enacted and each side set about to complete the task of training Iraqis on their own. I could not let that happen again in our new MiTT venture.

Eventually, even Captain Yamamoto had had enough of the back and forth. He stipulated that we would train the Iraqis in the fundamentals and not in area-specific missions. Even after Yamamoto adjourned the meeting, my eyes did not leave Gunny Babineaux's chest. What exactly erupted out from my lungs, I don't know. I just know that whatever noise I made cleared the room of everyone else, and I was quickly nose to nose with the gunnery sergeant.

"Gunny, you are fucked up! You have no right undermining the captain and our mission that way. You have consistently forgotten your place in all of this," I said.

"Sir, you can't talk to me like that, you ..." Babineaux stammered. His face was red, and I could tell he was getting embarrassed. Our voices carried out into the hall for everyone to hear.

"Bullshit, Gunny, you have forgotten who you are and where you come from. You are a fucking Marine! You do not question orders! If you ever pull that shit in my presence again, I will personally crush your balls!" I screamed into his face. My outburst surprised even me. I was out the door before he could respond.

The point of highlighting such a "conversation" is neither to place an inordinate amount of blame on Babineaux's actions nor to emphasize myself in any way, but rather to illustrate how important the advisers' personalities were to the mission's overall success. Gunny Babineaux had come to believe that because the drifters were a small team and not a regular Marine unit, he did not have to act according to Marine standards. He believed we were something akin to a special operations team and the normal rules did not apply. So, his interpretation of the mission caused tension and conflict and interfered in the conduct of that mission.

The gunnery sergeant was just the latest example of this phenomenon. The people back in SKETCHY had their own ideas about the mission and what type of training we would need for it. The generals all had their own interpretations that lead to the simultaneous setup of an NCO academy, recon platoon, and weapons school on the same base all while a basic infantry battalion was supposed to become fully operational. The president, back in Washington, D.C., probably had his own ideas of what training the New Iraqi Army entailed. None of these interpretations appreciated the true nature of the mission or, more important, the people we were trying to train.

Eventually following my outburst, our meetings simmered down. My shouting had the effect of limiting the dissension of Captain Yamamoto's subordinates. The Iraqis were presented with a comprehensive training plan that tried for the first time to take the 9th Battalion and mold it into an actual fighting unit.

The fact that we were only now, some three months after we deployed into a combat zone in Fallujah with those same Iraqis, starting to train the Iraqis in an organized way was never mentioned. But this fact lingered on my brain as we sat there trying to sell Colonel Mehgid and his newly invigorated Battalion Staff on the training plan we had put together. We again tried to use the Jedi mind trick.

"You will like this plan. This plan is a good one."

"Yes, yes, mister, we will like this plan. This plan is good." The Iraqi colonel said, and his staff all nodded.

Even after the plan was put into place, I wondered if we drifters could use a Jedi mind trick to deceive ourselves. "You will not notice that you are training the Iraqis *after* you already deployed with them. You will not care. You will like this plan. This plan is good." But no such wave of the hand was available. Our memories were too cruel.

THE HABBANIYAH ROUTINE

Cruelty is a relative term. This fact was consistently driven into my brain during my deployment. Whether an Iraqi complained about the American Port-O-Jons not being conducive to his squatting action or a U.S. soldier questioned why none of the Iraqi jundees ever listened to him or Gunny Babineaux pointed out that one of the new Jordanian terps couldn't really speak English, I was reminded of my own conception of hell: a constant barrage of nonsense. Habbaniyah was overflowing with the sorts of inane, petty, and often dangerous circumstances that drove lesser men to the asylum.

Cruelty came in many forms. A spring heat wave was upon us, and the summer sun was fast approaching. The days became longer, the air hotter. And always the cruel ball of fire kept coming back for more. At some point there ceased to be any discernible difference between the end of one day and the beginning of the next. It was all one long day, stretched out over many long months. The desert was swallowing us, taking with us our sense of time. The polychronic mind-set was taking effect. We had gone native. There was no escape. We had lived in the Iraqis' Bizarro world for so long that at some point we just spoke the magic words Insha Allah and made ourselves comfortable amid the chaos.

In short, Habbaniyah became home. We settled into our new base, with our new MiTT members, our new mission, and our new neighbors. Between the mortar attacks from the towns nearby, the tensions with the 1st of the 506th next door, the continued refurbishment of the base all around us, and the Iraqi high jinks, the entire cacophony fell into its own rhythm, the Habbaniyah routine.

The town of Habbaniyah was located right in the middle of the two cities, Fallujah and Ramadi. Its most important feature was its position by the main highway that ran westward from Baghdad out through the Al Anbar Province. The 1st of the 506th's primary mission was to ensure that the highway remained open as a main supply and communications route.

On top of that critical mission, the 1st of the 506th also had over four hundred Iraqis on the other side of their base to worry about. They were supposed to support the Iraqis with supplies and joint training until the Iraqi side of the camp could function properly. Needless to say, they had a problem with this arrangement.

The Checkpoint Charlie was one example of the Army's discomfort. The 1st of the 506th had set up a guard post at the exact point where people could cross from the Iraqi side of the base to the American side and vice versa. Iraqis were not allowed across into the American side. Eventually we negotiated with the Army to let the Iraqis across for training or missions, but only if they were escorted. The young American guards at the post were instructed to be strict about access to their side. They didn't care who went over to the Iraqi side. Hell, a suicide car bomber could cross over to the Iraqi side and the guards would not have cared.

The guards sometimes even stopped us drifters. One guard actually asked the first sergeant for ID. That almost sent the first sergeant's head into a 360-degree spin. I could see the steam coming out of his ears from my view in the backseat of our Humvee. The first sergeant chewed out the poor guard, but that didn't end the games. The rules for crossing the unofficial border constantly changed. One day we had to have IDs, the next day we didn't. Once I noticed that the guard in the tower at the entrance actually had his weapon pointed toward the Iraqi side of the camp. Instead of looking for enemy snipers out in the neighboring town, the guard was concerned with the Iraqi Army, the same Iraqi Army the

Americans were supposed to be training and fighting with. Obviously, this situation sent our Iraqi partners the wrong message.

I partly understood why the 1st of the 506th didn't trust its neighbors. A mixture of fear and hatred drove the American soldiers. They had been fighting the insurgents for months now. At least ten of their battalion's members had been killed in that fighting. The sight of the Iraqis must've continually picked at the scabs on their wounds. This situation served to highlight the flaws in the MiTT program. While it was encouraging that commanders recognized that the adviser mission required much more manpower than originally assigned, the units now being tasked with filling those manpower shortages were not prepared to switch gears. Those units remained intent on finding and killing the insurgents, not with standing up a New Iraqi Army they considered comprised of many of those same insurgents.

The mistrust in the air was constant and palpable. The separation in this camp reminded me of the separation in Camp Fallujah. The Marines had also sent the Iraqis over to the far eastern side of the camp, away from their main buildings. They threw them in shabby tents staged open to the desert winds and posted guards on the service road that separated the Iraqi side from the American side. In Habbaniyah, we found ourselves right back where we started.

The most amusing part of this was that the time we had spent with the Iraqis had taught us one important point: they were far more dangerous to themselves than they were to any of the American units. The Iraqis were far more likely to shoot themselves than they were to try and turn on the Americans. But no matter how many times we tried to explain the situation, we could never get either 3/5 from the Marines or 1st of the 506th from the U.S. Army to believe us.

Of course, the mistrust directed at the Iraqis was also directed at anyone associated with them. Whenever we drifters mentioned we worked with the Iraqis, we got "the Look," which could only be described as one of disdain mixed with pity. While some of the Marines had flashed it during our operations in Fallujah, I distinctly remember the first time I noticed it at Habbaniyah. We were in the U.S. Army's chow hall. I was in line, and the specialist handing out rolls started to strike up a conversation with me.

"Hey, Sir, what're you doing here? We don't get a lot of Marines around these parts too often?" he said, with a cheery disposition and wide grin.

"Oh, I'm here with the Iraqis," I said off-handedly, forgetting that this was a big deal. The specialist's look said it all. His face turned to stone immediately.

"Oh, shit. . . . Well, sorry to hear that, Sir."

I looked around. All of the soldiers behind me in line were also giving me the Look. It was as if I had been contaminated by my contact with the Iraqis and was now carrying an infectious disease. No one warned us that when we went through this deployment, we might end up being ostracized. It was completely disturbing.

"Yeah, so am I," I responded, quickly taking my tray to sit in the corner with the rest of my contaminated drifter comrades.

I was still smarting from the specialist's comment when I noticed what the meal was. Sitting on my little cardboard tray was a steak and a lobster tail. I couldn't believe it.

"What is a lobster tail doing in Iraq?" I asked.

"I don't know, Sir, but I'm going back up for seconds," the first sergeant said, enjoying his small taste of the finer life.

Not twenty minutes later, the same question was put to me and the others as we crossed through Checkpoint Charlie back to the Iraqi side.

"Now, Sir, they ask what is this?" Snoop was translating for Colonel Mehgid and pointed to a lobster tail he held up on a plastic plate.

The Iraqis had been forced to eat American food for the time being. There was a plan to construct a new and improved chow hall on the Iraqi side of camp that would serve Iraqi-style cuisine, but like all the other plans, that one had been delayed because of poor planning and even poorer workmanship.

As had been the case for most of my conversations with an Iraqi, I had an audience. A group of jundees hovered around us. They all pointed to the lobster tail like it was a piece of an alien, from another world. They had never seen lobster before.

"Well, I can understand their apprehension," Captain Yamamoto chimed in.

"How do you mean?" I asked.

"Well, it does kind of look like a giant insect."

"Mister," the jundee emphatically pointed to the tail of the sea insect, "no good!" He kept pointing and shaking his head. His friends agreed and voiced their opinions. The colonel's face was stuck in a grimace. He stared at the lobster tail until we took it away from him.

"OK, OK, we're sorry. We'll tell the chow hall no lobster tails," Major Lawson finally decreed.

"That just means more for me," the first sergeant blurted out.

"Hey, and Snoop, tell them, where we come from that is considered a delicacy," I added. Even after Snoop translated, the colonel and the jundees did not understand. They kept shaking their heads.

"No, Mister, no good, no good!" the colonel said, still grimacing.

The first sergeant didn't seem to mind. He grabbed the lobster tail in question and started to eat it. He finished just in time for us to leave. We all made mental notes to monitor the Iraqi chow hall's menu from then on. The Iraqis were concerned about what went into their mouths, so we would have to be also. Such concerns, however, paled in comparison to others. Our most critical concern was still what came out their other ends.

Following the move and the unfortunate incident with the jundee squatting behind the Port-O-Jon, the problem of where the Iraqis would go to the bathroom did not go away. In fact, it only intensified. The "change of context" concept was alive and in full color.

Over the course of our time in Fallujah, we had started to get the Iraqis into a routine. They were progressing—not as fast as we would have liked, but there was progress nonetheless. Then we moved the battalion, and as soon as they left the scenery of the city, the jundees forgot the routine. Once on the ground in Camp Habbaniyah, the Iraqis seemed to roam around, lost.

The bane of my entire Iraq experience could be summed up in one word: shit. Iraqi shit. It followed us everywhere we went, including to Habbaniyah.

To review, our living area was confined to the collection of buildings on the eastern edge of the designated Iraqi side of the camp. Only the group of four buildings was considered livable. All of us, the hundreds of Iraqis and the ten drifters, were squeezed inside those four buildings. Except for the four buildings, the command post for Colonel Mehgid and his officers, and the Iraqi chow hall, the rest of the Iraqi side was deserted. The renovation of the other buildings on the Iraqi side was moving at a snail's pace. It would be months before anything else was functioning. Thus, the Iraqi soldiers could always find an empty building to try and fill up with their waste.

Instead of using the plastic Port-O-Jons or even the wooden Turkish shitters, the Iraqi battalion decided it would be better to relieve themselves in the neighboring, empty buildings. Add in the copious amounts of water they used to wipe their behinds and we had a serious health hazard on our hands. Germs and diseases could easily have taken root in our cramped living quarters and wreaked havoc on the entire unit.

We found evidence of their avoidance of the Port-O-Jons all over the camp. The problem became so bad Major Lawson had to bring it to the attention of Colonel Mehgid. Mehgid, in turn, had to call for a battalion formation. Picture the entire Iraqi unit standing at attention while a colonel ordered it to use the proper facilities or face military punishment.

The realization that we were going to have to teach them everything all over again was almost too much to bear. We were back to square one. Shit here. Don't shit over there. It was all part of the same mind-numbing sequence. Insha Allah was a completely appropriate expression in this scenario. I stopped fighting the fatalism and, instead, embraced it whole-heartedly.

The uproar over the alien lobster tails was not an isolated incident. The Iraqis were easily excitable and constantly complained. Mind you, this was while they were being paid and housed and fed all on the U.S. government's dime.

Disregarding the nerve of it all, we made every effort to smooth the transition to our new home in order to avoid further difficulties, whether mass desertions or unruly mobs. One way to do this was to build the Iraqis a soccer field. One afternoon, the U.S. Army MiTT members helped me construct the two goals in the midday sun. Did the Iraqis thank us for our efforts? Of course not. One of them actually complained that the playing field was too small.

Our hospitality spread into other more important areas. When the Iraqis complained about the way the Port-O-Jons were constructed, we brought in plastic Port-O-Jons that were designed for Iraqi use. I hadn't even known such varieties of portable toilets existed. Apparently the problem for the Iraqis was the way Americans used seats. The Iraqis didn't sit when they went. Instead, they simply squatted over a hole in the floor and took aim. The new Port-O-Jons had been designed with that principle in mind. They were taller and wider than American-style Port-O-Jons, had no seats, and had trap doors on the bottom of the booth. Finally, at least on this subject, the Iraqis seemed somewhat satisfied.

One day I caught Lieutenant Hamza coming out of a new Port-O-Jon still carrying his water bottle in his left hand.

"Ah . . . Nevarro. . . . Good. Zain, zain!" he said, pointing to the new toilets and giving me a thumbs up and big grin. I smiled and nodded in the affirmative. Then he tried to shake my hand. I had to pull away.

"Hey there, big fella, no, thank you. La, shukran," I quipped. Hamza shrugged and moved to leave. Before I turned I watched him as he discarded the water bottle he had been using in the toilet. He threw it into a large dumpster we positioned next to the toilets for that express purpose: the collection of the water bottles. The bottle came to rest on a pile of dirty water bottles approximately five feet high. Flies buzzed around the pile in the hundreds.

The water bottle was yet another mainstay of our time with the Iraqis. Everywhere we went, we gave water bottles to our new Iraqi partners. It was part of the logistical support that we provided because the New Iraqi Army had almost no way of supporting itself. And what did the Iraqis do with half those bottles? They used them to wash their asses. Furthermore, what did the Iraqis do with the bottles after they were done with them? They simply threw them in piles right next to the toilets so that they could attract swarms of flies that could potentially spread disease. The water bottles followed us everywhere we went. They became the evidence of an Iraqi presence. They were the harbingers of chaos for anyone visiting us.

The flies weren't the only things swarming around. Twice a day, a trio of Hungarian contractors drove by in what was called the "Honey Sucker" truck. They all had shaggy hair and three-day beards, and they bounced up and down in the truck's cab as they sped down the service road. Their job was to go around the camp and clean up all the Port-O-Jons. Who had hired them, no one knew, and we couldn't ask them because none of them spoke a word of English. They were simply three more additions to the strange cast of characters that filled our days. Over time their visits became just another part of the whole routine.

Other parts of that routine were even less palatable than the water bottles. After each training day and operation, the nights in Habbaniyah turned into an entirely different kind of strange. At twilight every day, hundreds of bats fluttered in the darkening sky. I was never sure whether they were the kind that sucked blood, but their presence lent a creepiness to the camp's atmosphere.

Once the day's cruel heat was gone, the Iraqis criss-crossed the courtyard and congregated in groups to socialize. Many of them walked holding hands. I knew this practice was an Arab custom, but some of the jundees' faces revealed other, less platonic motives. Snoop eventually confirmed for a second time that what went on at night in the corners of the billeting rooms was not something we should ever talk about. In short, homosexuality was rampant. I started calling the camp

Club Habbaniyah, but then I realized the place was much darker. Picture four hundred men in a confined space, with one big open courtyard. Now picture some of them sneaking off for all sorts of unsavory dealings. What did such a scene remind me of? Prison.

I was living in prison and had no way out. I was stuck there until my parole date, and even that was a floating target. Each day was a mixture of irony and danger. Over time it all started to feel the same. One day blended with the next, and to my horror, I was actually getting used to it all. I was giving in to the Insha Allah concept. I was reaching the same conclusions the Iraqis had. Everything was up to either Allah or, at least, someone other than me. I had no control.

Thus, when some Iraqis tried to make chi out by the side of one of their buildings and ended up starting a brush fire that threatened to burn the whole camp to the ground, I merely shrugged. When we found out one of the Jordanian terps was stealing drugs from Diktor Moussa's medicine supply and injecting his arms with whatever he could find, I again simply shrugged. It was all part of the same cycle of craziness. I was now completely at home in the center of this maelstrom.

Time and time again, Lieutenant Hamza and his Intelligence shop secretly talked to some of the Iraqi workers who came onto the base during the day to fix up some of the buildings. Time and time again, he relayed warnings that many of those same workers were working with the insurgents and that an attack on the camp was imminent. Each time, we took the necessary precautions and waited for the attack. Did we cease transporting the Iraqi workers back onto the base the next day? Of course not. Why would we do such a thing? It would make too much sense.

Someone relayed to me a definition of *insanity*: doing the same thing over and over again, even in the face of evidence that dictates one should change. Camp Habbaniyah was the perfect example of this, and once I figured that out I stopped fighting the Insha Allah philosophy.

A case in point was the situation with the mortars and rockets. Rocket and mortar attacks were a constant in Camp

Habbaniyah. At the northeast corner of our end of the camp was some swamp land. The Euphrates River snaked through this area, and tall reeds that provided the perfect concealment for the insurgents grew in the swamp. The enemy would sneak up through the reeds, set up a makeshift mortar or rocket tube, drop a few rounds into the tube, and be gone before the rounds even impacted.

Bam, bam, bam! Three rockets slammed into our camp on one particular day, early on during our time at Habbaniyah. I immediately jumped into action. I had my reaction time down pat. Flak jacket, Kevlar, shades, weapons, out the door—all in less than two minutes. Once outside, in the courtyard, I ran to the nearest Humvee. I wasn't the only one there. Captain Courageous was already in the driver's seat. Gunny Gonzalez was up in the gun turret. One of the MiTT soldiers was getting into the backseat. I hopped into the front passenger side, and we started rolling. We headed toward the northeast corner, where we had heard the firing.

In my haste I had forgotten about Captain Courageous and his driving skills. He had been my partner during our stunt driving training back in SKETCHY. He had a heavy foot and an even heavier brain back then. In the Humvee, racing through the rocket fire, he was no different. We skidded into each turn. We were going way too fast. The whirl of the engine was deafening. Boom! Boom! More rockets landed. They were getting closer. I banged into the side of the vehicle during a particularly tight turn.

"Jeez, Sir, you trying to kill us before they do?" I screamed out.

"Shut up and quit your whining!" He looked like a demon, possessed. His eyes were about to pop out of his skull. He gripped the wheel so tight the veins in his forearms were bulging out. His teeth were clenched in some sort of smile the devil must've been known for.

Boom! Boom! Boom! More explosions. These were even closer.

"I think they have eyes on us! They're targeting us!" I yelled out. I could see plumes of smoke rising where the rounds were hitting the ground. The Humvee rocked and bucked through potholes and unseen crevices in the road.

"Oh shit. Look out!" Gonzalez shouted from up in the turret. Everything was so confused. He had the best vantage point. If he was yelling out, we were in trouble.

"Forget it, forget it. Let's get to some cover," I said. Sweat was pouring into my eyes. I didn't know who was going to get us first, Captain Courageous or the enemy. I only knew one thing: I wanted out.

"I'm on it," said Captain Courageous. He seemed to suddenly realize how out of control he was. He slowed down then brought the vehicle to a complete stop inside a small cul-de-sac at the camp's northeast corner. We all hopped out at once and hurried into one of the empty buildings. There, a direct hit on the roof could hurt us, but we were safe from most other impacts. I hoped. We stayed away from the window openings and ignored a couple of turds that had magically appeared in the middle of the floor. The rockets were dying down now. The enemy couldn't see where we had gone.

The whole group of us summoned up some courage and rushed outside to another wall. From the new vantage point, we could see the reeds. I was hoping, praying for a human head to pop up from those damn reeds. With my rifle raised, I scanned the area. Nothing. The escape route was easily concealed by those same tall reeds. The enemy was already gone. My heart was pounding. My breath was on fire. I was wound so tight I wanted to explode in a stream of fiery lead and hate.

A few months later, I was walking toward a shower trailer. I was halfway through the courtyard when four rockets hit right in the center of our camp. Everyone exploded into reaction all around me. Iraqis hopped into Nissans and sped off to check on the damage. The 1st of the 506th sent their Quick Reaction Force over as well. I took one look at the plumes of black smoke rising into the sky and another look at the men buzzing all around me and then kept walking to the shower trailer.

Once inside, I calmly washed while I listened to the sounds of continued rocket and mortar rounds landing nearby. I could feel a couple of the closer blasts even as I dried off and wrapped the towel around my waist for the walk back to my room. I didn't have a care in the world. I was living in a place where Insha Allah made sense. And, I was used to the Habbaniyah routine by then.

Sarcasm, Shoot-outs, and a Wet Dream Riot

Even when the asymmetrical situations and threats that we were dealing with on a daily basis became routine, certain days and certain events definitely stood out. In fact, three different events adequately highlight the absurdity of our lives as drifters.

The first happened one day when I was standing in the courtyard with Major Lawson, Captain Yamamoto, Captain Courageous, and our brigade adviser, the Marine lieutenant colonel who had replaced Colonel Klink. The lieutenant colonel was in Habbaniyah to check on our progress, and we were all going to have breakfast together. We started to walk, five across, toward the Nissans. As was our usual routine, we would drive to the American side, eat chow, check e-mail, call home, drive back to the Iraqi side, train, patrol, shit, shave, shower, and so on.

"So, Sir, how are things going back in Fallujah?" Yamamoto asked.

"Things have started to heat up now that more and more people are coming back. We just had an IED take out a couple of our jundees the other day," the lieutenant colonel answered. He was chewing on a big, fat cigar. As was everyone I met in Iraq, this man was more of a cartoon character than a real person.

As we approached the makeshift parking lot, we heard a huge explosion rock the camp. I could feel the ground shudder underneath my boots. I recognized that the sound had been too big to be one of the daily rocket attacks, and I stopped in my tracks. The four senior officers continued their conversation and kept walking toward the Nissan.

"Uh, Gentlemen, shouldn't we go see what that was?"

"Nah, it's probably just another rocket," one of them said and dismissed it with a wave of the hand.

"I'm not so sure," I said, careful not to directly contradict a senior officer. I looked back to see a huge plume of smoke rising from behind the buildings that were in the southeast corner of the camp.

"Gentlemen?" I asked again. They all turned around, annoyed. I pointed to the smoke.

Bang, bang, bang! Bang, bang, bang! Three round bursts from an AK rang out. Rat-tat-tat! Rat-tat-tat! Automatic weapon fire followed from one of the guard towers and echoed off the buildings. Hearing this, the senior officers started rushing back to the barracks. I was one step ahead. All the drifters were scurrying, criss-crossing the courtyard, going for their gear. I was in and out of my room in a few minutes.

Soon I was running between the buildings. Bang, bang, bang! More gunfire rang out, leading us to the source, the enemy. Moving carefully, I jumped from one building to the next. My senses were firing on overdrive. My veins pumped with adrenaline. I carried my rifle in tight hands, careful to keep it pointed to the ground as I moved. I could raise it to my shoulder and cheek in an instant. I was a hunter, a predator, using all my senses to find my prey.

Rat-tat-tat! The guard tower was letting loose with more machine-gun fire.

Realizing I was an easy target out in the open, I raced across a clearing until I made it to some cover behind the next building.

Pop, pop, pop. A series of single gunshots rang out from right across the way, from inside the neighboring town.

I needed to find higher ground to have a better vantage point, so I raced inside the building and ran up a crumbling stone staircase, which had no banister. The continuing gunshots rang around inside the building; it was as if I was in an echo chamber. I peeked out through a window opening. The building's renovation had not yet been completed, so there were no windows, just square holes. I stayed several feet from the opening to prevent the enemy from seeing my weapon pointing out of the hole. I could see over the short fence that marked the border of our camp and into the town. The town was composed of typical short, irregular-shaped houses with courtyards and rooftop patios and countless windows or doorways, all creating a perfect perch for a sniper.

Bang! Bang! He was shooting from literally right across the street, but I couldn't pick him out from the urban jumble.

"What's going on? Where is he?" Captain Courageous asked, rushing up the stairs with that crazy look in his eyes again. The major, lieutenant colonel, and Snoop all gathered into the space behind him. Snoop poked his head out of the window opening.

"Snoop, what're you doing?" I yelled.

"Looking for enemy, Sir," he said, as cool as a cucumber.

"OK, good, but stand away from the edge, so the enemy can't see you looking out of the window."

"And pop one right into your grape!" the major added, finishing my thought. Despite the Marine jargon, Snoop got the message. He backed away and lit up a cigarette without a care in the world.

"I'm going up to the roof to getter a better view," Captain Courageous shouted.

"I'll go with you." I wanted to do something. I was pumped up.

A thin ladder led up to a hole in the ceiling that would allow us to climb out onto the roof. Once on top of the building, we hoped we'd be able to see over any cover the shooters were hiding behind.

The captain went first, while I held the ladder. He reached the top, peeked around, then climbed over the threshold, and disappeared from my view. As soon as he got up there, I heard, "Bang, bang, bang!" Another burst of AK fire erupted.

"Hey, they're shooting at us!" he yelled out.

I thought about that statement for a moment. "No shit, Sir," I said. My sarcasm in the face of violence surprised even myself. I thought about the situation. The captain had rushed to the roof without fully considering the circumstances. He was pinned down, but the short wall ringing the rooftop provided him some cover so he was relatively safe. There was no sense in me going up there. Then two officers would be out of the fight.

"I'm not coming up," I shouted up to him.

"Pussy."

I paid him no mind and went back by the windows. The only way to help the captain was to eliminate the threat, so I scanned the area again. Smoke was still rising from a building to the southeast.

"We've got one on the roof with a weapon!" I said as I spotted a man running around the roof of the smoking building a few hundred meters away.

"Drifter Five, this is Drifter Six." Major Lawson was calling Yamamoto on the radio.

"This is Drifter Five."

"Roger. We've got a military-aged male with a weapon on the roof of a building. Do you have any idea what that building is? The one that is smoking?"

We waited for the response, which would determine whether the man lived or died.

"Drifter Six, this is Drifter Five. Be advised, the Army, the Americans, are telling me that building is the Iraqi National Guard building. They're saying that was the target. It was car-bombed. It looks like that building is friendly. Repeat, those are friendlies. How copy? Over."

"Roger. I copy. Out." The major clipped his radio back to his vest.

I had my aiming dot squarely on the man's silhouette. Damn. He was on our side, whatever that meant. I exhaled and continued my scan. Two women started to cross one of the streets. They were dressed in big, black burkas. "Could they be the enemy?" I wondered to myself but quickly shook the thought off. I continued scanning. The rooftops were clear.

A road on the other side of the town allowed the civilians access to the main highway. The 1st of the 506th did not want to close the road for fear of angering the citizens. As a consequence the road provided the enemy with an easy escape route. By the time the Army sent its Quick Reaction Force out into the town to try and trap the attackers, they were long gone. The enemy had only to sneak down the back alleys between the houses, hop into any vehicle, and pretend to be driving to the store to pick up groceries for their families. We spent the next twenty minutes desperately searching, in vain. By the time we concluded our search, Captain Courageous could finally climb back down the ladder.

"What happened to you?" he asked me.

"There was no reason for both of us to be taken out of the fight," I said. He nodded in begrudging agreement.

"Besides, 'Hey, they're shooting at us?' What was that all about?" I cracked.

"Hey, I was trying to inform you guys of the tactical situation," he countered, only half serious. Having lived through so many similar situations, we were able to make light of this dangerous episode. We had learned to expect the unexpected. We had also totally succumbed to the Iraqis' way of thinking. We had given up control of our own lives and let them fall into God's hands.

The attack provided yet another example of the overall problem with our American approach to the mission. Upon getting attacked, all of us simply hurried over to the source of the shooting. We had no plan in place for our reaction, and we had no real idea what we were going to do once we arrived at the scene. And what about the other parts of the base? Were Americans moving to those lightly guarded corners? What if this initial shooting was a diversion? We took none of these questions into consideration. This disorganization reflected the entire adviser mission. Everyone felt they had to be involved, but they never coordinated their efforts into one cohesive plan.

Most important, the attack and the enemy's subsequent escape illustrated that we still did not have a clear picture of our area of operations and that the 1st of the 506th did not have complete control of that area. The U.S. Army was keeping the main road open for the Iraqis to use, and thus it afforded the enemy a way to attack us and leave in too short a time to mount an effective response. Additionally, the 1st of the 506th still hadn't briefed us in full on the area. We didn't know who else was there or what all the potential threats were. Consequently, we had trouble picking out who was our friend and who was a foe.

Given the number of competing forces in Camp Habbaniyah, this was not the first time such difficulties had arisen, and it certainly was not the last. Sure enough, some months later an even more dangerous episode occurred shortly after new intelligence reports came in indicating the enemy was planning to target the civilian workers who came to the camp each day to continue refurbishing the Iraqis' buildings. We were using local workers for the renovation to build up the local economy and garner goodwill among the Iraqi citizens. We thought that if we could get the locals invested in this base and the New Iraqi Army, they might believe the U.S. occupation and the new Iraqi government were headed in the right direction.

The civilians gathered outside the main gate of the Iraqi side of Camp Habbaniyah every morning. They were greeted by a mixture of American and Iraqi soldiers and also a crew of American civilian contractors. The contractors were a strange group of former military men who were getting paid large sums of money to escort convoys and provide security to installations across Iraq. For all intents and purposes these guys were mercenaries. They lived in a previously abandoned part of the camp that back during Saddam's time was the housing quarters for the senior Iraqi officers and kept to themselves. Their job was to search the Iraqi civilian workers before they entered our camp's gate, escort them to the designated work area for that day, and continue to monitor them for the duration of their time on the camp.

Every worker had to be carefully watched. While some intelligence reports said the enemy was interested in killing civilians, other reports said many of the workers themselves were members of the insurgency. As with everything else in Iraq, each threat had many different sides. We had to continuously look in all directions.

The insurgents were definitely interested in sneaking their

way onto the base and doing as much damage as possible. The chow hall was their number one target, as bombing it would produce the maximum number of casualties.

Sometimes we used the Iraqi troops to escort workers back out into the town. Sometimes, we'd use them to talk to individual workers to get a feel for who might be an infiltrator. Because most of our jundees were Shiites from the south and most of the civilian workers were Sunnis from the neighboring towns, trouble was bound to crop up. Whenever the two groups brushed up against each other, I saw the glares and heard whispers that confirmed their mutual ethnic hatred. The camp's tension levels were rising.

So, we had threats from all different directions. We had ethnic tension among Iraqis. We had tension between Americans and Iraqis. The camp was a powder keg.

By that point, several months into our time in Habbaniyah, I was not surprised when I heard the first burst of gunfire. Rat-tat-tat-tat! It was AK fire in the not-far-enough distance. Rat-tat-tat-tat! There it was again.

"Where is that coming from?" Major Lawson asked.

"It sounds pretty close," I replied.

Rat-tat-tat-tat! The automatic fire rang out again. Then, we heard, "Bang, bang, bang!" It was different kind of gunfire, from neither an AK nor an RPK.

"Is that what I think it is?" I yelled out. The major nodded, still trying to listen.

More shots, a mixture, went back and forth. I finally realized what was most troubling about the shots: some were American and they were coming from inside the camp. A gun battle was raging on our base, inside our own wire.

The major and I immediately sprung into action, gearing up and racing toward the apparent gun battle in a Nissan. It was a short distance from our own buildings, right down the camp's service road. A fallen tree blocked our path so we exited the vehicle and proceeded on foot. The major was in the lead. I was right behind him and just off to the side. I was his wingman. We moved in a hurried semicrouch. I raised my rifle, preparing to enter the fray. We walked down the service road as more gunshots ricocheted in the distance. With each step more questions raced through my mind. What the hell was going on? Were we being overrun? Where was the enemy? How many were there? What direction were those shots coming from? Who was firing back?

We approached a medium-size courtyard that was surrounded on three sides by two-storied buildings and on the fourth side by a smaller, one-story structure. The setup was rectangular. There were four of the big buildings, two on our right, one on the top of the rectangle, and one on the bottom. The one-story unit was to our left.

When there was a lull in the gunfire, we rushed into the middle of the situation. We had no idea what was going on or who was shooting at whom, but there was only one way to confront such a scenario, push on, always forward.

"What the hell?" Major Lawson yelled out.

A couple of our Iraqi soldiers were peeking out from one of the second-story windows. I caught a flash of an AK. Bullet holes were all around the window.

"Stay down! Stay down!" yelled an American contractor from inside the one-story building to our left. He was moving around inside the building, ducking behind whatever he could find for cover. He wasn't talking to Major Lawson and me. He was pointing and directing his fellow contractors, who were all hiding inside the small building. They had their weapons pointed across the courtyard at the building I had just seen our own Iraqi soldiers peek out of.

"What the hell is going on here?" I said out loud. The major looked at me like he was wondering the same thing. We cautiously approached the room where the contractors had taken up defensive positions.

"Americans coming in. Don't shoot. Americans coming in," the major said.

We managed to enter the building without one of them accidentally shooting us. They were all crouched near the window openings, pointing their weapons at our Iraqi soldiers.

"What happened?" the major asked one of the contractors. He replied with a garbled explanation that didn't make any sense. The guy had long hair and a beard. He looked like

Jesus. He held out an American-made pistol. "Iraqi soldiers ... shooting ... fired back ... confrontation ..." That's about all he could say. He was freaked out. The fog of war was filling his eyes.

Iraqi jundees started spilling out of the buildings. We were receiving fresh Iraqi troops every other week as part of the buildup on the base and had started to move some of our soldiers into these newer buildings to accommodate our growing numbers. The problem was these buildings were still in the process of being refurbished. Thus, the civilian workers and our jundees were in close contact for a good part of the day. I was starting to understand what had happened.

The jundees continued to spill out of the entrances. Others were hanging out of the windows. They were screaming, some at us, others at each other. They were working themselves into a frenzy.

"Alright, no one fires another shot! Got it?" Major Lawson said to the contractors. I couldn't tell if they had heard him. They were too focused on the growing number of Iraqis shouting insults and threats at them.

The major walked back outside, and I was right behind him. I scanned the growing crowd for any threats. I recognized many of our soldiers. Mohammed was there. So was Saleh. The Ninja Shitter was there too. But they were all far too mad to acknowledge me at this point. They were pointing at the contractors, screaming until their spit flung out into the air. The major and I stepped right into the open, into the center of the courtyard and the center of the storm. Finally, the Iraqis noticed us. They recognized us as the "good" Americans and started shouting at us. They weren't angry with us; they were only trying to tell us or show us something. I couldn't make out anything coherent. Too many of them were trying to speak at once. They were pointing toward one of the doorways, which, I noticed, was framed with bullet holes. They kept pointing to something or someone.

"Mister, Mister, Mulazem Awal, Mulazem Awal" was all I could make out. I followed their fingers to two jundees. They lay by the side of the building, writhing and moaning in agony. Some of their fellow jundees were trying to calm them down and tend to them. They had been shot.

"Fuck!" It was the only word I could manage. Even though I knew by then to expect the unexpected, this situation was as asymmetrical as one could get.

"What the hell happened?" the major asked. Before he knew it he was surrounded by excited Iraqis all trying to talk to the American officer in Arabic. He shook his head at his own mistake, pushed past them, and went to the two injured Iraqis' sides. One had a bullet hole in his hip. The other had one right in his ass. They were moaning and had their eyes squeezed tight in pain.

At that point the shit storm grew. A Navy corpsman came out of nowhere and immediately started tending the wounded. I had no idea who he was or what he was doing there. The major was on the radio calling for a medical evacuation. Captain Yamamoto pulled up in a Humvee as though he was coming from right around the corner. A Marine corporal I had never seen before was standing in a doorway with his pistol pointed up at the window the Iraqis had been shouting from earlier, the one with the bullet holes around it. Captain Courageous came running into the courtyard ready to save the day. Soon, he was talking to the Jesus contractor, getting his side of the story.

Then came our friendly neighbors, the 1st of the 506th, rumbling into the courtyard with four heavily armored Humvees from the Quick Reaction Force, thinking the base was being overrun.

"Where's the enemy? What's going on?" one of the gunners yelled out. No one bothered to answer.

The Iraqis, nearly the entire battalion, soon filled the courtyard. They gathered in crazed, nearly riotous groups of ten to twenty and stared at us. Colonel Mehgid was standing in the middle of their ranks with his most trusted sidekicks whispering into his ear, relaying the latest gossip about what had happened. He was looking right at me. I looked to both sides. Major Lawson was gone. So was Captain Yamamoto. I was the only drifter officer around.

"Where'd they go?" I asked Captain Courageous, who was still trying to piece everything together.

"They went with the wounded."

"Both of them?!" I shook my head. Snoop appeared out of nowhere.

"Now, Sir, the soldiers, I talk with them. They say they going to kill the contractors," he stated matter-of-factly. When would this end?

"Dude, they can wipe us all out if they want to," Captain Courageous said, making his bid for the title Master of the Obvious.

I saw that Colonel Meghid was still looking at me. The entire courtyard was filled with people. The crowd was seething and writhing. It swirled around us. I took a deep breath and approached the Iraqi colonel.

Suddenly an American Army colonel came out of nowhere. I wasn't sure who he was or what his business was. I thought I recognized him as an adviser from another unit who was visiting the base for no particular reason. He was very short and had a Hitler moustache that I wanted to tell him went out of style right about the time World War II ended—but I had bigger things to worry about. Our campmates were about to kill each other.

"Alright, alright, what the fuck is going on here?" The colonel was barraged with responses in all different languages from fifty different people before he stopped them with a hand held up into the air. "Who is the senior adviser here? Who is in charge?"

I looked around at a mix of Iraqi officers and jundees, U.S. Marines and soldiers, a few Navy personnel, heavy weaponry, and all of my drifter team except Yamamoto and Lawson. The whole circus was in town.

"Who is in charge here?" Little Hitler asked again.

Whether I was getting pulled into an office and told to prepare to go to Iraq or getting attacked an hour into our first combat operation or driving an injured jundee through the streets of nighttime Fallujah, or being called out by the commandant for questions, I was always being put to the test. Whether by design or happenstance, I always seemed to be in the middle of things. Was this a coincidence? Or, was this part of a plan? Was this the result of Allah's will?

I took a deep breath and swallowed before opening my mouth. "Sir, I am in charge."

Little Hitler took one look at me, then all around him at the cast of assorted characters that surrounded him. He snorted under his breath, shook his head in disbelief, and walked off the stage.

I chuckled to myself and then tried to show Colonel Mehgid the wisdom of gathering up all the ammunition from each and every Iraqi jundee so that they wouldn't be able to kill us all. He agreed.

I exhaled and watched as the situation came down to a slow boil over the next few hours. Brokering a cease-fire agreement between the contractors and our Iraqi partners took several days, and the tensions between the groups never dissipated.

The standoff was yet another example of how uncoordinated the adviser effort was. Too many pieces were being thrown into the puzzle and none of them fit neatly together, no matter how much the president or the generals wanted them to. American contractors, Iraqi civilians, Iraqi soldiers—all were mixed together with Marines, soldiers, and sailors from a multitude of different units. No one person was in charge of it all. We were living with a complete breakdown of command and control in a combat environment.

The shoot-out also illustrated the various angles from which threats presented themselves to us. Discerning who was friend and who was foe was always difficult. No clear delineation between the safe zones and the combat zones existed. There was no front line. Instead, we lived in an environment where death lurked everywhere. We were surrounded by Iraqis and other strange actors, and the danger could be in any room or down any road, whether it was outside in the town or inside the confines of our own base.

Given the twenty-four-hours-a-day nature of the threats, I went through the entire deployment with my pistol either under my pillow or placed on the floor right under my bed. I even practiced reaching for the gun and bringing it up to bear on the door to my room. I wanted to be ready. Unfortunately, this preparedness waned as the Insha Allah fatalism took root in my thoughts. Although I would normally carry a weapon with me at all times, sometimes I found myself not bothering to when I went to take a shower or went to use the Port-O-Jon. I figured that if it was my time to die, I could do nothing about it.

Not too long after this mentality had invaded my thoughts God seemed to test my theory. I was standing in the court-yard, unarmed, wearing camouflage trousers and a green skivvy t-shirt. The courtyard was empty except for a couple of Iraqis walking hand in hand to the shower trailer. By that time, I could shrug off the man-love.

The shower trailer—one of four old, unused trailers that had been sitting abandoned in a corner of the camp—was courtesy of some Navy Seabees who were helping to refur-bish other parts of the base. Somehow the Seabees had hooked up the proper piping and water tanks to get the showers running. The trailer had ten shower stalls and some sinks to shave over.

One trailer was better than none, but when you realized there were over five hundred dirty bodies on camp to wash, it didn't seem as good. The trailer was used by both the Ameri-cans and Iraqis, and a schedule was instituted so that water could be conserved. To ensure that the schedule was adhered to, a lock was placed on the trailer door. One key was given to the Americans, and another was given to the Iraqi logistics shop. In theory the Americans and the Iraqis could each moni-tor key use and thereby monitor shower use.

Standing in the courtyard that day, I watched as the theory went bust.

A small group of jundees had gathered across the way, just outside their building. One of them was angrily shouting while his friend listened intently. Once they heard what the agitated one had said, they all started raising their voices, jab-bering back and forth to each other.

I watched this interaction, mildly amused. By then I knew almost every single Iraqi, if not by name then by face. I knew who were friends and who didn't like each other. Snoop was excellent for gathering intelligence on the inner dynamics of the Iraqi battalion. He hung out with everyone, from the officers to the jundees, and could help us keep our ears to the ground.

The jundee who had started the commotion was tiny, maybe five feet tall. He had a flat face, without the usual Saddam moustache, and beady little eyes. I recognized him and his friends as a group of troublemakers who always complained. First they complained about vacation. They didn't get enough time with their families. Then they complained about the amount of pay they were receiving.

As an aside, there were rumors of kickbacks to the officers and other financial dalliances. One rumor that refused to go away had it that Colonel Mehgid had stolen over one million new Iraqi dinar from some houses in Fallujah. I wasn't sure exactly how much that was in dollars, but it was easily more than ten thousand. Since we had no evidence to back this claim, we couldn't do anything. Insha Allah.

The jundee continued to carry on, and his friends were getting louder and louder. They all started to move with an aggressive manner toward the next building, where most of the officers were staying. Sure enough a group of officers and senior NCOs walked out just in time to meet the band of angry jundees. I could see where this was going, fast.

The two groups started yelling and screaming at each other. The tiny jundee was incensed. He couldn't contain himself. He was trying to push his way through the crowd to get at one of the senior NCOs. Others were holding him back, which made him even more frustrated. He broke contact but only to run around the crowd to approach his target from a different angle. The NCO he was after was one of the good guys as far as we drifters were concerned. He was a little overweight but was good at his job. He was in charge of the logistics from the enlisted side of things. He had a big smile that he flashed whenever one of us Americans said hello to him. I couldn't imagine what he had done to rile up the jundee.

The courtyard had a strange acoustic effect on every sound. The echoes could be heard by almost everyone in every room of the four billeting buildings, and soon the fighting Iraqis had an audience. The two groups of Iraqis had begun to push against each other. The tension in the air was rising. Many were screaming nose to nose. One of the troublemaking jundees ran into his building. When he came out not two minutes later, he had twenty others behind him. The reinforcements added some real punch to the jundees' side, and the small group of officers started to feel the pressure.

The whole battalion had spilled out of the buildings and filled the entire courtyard. Some jundees stood by and watched, trying to figure out, first, what was going on and, second, whose side they were going to take. I was sure most would've immediately supported their fellow jundees if they hadn't feared the officers' retribution. While many entered the fracas, even more sat on the sidelines, waiting to see how the situation played out.

Tension had been building between the officers and the soldiers for months. Most of the officers, products of Saddam's era, were not good. They had either bribed their way into their rank or simply came from a powerful tribe or family that had connections in the Ministry of Defense. Most didn't know half as much as they said they did, plus they sat around while their soldiers did all the work. They took long breaks in the middle of the day to lounge around, and they never liked when one of us Americans gave them a task. The Iraqi lieutenants were the worst. They were the junior officers and knew even less than everyone else, but they still felt entitled to privileges due an officer's rank. I once saw a lieutenant address his platoon wearing only pants and a sweaty brown t-shirt. The rest of the unit was in full battle gear. They had their helmets and flak jackets on and their weapons slung over their shoulders. They were about to go on a five-mile hike in the afternoon sun. The lieutenant didn't see anything wrong with his attire. He didn't think he had to lead by example. He simply had to order his men around, and they would have to do as he said.

This mentality led to the conflict I was witnessing. The situation had definitely metastasized into a full-scale riot. The tiny jundee that started it all was driven out of his mind by his inability to reach the subject of his ire, the normally jovial S-4 NCO. The jundee ran into his building and came running out with a small metal ladder from his bunk bed in his hands.

He swung the ladder back and forth wildly in the air, screaming at the top of his lungs. His friends were lunging at their opponents, clutching and grabbing. Some were swinging their fists. The officers were not backing down either. They had their own reinforcements and were pushing back against the crazed jundees.

Those on the sidelines added their two cents. The entire courtyard was like a bowl, filled with invectives and cliquish hatred. The prison metaphor came back to me because I felt like I was in the yard with rival gangs fighting over some unknown beef. The rest of the drifters were out of their rooms and watching as I was. We had learned when to get involved and when not to. This was definitely a time not to get involved. This was an Iraqi-on-Iraqi problem.

So, I stood there, unarmed and alone, in the middle of the riot. But that was the thing: while one side of my brain was telling me to run and get my pistol, the other side, the fatalistic side, said, "Oh, well. If we die, we die."

"Insha Allah," I said, but no one was paying attention to me. As Iraqi fists were flying and more pushing and shoving and shouting swirled all around me, I shrugged and watched the riot roil to a new level.

Colonel Mehgid came striding out from his room. He was like an emperor, surrounded by his own set of bodyguards, the Praetorians, as he made his way through the crowd. Whenever a jundee or another officer saw the colonel coming, he made way. It was like watching the parting of the sea. However, this time, even when the colonel reached the epicenter of the fighting, the pushing and shoving did not stop. His bodyguards had to put up defense when a couple of wild punches came too close to the colonel. The scene was becoming too chaotic to catalogue. I scanned the courtyard and saw little arguments flaring up all around. The situation was spiraling out of control.

The tiny, angry jundee took his metal ladder, his weapon of opportunity, and flung it into a crowd around the S-4 NCO. That, of course, provoked an equally violent reaction and fists flew in earnest. A couple of bloody jundees backed out of the crowd, clutching their heads or mouths.

Colonel Meghid was yelling at the jundees like a father would scold his children. Some of them backed off, but others actually shouted back. Something had triggered their anger, and they were not going to let it go. At least that was the meaning I attached to their gestures. I was simply a bystander, completely disconnected from my body. I felt no fear, no preoccupation. I felt like I was watching a foreign movie with no subtitles. I had to piece together the meanings from only what I saw.

The colonel, having arrived after the fighting had started, was trying to figure out what was going on. He was having little luck with this because the jundees were shouting so incoherently he couldn't figure out what their problem was. He knew who they were after, though, because the angry jundee kept pointing at the fat S-4 NCO.

At some point in the chaos, one of the lieutenants, one of the real shitbirds, seemed to have enough of the dialogue. He felt it was beneath the officers and especially his colonel to even talk to the jundees. The soldiers were there to do the officers' bidding, period. The lieutenant was armed. He had a Russian-made pistol in a holster slung around his shoulder, and he reached for the weapon. He was going to teach these jundees a lesson.

Colonel Mehgid happened to notice the pistol flashing in the sunlight. He immediately broke contact with the jundees he was talking with and turned to the younger lieutenant. He started screaming into the junior officer's face. I didn't need a translator to tell me what he was saying. Mehgid recognized the danger of ratcheting up the level of violence in this situation. One pistol could result in a full-scale cannabalistic bloodbath. The jundees outnumbered everyone else more than three to one. With sheer numbers they could've crushed us all. The colonel grabbed the pistol out of his foolish lieutenant's hands and waved him away with the back of his hand. The lieutenant cowered out of sight. That seemed to do the trick. I wasn't sure if he intended to do it, but the colonel had shown both his strength and his fairness. No one was going to challenge him. It took an hour to calm everyone down sufficiently to get them to return to their rooms. The jundees who had started it all were nowhere to be seen.

Mohammed walked by me as the situation was returning to a simmer. I hadn't seen all that much of him since we moved to Habbaniyah and he started training for the SEALs' recon platoon. I gave him a nod of recognition, but he did not smile.

"You come and say you change Iraq. You change things in my country. Where is change?" he asked, angry.

"What do you mean, Mohammed?" I replied, on the defensive.

"You say new army be different from old Saddam army. But nothing change. Nothing change. This all same as old army." He looked around at the simmering aftermath. The Iraqis were filtering back into their rooms to stew about everything.

I looked directly into Mohammed's eyes. "Mohammed, this is an Iraqi problem. You and your friends must change this." As I said this, I pointed all around us.

"No. This no change. I think this stay same, forever. Iraq no good." Behind the anger and disgust I saw sadness. Mohammed felt hopelessness I could do nothing about.

"What is it you Iraqis like to say?" I asked, and Mohammed looked at me inquisitively. "Insha Allah," I said. He didn't like that response. It seemed that when confronted with the Iraqis' way of thinking, he could only shake his head in disagreement. Apparently, God's will was only useful when it was good for the Iraqis.

Mohammed did not have anything left to say. We looked at each for another moment before silently breaking away. I wondered if our friendship was over. But I didn't have time to worry about hurting peoples' feelings. I needed to find out what the cause of the riot was. I had to talk to Snoop.

"Now, Sir, the jundees say that they have been insulted. They cannot let it stand," Snoop said.

"OK. So, what does that mean?" Yamamoto asked.

"Now, they going to do something about it for themselves."

"What are they planning?" I said, but I already knew the answer.

"Now, Sir, they plotting to kill the officers that insulted them. And the officers they trying to get soldiers discharged from army," Snoop said.

"This is not good," said Captain Yamamoto, once again stating the obvious.

"I don't mean to be belligerent here, Gentlemen, but do we even know what this was all about?" the first sergeant interjected.

Snoop started chuckling. He couldn't help himself. In fact, once we all heard the explanation for the violence, it was hard for any of us to take it seriously either. Apparently, the fight centered on the fact that the small jundee needed to take a shower. As Snoop told the story, when the jundee approached the fat S-4 NCO and asked for the key to the shower trailer, he was thoroughly rebuked. The jundee, however, would not take no for an answer. He was emphatic that he absolutely, positively needed to take a shower. This was the world's most important shower ever.

In this case, it turned out, the devil was in the details—literally. The jundee was so crazed because the night before the riot, he had had a dream. And it was not an ordinary dream. When he awoke the next morning, he realized his dream had resulted in a nocturnal emission. An American would've merely shrugged had this happened to him, but for a Muslim, the occurrence had an added significance. As Snoop explained, a nocturnal emission was a sign that the devil had come and visited the dreamer in the night. To cleanse himself of the satanic spell, the Muslim had to literally clean himself up immediately.

Thus, when the NCO refused his shower request, the jundee faced eternal damnation. The jundee was incensed that the NCO was essentially sending him to hell by refusing him the key. Considering the religious connotation of the exchange, a confrontation was almost inevitable.

On hearing this tale, we Americans could only throw up our hands and walk out of the room shaking our heads. We had now seen it all, including the world's first wet dream riot.

THE PATROL PACKAGE

Despite the repeated mortar attacks, the riots over seafood and nocturnal emissions, the continued tension between the Iraqi and American sides of the base, and ongoing Iraqi vacations, the training plan gathered steam and continued on a steady pace. The MiTT was firmly in place, and classes and practical exercises were implemented on a daily basis. The Iraqi shitting problem, though it took some time and increased effort to solve, was also eventually brought back under control.

Acclimating the 9th Battalion to its new home in Habbaniyah had provided the best example yet of the Iraqis' problems with changes in context. Once they arrived in Habbaniyah, learning the rules of the new context, the new area, took them a significant amount of time. Through adherence to a set training plan we eventually brought some semblance of order to their new world. By instituting a rotating system of responsibilities we kept them focused on their daily tasks.

In addition to teaching the Iraqis the fundamentals of military operations, the three training blocks—basic training, standing guard, and patrolling—sought self-reinforcement. For example, many of the basic training classes centered on how to stand guard and how to lead a patrol as an NCO. Our intention was to run the jundees through the rotation several times, with each subsequent block of training building on the lessons of the previous block. Furthermore, during each rotation the Iraqis were given more responsibility. We started by focusing on the Iraqi squad leaders and sought to work our way up through the units. Next we would focus on the Iraqi platoon commanders or platoon leaders, as they called them. From there, we would attempt the unprecedented step of conducting a full-size company-level operation. We forced both the company commanders and the Battalion Staff to be involved in every step of this plan. We wanted to place as much responsibility we could onto their shoulders so that they would actually start running the 9th Battalion.

The plan, as ambitious as it was, hit several obstacles along the way. The Iraqi leave policy was still in effect, which meant that training often shut down while the Iraqis went home to see their families. The MiTT members had philosophical differences as far as the specific classes that should be taught. Plus, the level of partnership between the 9th Battalion and the 1st of the 506th had an ever-evolving benchmark.

Taken as a whole, however, the setup was working. The Iraqis were improving at a modest pace and our footprint in the area of operations was increasing. Nowhere were these developments more readily apparent than in the patrolling package.

As they had been in Fallujah, patrolling and guard duty were the two principle missions that the Iraqis were expected to conduct. The two worked hand in hand. The Iraqis had to be able to provide security for themselves and to go out into the neighborhood, among their own people. Foot patrols showed the Iraqi civilians that the New Iraqi Army was on the scene. The patrols were tangible evidence that the new Iraqi government was working to secure the streets. In addition, they could be an effective means to combat the insurgency. The Iraqis knew the area and the people better than the Americans did and could help figure out who was an insurgent and who wasn't. Finally, by patrolling the Iraqis gave the coalition a larger footprint on the battle space. If the Americans could count on the Iraqis to police certain areas, they could focus on different areas. The two forces could work in concert and spread throughout the area of operations.

The pressure to bring the Iraqis up to speed enough to conduct their own independent patrols was always present. As the adviser for the 9th Battalion's assistant operations officer, I was in charge of developing the entire patrol package. Captain Omar, my Iraqi counterpart, seemed limited in his understanding of the operational plan, so I was able to comprise a plan on my own. As long as I briefed him on the plan in a manner that suggested I was asking for his approval, I could construct the plan however I wanted to. In this task my ability as an adviser to appear to ask instead of order was of prime importance.

The plan I devised was both simple and complicated at the same time. We would focus on two aspects of the patrol. One focus would be the jundees' actions on the patrol, including their basic formations, their movement through an urban area, and the immediate action drills, including reacting to a sniper or an IED. Eventually, we would start throwing in more skills such as how to conduct a snap vehicle checkpoint (VCP) and how to transition from a patrol into an assault. The second and more involved focus was on the patrol leader himself. The patrol leader was the one man most responsible for the way each patrol was run. Since the patrol leaders were also training to be either Iraqi NCOs or officers, this focus contributed to the Iraqi leadership's training. Each patrol leader was expected to be able to navigate the terrain and control the patrol formation. In addition, he was involved in planning the patrol.

I wanted each Iraqi leader to receive instruction on how to plan the patrol, how to brief his plan to both his higher commanders and the members of his patrol, and how to then make his plan happen. Toward this end, we exposed the Iraqi leaders to a much greater level of detail in instruction than they had experienced before. Viewing Habbaniyah via satellite imagery, I designated names for each street in the towns surrounding the base. Using Snoop and some ingenuity, I named the streets after numbers and months of the year so that they could be easily translated to the Iraqis. This forced the patrol leaders to plan their patrol routes with specific detail and draw them on overlays that matched the maps created from my satellite pictures. The patrol leaders submitted their overlays to the battalion operations center, located in the command post building. They would brief the watch officer in the operations center on their route and plan and ensure they had a solid communications link back to the op center.

The patrol leader was also expected to review his plan with his patrol members. He was supposed to inspect his men to ensure they were wearing the proper gear. Then he conducted rehearsal drills to make sure the jundees were prepared for anything they encountered while on patrol. During the patrol, the leader had to report in when he was leaving and when he returned to the friendly line. He also had to report when his patrol had reached different, pre-designated checkpoints so that the battalion's op center knew exactly where its soldiers were. We created a Quick Reaction Force that would remain alert and ready to reinforce the patrols should they receive contact with the enemy. And because I was also working with Lieutenant Hamza in Intelligence, we started attaching at least one intel jundee to each patrol to talk to the Iraqi citizens in town, to try and find information about the enemy. In short, the patrolling package was a comprehensive effort.

That is not to say, however, that there were no potholes on the road to independent patrols—far from it. Many of the American soldiers had doctrinal philosophies that differed from the Marines' philosophies, and this caused much friction. For example, as part of this ongoing patrolling effort I created a patrol checklist based on the official Marine Corps patrol checklist. Each MiTT member who accompanied the Iraqi patrols was given a checklist to use to evaluate the patrol leader's skills. I even had Snoop translate the checklist into Arabic so that Captain Omar could issue the checklists to the patrol leaders. Thus, the Iraqi NCO or officer knew exactly what skills he was expected to show proficiency in. The checklist was a great teaching tool.

Unfortunately, not every American bought into the concept of filling out written evaluations. Some soldiers were of the mind-set that because we were at war, and in a combat zone no less, we should not be trying to run a school. While I could understand this point of view, I accepted the necessity of a training school as just one of the fundamental flaws in we Americans' adviser mission. We were in Iraq to stand up a completely new military force. This was not a short-term project. If we wanted to create a stable and self-supporting force that could continue on even after the Americans left, we were going to have to start from the ground and build a sound foundation based on core competencies. Only with this foundation would the New Iraqi Army eventually stand on its own two feet and take over from the coalition forces.

Again, not everyone agreed. Lieutenant Grissom, one of the U.S. Army MiTT members loaned to us from the 1st of the 506th, was one of those who disagreed. Strangely, he decided not to voice his disagreement but rather secretly undermine the whole process. During a weekly operations meeting we discovered that none of 2nd Company's advisers had filled out an evaluation checklist for any of the company's patrols. Only when I confronted Grissom about this deficiency did I learn that none of the checklists had been completed because Grissom didn't agree with the checklist approach. He felt the checklists were too detailed and unfair to the Iraqi patrol leaders.

Needless to say, I met his disagreement with hostility. Not only did I think he was wrong, not only did I believe we should hold the Iraqis to higher standards and train them to meet those standards, but I also felt the manner in which Grissom had decided to subvert the training process went against every fiber of my professional military upbringing. In fact, his behavior reminded me of that of the Iraqis, who were known for nodding "Yes, yes, Mister" and then ignoring whatever they had been told to do. As we questioned Grissom about his actions, I almost expected him to simply shrug and say, "Insha Allah." When this response did not come, I could only assume that Grissom hadn't yet learned the Iraqi explanation for everything. I was confident he would know those two words well in time.

The doctrinal differences illustrated by Grissom's refusal to fill out patrol checklists were not the only difficulties we faced during the buildup of our patrolling capabilities. Bringing the Iraqis up from where they were to where we wanted them to be required time, effort, and much patience on our end. Two specific patrols showed me that this patience would have to be extended toward not only the Iraqis but also many of my fellow Americans.

As adviser to the assistant operations officer I also helped supervise the conduct of the battalion's operations and ensured that the Iraqis were indeed learning. One of the best ways I could do this was to periodically accompany Iraqi troops during missions to observe how they were progressing. This always provided a mixture of comedy and terror. It also provided important lessons—some I did not want to learn.

I went out on one patrol with a squad from 3rd Company, during which we rode out of the camp in the back of one of the Ashook Leland trucks. Unfortunately, the driver got lost on our way to the exit point. Apparently, the Iraqi patrol leader had not done an adequate job of briefing his movement plan to the drivers. When I asked one of the Jordanian interpreters to tell the driver to turn around, the terp couldn't understand a word I said. "I no understand," the terp repeated again and again. This was not a good start to the patrol.

When we finally found the right exit point, the Iraqi patrol leader almost immediately exposed himself as substandard. First, his confused looks made it obvious that he couldn't read a map. His map-reading deficiency caused the entire patrol to become lost and stuck in some ten-foot-tall reeds with swamp water up to their knees. The marshlands, a product of the nearby Euphrates River, were completely impassable. Eventually, the patrol leader figured this out and turned the patrol around. I marked down his deficiencies as we went: poor navigational skills, lack of knowledge of the patrol route, etc.

Eventually we arrived at our originally intended destination, a part of the town right next to our camp that was completely abandoned. Once there, the patrol leader, who still had no idea where he was going, started walking with his map held out in front of him. This was not exactly tactically sound, as any enemy could easily have pegged him as the patrol leader and could have rendered the unit leaderless with one shot.

This patrol occurred during the later spring months, and the heat was growing in intensity. I made sure I was hydrating as much as possible. I drank enough water to prevent any dizziness from setting in. When I looked around at the Iraqis, I noticed that none of them were drinking. In fact, most of them hadn't even brought water bottles with them. Apparently, since the patrol leader had not told them to bring water, none had. Of course, not ten minutes into our patrol of the abandoned buildings one of the Iraqis dropped to the ground from apparent heat exhaustion. When I examined the downed jundee, I could see that he was much older than many of the others. He had wrinkles and graying hair. Eventually, I learned that he was almost forty years old. He should not have been sent out on this patrol. When he complained of legs cramps, we threw him into one of the Humvees that had come along with us and continued on.

Later in the patrol, half the Iraqis started swaying, as they too suffered the onset of heat exhaustion. Many of them told their patrol leader they had to sit down. I couldn't entirely blame them. We were in full gear. The temperature was close to 105 degrees, and there were no clouds in the sky. My brain felt like it was being scrambled, with my Kevlar helmet acting as the frying pan. Sweat was pouring down my back with a squish, squish, and my feet were on fire. We were baking. The patrol turned around not five minutes after men started asking to rest. The Iraqis couldn't take the heat any longer. They were simply too dehydrated because their patrol leader was not competent and had failed in his leadership duties. He had not properly briefed his plan and had not inspected his troops to ensure they brought water for the patrol.

On our way back to base, we encountered gunfire coming from just beyond the tall reeds. When we investigated the marsh area, we found no one. The reeds had once again allowed the enemy to escape.

All in all, the patrol was as unsuccessful as any patrol I could've imagined. It merely reinforced my conclusion that patience and perseverance were required if any adviser mission was to enjoy even a modicum of success.

The adviser mission also required advisers who were professional and competent. The adviser team was the backbone against which the soft tissue of the Iraqi unit would have to lean. If that backbone was not capable of doing its job then the entire body would collapse. I became concerned about certain parts of, certain advisers in, the support structure we were providing after a particularly strange and infuriating patrol I later dubbed Operation Masquerade.

The operation started out as any normal patrol would have. A squad of Iraqis led by a squad leader was driven to a part of the local area a few miles from our camp. Two members of the MiTT were there to act as supervisors and to report back via radio transmissions to both Drifter Base and the 1st of the 506th in case of any serious engagements with the enemy. I shadowed the patrol, acting strictly as an observer. I was there to evaluate how the Iraqis conducted themselves and to ensure that the Americans were teaching the Iraqis the right techniques.

Once we arrived at the drop-off point, we jumped out the back of our trucks, got in the proper patrol formation, and stepped off into our assigned sector. We had a preplanned route set, and we were ready to search through a specific area of the town. Three of us Americans were on the patrol with the Iraqis, and we walked at three different points in the Iraqis' formation so that we weren't all hit by a single mine or IED.

The lead American for the patrol was Staff Sergeant Buckfield, one of the 1st of the 506th's MiTT members. He was tall and very thin and had a scraggily moustache and glasses. For some reason he was walking with a sniper's rifle with a big scope that could zoom in on targets. And, perhaps most important, he seemed to be constantly on edge. His eyes darted around too quickly. His partner, another MiTT member, was a short black soldier who had a good head on his shoulders. He was soft-spoken but knew what he was doing, and he was laid back enough to handle Buckfield.

Patrolling in Habbaniyah was much different than it had been back in Fallujah. Whereas Fallujah was a series of streets and avenues and buildings, the area around Habbaniyah was lush from the nearby Euphrates River. Fields of green swept across our view, marshland lay near the riverbed, and tall palm trees rose up everywhere. The houses were spread out as well. Many of them had small personal farm patches in which the civilians tried to grow food or kept a couple of animals. Cows, llamas, and a donkey were often seen in the area.

We stepped through the lush green lands with our rifles at the ready and our eyes scanning back and forth, but we knew we were sitting ducks. Any sniper could've taken clear aim at us. We could only hope he wasn't a good shot.

The civilians came out of their houses to watch the patrol pass by. We were curiosities. The civilians still didn't know what to make of the Iraqi soldiers. Sometimes the Iraqi patrol leader would stop and talk to the man of a house. We had one of the Jordanian terps, the one who looked like a heroine addict, along with us on this particular patrol. I hoped he wasn't high. We would need him if we were going to talk to any of the Iraqis.

We walked by a house that, for whatever reason, Buckfield and the Iraqi patrol leader decided to go inside. Entering houses wasn't part of the original plan. We were there to patrol the streets and fields and simply show our presence.

Two cows were tied to a post near the front of the house. They were emaciated and easily startled. When they backed away from me, the bell that hung around the neck of one of them jingled. Three young children stood just outside the door as I walked inside. They didn't know what was going on. They stared up at the giant American as I went in the front door. Once inside I saw the Iraqi soldiers going through everything. They were looking through all the rooms, all the furniture in each room, all the closets. The man's three wives looked on. Buckfield, the Iraqi patrol leader, and the strung-out Jordanian terp were all talking to the man of the house.

"What's going on, Staff Sergeant? I thought we were supposed to be patrolling," I said to Buckfield.

"Sir, we are, but this guy, I thought he was acting a little suspiciously, so we're checking his place out."

"Alright, what does he have to say for himself?"

"He claims to know where a big-time insurgent lives. The name he gave is on our high-value target list. I already called it in and got confirmation." He was clearly excited about this last bit of information. His eyes glazed over when he said "high-value target."

"Well, what does he say? Where does the guy live?"

"He said the guy lives in a house by the mosque in town. The house has a blue front door."

"OK, let's mark that info down and move on." The patrol was on a time schedule. The trucks would be returning to pick us up in an hour or two at most.

"Sir, I think we should pursue this lead. I don't want to wait," Buckfield pressed.

"Hey, Staff Sergeant, this is your show. I am here to observe. I would caution you, though, not to go off on some wild goose chase. We have gathered some information and we can investigate, but I wouldn't press it." I wasn't sure if he heard my warning. He just nodded and grunted.

We were out the door and on our way to search for the house by the mosque with the blue door. The main mosque in the area was located in a small town about two miles up the road. Since the civilian didn't want to be seen helping the Americans, he didn't come with us to point out the exact house. So, we continued on our own. I remember having a bad feeling about where the patrol was headed. I should've listened to my instincts.

We trudged through more green fields and palm trees until we came to the more built-up area. When I say "built-up" I mean the area had more houses closer together. It still was nothing but a shantytown. Half the houses looked decrepit and crumbling, and the streets were filled with debris and the occasional donkey. According to the other MiTT sergeant, the place was called Coolie Town, but there was nothing cool about it. The people on the streets stared at us as we passed. They were not all friendly looks. The suspicion, on both sides, was palpable.

"Staff Sergeant, do you know where we are going?" I finally asked. The hunt for the house with the blue door was turning into an exercise in futility. I admired Buckfield's initiative, but our actions had to have a clear purpose.

"Sir," he said, annoyed that he had to explain himself to me, "we are looking for the house with the blue door."

I scanned the houses carefully. They were the usual irregularly shaped variety. They had small walled-off courtyards with double metal doors as entrances. I quickly noticed a problem.

"Hey, Staff Sergeant."

"Yes, Sir?" He was getting even more agitated.

"Do you notice anything about the doors of these houses?" I asked. He looked around, then shook his head.

"No, what, Sir?"

"Well, you said we are looking for a house with a blue door."

"That's right."

"Well, almost every house has a blue door."

He hesitated. "Roger, Sir." That was all he could manage. His spirit, though, went unbroken. He was going to find the right house. He was committed. He walked off and took the Jordanian terp with him.

Time had flown by, and right about then our return rides arrived to take us back to the base. They met us on the main street that ran through the center of the shantytown. The Leland trucks and American Humvees came to rest in a single-file line in the middle of Coolie Town. The Humvees were equipped with the usual Mark 19 grenade launchers and heavy machine guns. The Iraqi trucks had gunners up on top manning the PKC medium machine guns. The firepower would help guard against any crazy insurgents taking pot shots at us on the street.

I took a seat in the back of one of the Humvees. I needed to get away from Staff Sergeant Buckfield. He was starting to annoy me. As I settled in, the other MiTT sergeant opened the opposite door, took a seat across from me, and shook his head in frustration.

"What's up, Sergeant?"

"Sir, has our mission changed from a patrol to a targeted raid?"

"What do you mean?" My ears perked up. The sergeant exhaled.

"Sir, the staff sergeant . . ." He hesitated.

"Spit it out, Sergeant."

"Sir, he found another Iraqi civilian who says he knows where the house with the blue door is."

"OK, so?"

"So, that guy was afraid to be seen with the Americans. The staff sergeant, I think he's going a little crazy. He really wants to find this high-value target. So, the staff sergeant told the civilian we would disguise him so that he could show us where the house is."

"What do you mean, disguise?" I didn't like where this was going. I looked out through the windshield for Buckfield, but my view was blocked by another vehicle.

"He had one of the Iraqi jundees give the civilian, the informant, his uniform."

"What?!" The other Americans, the escorts who were picking us up, were paying attention now. This was getting interesting.

"Yeah, he had the civilian dress up to look like one of our soldiers, and now they are going to go look for the house."

Operation Masquerade had begun.

Not more than two seconds after the sergeant finished telling me the incredible news did the lead vehicle in the convoy, an Iraqi Nissan pickup, peel out, and start racing down the road. The chain reaction that followed was a natural result of the pickup's sudden departure. The next vehicle in the chain, an Iraqi Leland truck, followed in the pickup's path. Then an American Humvee moved out, with another one close behind. Soon the entire convoy, American and Iraqi vehicles alike, was on the move, racing through the dusty streets of Coolie Town. Only the lead vehicle knew where we were headed.

The tan dust kicked up and obscured our view of the vehicle in front of us. We were all moving at a high speed. Our driver did not know where we were going, he concentrated only on staying with the vehicle in front of him. The gunner up in the turret was swallowing a bunch of dirt and sand. I could hear him coughing.

"Hey, didn't we just pass that house?" I said, as I recognized an intersection.

"Yes, Sir, I think you're right," one of the others agreed.
We were going in circles.

"Does anyone know where the fuck we are going?" I yelled out to the whole Humvee. No one answered. I had to find out what was going on. I sent an exasperated radio call. "Hey, all stations this net, all stations this net, does anyone know where we are going?"

"Roger, Sir. We are going to the target house," said Buckfield. "Sir, where are you?" he continued.

"What do you mean? We are right behind you in the convoy."
His response followed a long pause. "Sir, why did you leave?"

"What do you mean? You started moving so the convoy followed you." My blood was beginning to boil. This mission was turning into an episode of Keystone Cops. The road was racing by us. We looked to be on our third lap through Coolie Town. I could see the main street and the Iraqi police station.

The radio garbled to life a second later. "Sir, I left the terp and the soldier back in the police station."

"What do you mean you left them at the station? What are they doing there?" Blood was filling my eyes, steam coming from my ears.

"The terp is watching the jundee." Everyone could hear our back and forth over the radio. We still had not seen the Iraqi Nissan carrying Staff Sergeant Buckfield and his informant. They were lost in a different part of the town.

"Why is the terp watching the jundee?" I waited impatiently for the answer. Even as used to Iraq as I was by now, I did not expect what came over the radio next.

"Sir, because the jundee is naked."

My brain didn't fully comprehend what Buckfield had just said. I looked around at the rest of the guys in my vehicle. They all had the same look on their faces. Whisky Tango Foxtrot. I suddenly had a picture of the Jordanian terp, looking all strung-out, standing there in the Iraqi police station smoking a cigarette and next to him the poor Iraqi soldier sitting there naked.

"That's it, that's it. This operation is over!" I screamed, loudly.

"Driver take us back to the main part of the town now!" I was done. I keyed the radio again. "This is Drifter Two, this is Drifter Two. I am pulling the plug on this. Everyone rally back at the police station on the main strip in town. Over."

We were back in the center of the shantytown only a few minutes later. Sitting right outside the police station was the Jordanian terp. He took a drag from his cigarette as though he didn't have a care in the world.

"Where's the jundee?" I shouted at him. The terp pointed inside and shrugged his shoulders. "Staff Sergeant, this is Drifter Two. Get your ass back to the police station now!"

As we waited for the Nissan to come back, no one wanted to make eye contact with me. Finally, the Nissan came rolling down the street. I immediately approached as Buckfield stepped out.

"Staff Sergeant, this mission is over!"

"Sir, we found the house. We've got pictures."

"I don't care. This mission is over. The United States military does not engage in costumes and disguises and whatever else you have been pulling here. This ends now! Get the jundee dressed again, collect the terp, make sure everyone is accounted for, and let's get going." My eyes were locked in to his.

"Roger that, Sir." He blinked, but his tone was sarcastic.

Getting the right clothes in the hands of the right people took some time, but we were eventually off and on our way back to the base. We arrived at the camp close to three and a half hours after we had started the adventure. The patrol was originally scheduled to take one and a half hours.

With the misguided attempt to capture an imaginary enemy finished, I took a look at the digital pictures the staff sergeant claimed showed the target house. The pictures were of a wall. Nothing else, just a wall.

Operation Masquerade was over and with it went a great deal of the respect I had remaining for all our efforts in Iraq. I had expected that we would all need a lot of patience to deal with the Iraqis during the patrolling package. I had expected them to take two steps forward and one step back. I was prepared for that slow, frustrating grind. What I was not prepared for was the mounting evidence that we Americans were as bad at our jobs as they were.

Toward the end of our time with the Iraqis, someone asked me if I thought the Iraqis would ever be able to run all of their own patrols. I took one look at the Iraqis assembled for the next mission and then one look at the Americans gathered around some Humvees across from their Iraqi partners. My response should be easy to guess. Here's a hint: it was two Arabic words.

OPERATIONAL EXPERIENCE

Once the Iraqis were settled into the training rotation, their lives fell into a routine. The consistency of their schedule helped us keep them on track so that they started to learn and develop as a unit. The patrol package was used as the evaluation piece to judge, one patrol at a time, how much they had learned from the classes and practical exercises. The fact that these patrols took place in a real live combat zone added to the authenticity of the entire training regimen. Live rounds fired by real enemies had a way of getting everyone's attention.

Over time the jundees learned how to conduct themselves in a more professional manner, and the small unit leadership, the NCOs, and the junior officers also learned how to better control their men. Keep in mind that this progress was all relative to how lacking in basic skills and discipline they were at the beginning of the training. The final piece, the Battalion Staff, was also being developed by the adviser dedicated to each specific department and by their actual involvement in the planning and executing of both the training and the patrols.

The culmination of all of this effort was to bring the overall level of competence up from the small unit level to at least the company level. Our goal, toward the end of our time with the 9th Battalion, was to have the battalion not only conduct joint operations with its American partner unit but also ultimately plan and execute its own independent company-level operation. When I considered how inept the Iraqi forces had been when I first met them in Fallujah, I was amazed that we had reached a point at which we could contemplate such an operation. The fact that we were pushing head first toward this objective only served to highlight how far we'd come. What prevented me from declaring our performance a true success, however, was the little voice inside my head that reminded me of all of the other times during the mission when my hope had been dashed. "Insha Allah, Insha Allah, Insha Allah," the voice repeated over and over again.

The voice did have the ring of past experiences and truth, I had to admit. When the time came to begin the formal process of partnering with the 1st of the 506th for joint operations, many of the obstacles we'd encountered throughout our deployment presented themselves once again. The Iraqis, especially the leadership, still had much learn, and the Americans still either distrusted the Iraqis or had not yet bought into the entire partnership venture.

The cordon and search operations were prime examples of these difficulties. When the 1st of the 506th conducted missions, it picked the mission's venue based on which town near Camp Habbaniyah it had the most recent and accurate intelligence of enemy activity for. The soldiers would convoy their forces over to that town, unload them, and then create an outer seal, or cordon, to surround the designated area and keep others from entering. The forces within the cordon then swept through the entire town, house by house, in search of suspected insurgents and weapons caches. They would question the townspeople for information about potential insurgent activity. After the town had been searched, they would reboard their vehicles and return to base.

The planning for an operation that involved much of the battalion required several days. It also required an operations order brief a couple of days prior to the evolution. During those briefs the 1st of the 506th, and specifically its colonel, to my surprise, brought in the Iraqis' battalion commander, Lieutenant Colonel Mehgid, or a senior member of his staff, such as the operations officer, to take part in the plan. This was an important first step in cooperation between the

American and Iraqi armies. From the brief, the Americans could plan how the Iraqis would be employed during the cordon and search mission.

Following the mission brief, the Iraqis went back to their command post and started planning their own part of the mission. The MiTT members attached to whichever Iraqi company was going out on the mission would advise the company commander and the rest of his leadership throughout this process. How many jundees were going out on the misson? What time were they going to be picked up? What did they need to bring with them? All of these elements were considered.

Of course, much of the interaction between the American army and the Iraqi leadership was for show. The Iraqi colonel and his other leaders had no real say in how his forces were going to be used. He also had no say in how many of his troops would be needed for the operation. Since Mehgid was not a complete fool, he quickly realized that he was invited to the briefing as a courtesy. He played along and seemed to enjoy at least being treated with some degree of respect by the U.S. colonel and the rest of the 1st of the 506th. Still, the one-way nature of the planning relationship was indicative of the nature of the overall command relationship. This was obviously a partnership in name only.

Although I had previously advocated a relationship dynamic in which we advisers were in command of the Iraqis we were attached to, that dynamic was not put in place. Thus, I found it hard to watch the 1st of the 506th attempt to take command of the Iraqis on their own accord. I admired the Army's moxie, but questioned whether it would eventually backfire. What effect would not treating the Iraqis as partners have down the road? This important consideration was brought into focus almost immediately, during one of the first joint cordon and search missions. The answers to the question would have far-reaching ramifications for our entire effort in Iraq.

As the adviser to the Iraqi Battalion's assistant operations officer, I periodically went out on the joint missions in order to evaluate how our soldiers were performing and also how the 1st of the 506th was employing our soldiers. The first joint mission was a key step in the process of training the Iraqis, so I volunteered to join the Iraqis and their MiTT members on the mission to observe and critique. I never expected to return with a harsher critique of the Americans than the Iraqis.

The summer was close at hand, and the heat was there to stay for a while. The sun affected everything and everyone, whether machine or man. Even the insurgents took some time off around noontime to cool down. The rockets and mortars didn't start falling until just after five in the evening, about the time the temperature started dropping significantly for the night. Given this harsh environment, we had to move out on that first mission as early in the morning as possible.

I peeled open my eyes the morning of the mission at the sound of a knock on my door. An Iraqi jundee leaned hesitantly into the room.

"Mister, Mister," he whispered. He didn't know I had my pistol in my hands, just in case he was an infiltrator.

"Yeah, yeah. Shukran," I said.

"OK, OK." He left, and I got up, dressed, and stepped out the door ten minutes later. It was still dark out, the painful sun had not yet creeped over the horizon.

As I previously mentioned, I was going along with the mission to act as an observer. However, a secondary duty of mine during this mission was to act as go-between for the 1st of the 506th and the Iraqis. Using an interpreter and my prior advising experiences, I was going to try to facilitate better communications and understanding.

The partnership itself was driven by two main factors. First, the generals had ordered the 1st of the 506th to link up with and train the Iraqi forces. Preparing the New Iraqi Army to protect its own country was now the main effort for all American forces in Iraq, and the units that had been fighting the insurgents on the front lines would have to transition to the advising role whether they liked it or not. Of course, the American units, including the 1st of the 506th, transitioned begrudgingly and much more slowly than was advantageous to the operation. Instances like this particular cordon and search mission were a step in the right direction, though, I hoped.

The second driving force was more practical in nature. As previously mentioned, the Iraqis, with their ability to speak the language and understand the culture, were better equipped to lead the searches of peoples' houses. The theory was that the civilians would be less agitated if Iraqis rather than Americans searched their houses. Also, the Iraqis were better than us at picking out the insurgents from the crowd. They knew who belonged and didn't.

I stepped outside that morning, ready to meet up with the platoon of Iraqis I was going to shadow for the operation. The courtyard was alive with activity. The Ashook Leland trucks were fired up, and the jundees were climbing up into the flat bed backs of the vehicles. I made sure they had water bottles with them. I climbed into the back of one of the trucks with the jundees, and the driver took his place in the convoy line. We had a U.S. Army escort through Checkpoint Charlie and over to the other side. Once there, we linked up with the rest of the American forces, boarded new vehicles that were armored at least to a degree, and then headed outside the wire and toward our objective.

The objective that day was one of the small towns that lined the sides of the main highway through Habbaniyah. The town was called Khaldea. Several IED and small arms attacks had occurred in the previous three days. Intelligence suggested the townspeople knew who was responsible. Our job was to make sure the townspeople understood that hiding the enemy from us was a big mistake.

We—over half the Army battalion plus about a company's worth of Iraqis—rolled up from the main road. Our force was over three hundred personnel strong. We had Bradley fighting vehicles and tanks position themselves on the main roads to cut off access to the town. Armored Humvees with fifty-caliber machine guns and Mark 19 grenade launchers filed into the small side streets to watch for anyone trying to escape down the alleyways. We arrived at the town with the subtlety of a sledgehammer.

I jumped out of the truck and found my bearings. The sun was starting its murderous ascent; its light caressed the tops of the tan buildings. Power lines draped every which way from one house to the next and back around again. There was a jumble of dozens of similar lines above every intersection. A stray dog, one of legions, quietly darted down one of the streets. The gutters were filled with the usual filth. If you've seen one Iraqi town, you've seen them all.

When I turned to make sure the Iraqis were all accounted for, I noticed that one of the Iraqi squad leaders already had his men in an orderly formation. I was impressed. We moved out, crossed a road, and stepped down another dirty street. The Americans from the 1st of the 506th quickly joined up with us. They were squawking into their headset radios. Their squawks and the whine of vehicles moving into place were the only sounds. The town was quiet; its inhabitants were still sleeping.

Each block of the town was assigned to a specific American platoon, and the Iraqis were broken up into smaller teams to lead the house searches. I stayed with my Iraqis as they approached the first house on our assigned block. It had a set of twin metal blue doors jimmied together, and not one light was on inside. The Iraqis hesitated. No one had given them specific orders. The Americans hadn't bothered to tell the Iraqis' leader what he was supposed to do. And no interpreter had been provided. What I gathered from these initial moments was instead of treating the Iraqis like a normal military unit the Americans were using them simply as bodies.

"Well, come on! That door ain't going to open itself up!" a U.S. soldier snarled. He was the platoon sergeant in charge of the clearing of this sector. The Iraqi, of course, didn't know what he was saying, so he just stood there.

"Hey, Sarge, these guys don't listen," an anonymous soldier chimed in.

The platoon sergeant huffed then kicked the door himself, making a loud whacking sound in the morning air. With another swift kick the two sides were separated. The Iraqis just stood there, unsure what came next. Even though they had already been trained in search techniques, they were too confused by the language barrier and the lack of clear directions to spring into immediate action.

"Well, let's go. Get in there. Shit!" The platoon sergeant couldn't say anything without that snarl on his face. He didn't try and hide his displeasure.

I waved the Iraqis in. Once they saw the hand motion, they understood and rushed into the house. They spread out like water filling cracks in the pavement; they ran into every room. I was briefly worried that they would shoot anything that moved because they were so amped up.

The house, like every other house in Iraq, had a small inner courtyard. The toilet, in an outhouse area, was off to the side of the courtyard. I could smell it from five feet away. I didn't move any closer. A mine detector was brought in to scan for hidden weapons and bomb-making materials. Everything was turned upside down.

The jundees found an older civilian and brought him out of his room. He was the man of the house. This man was followed by the rest of his family: a woman, two other grown men, and three young children. The family looked up at us with bleary, bloodshot eyes. They didn't know what was going on.

"There, get them over there," ordered the platoon sergeant, pointing to a corner of the courtyard. The Iraqis did as told. The older man, looking disheveled in his clothes, watched as his house was searched from top to bottom. He didn't make a sound. It looked like he had been through this before.

"Nothing's here, Sarge."

"Alright, let's go. We've got the whole block to get done in an hour or so."

We were out the door in a matter of minutes, leaving the family to clean up. I looked back and caught the eyes of one of the children, a young boy. He didn't look at me with hate, as I expected, just curiosity. He didn't know why we Americans did what we did. I was starting to wonder about this myself.

The same routine repeated itself over and over as we moved through the block. The jundees were ordered to bang and open the doors and begin the search of the houses. The inhabitants of each home were roused out of their sleep, out of their beds, and made to watch. If one of the few interpreters was around at the time, he would ask the family members if they had seen any of the insurgents in the town recently. All of them would shake their heads no.

Once the soldiers had their routine down, I stood back and observed. I was to report back to Major Lawson about the operation, about how our Iraqis were treated, and about any improvements that could be made to better train and employ the jundees. My list of improvements was growing by the second.

We went up to another metal-doored house, banged, and waited for someone to open the gates. If we didn't have to break the doors down, we didn't want to. A sleepy civilian shuffled his feet and opened the gate from inside.

"Get over there," an American soldier said. The civilian didn't move. He just stood there. "Get over there!" the soldier repeated, shouting this time. The civilian kept looking around, watching the other Americans and jundees pass him and walk into his house.

"Goddamnit, move your ass!" The soldier was screaming right into the guy's face. No reaction. The soldier turned to one of his friends. "Why don't these people ever listen?" he asked.

My brain was swelling. I couldn't take the lunacy any longer. "Because *they don't speak English!* You friggin' idiot!" I didn't say this out loud. It wasn't my place. I was not in charge of the soldier or his buddies. The problem wasn't the individual anyway; it was the mind-set. I finally realized something that had threatened to breach the surface of my consciousness since my arrival at SKETCHY: our American misconceptions were as much to blame for the situation in Iraq as the native Iraqis unprofessionalism and poor training.

The ramifications of the entire mission in Iraqi were coming into focus for me. Maybe I didn't want to admit that we could be responsible for our own failures, but after I witnessed this soldier's ignorance, I could ignore the evidence no longer. We might have had the best of intentions, but we had no idea what we were doing in this country. We had no idea who we were dealing with or how to deal with them. Unless we recognized these deficiencies, we were doomed to fail.

The operation continued along that same pattern, and we found nothing but sleeping people and empty houses. The entire town, somehow, was clean. A few suspicious people were taken in for questioning. Aside from those people, we had nothing to show for our day. The town had been awakened, and the civilians filled the streets. They watched us like we were invading aliens. They wore blank expressions on their faces, but tension was in the air. The kids, oblivious to everything, kept asking us for candy.

Eventually the battalion saddled back up and rolled out of the town as if nothing had happened. We had arrived hoping to find the people responsible for many local attacks and gather valuable information about other enemies in the area. Instead, we pissed people off and then simply left.

The townspeople had zero incentive to help us. The word we received from our intelligence shop after the operation was that the enemy had intimidated most of the town into cooperating with them. That seemed obvious to me. Our forces merely went in and out of the town without keeping a meaningful presence there full time, but the enemy likely left when they knew we were coming and then returned once we'd gone to make sure no one was working with us, the infidel.

When we returned to the camp, I gave Major Lawson my honest assessment under the intense heat of the midday sun. Lawson was most concerned with how our Iraqis were employed. The sad fact was that the 1st of the 506th, at the platoon and squad level, hadn't bothered to work with the Iraqi leadership. All they wanted were Iraqi soldiers at the front of their mission so that they could say that they were complying with their higher command's orders to involve the Iraqis. They were also exploiting the Iraqis for manpower purposes. The deficiencies of this relationship had to be addressed with the 1st of the 506th colonel and markedly improved if we ever hoped to bring the Iraqis up to full speed.

"Sir, I don't get it. How can we expect the Iraqi Army to act like a professional military unit if we don't actually treat them like a professional military unit?" I asked, summing up the nature of the contradiction.

He had no answer. I guessed no one but the Iraqis had the answer, and I was tired of hearing those damn two words. Over time, however, after many subsequent joint operations, the U.S.-Iraqi relationship and the Iraqis' performance slowly progressed. Through assessments and addressing the deficiencies identified in the assessments, we were able to tweak the working relationship between the two armies. We were also able to further develop the Iraqi leadership. Additional obstacles continually presented themselves. During another cordon and search mission, for example, the American combat engineers found a large weapons cache buried by the side of a road. While the 1st of the 506th setup the charges to blow the cache in place, they had me and the Iraqis wait in one of the neighbors' homes. In this case they seemed to be suspicious of the Iraqis seeing how they prepared their explosive charges. The distrust, even after many missions, remained.

Even when the Iraqis graduated to conducting their own missions, we experienced the expected hiccups. At the tail end of one cordon and search mission, after the Iraqi soldiers had completed their search of a suspected insurgent's house in the nearby Civil Camp area, they jumped back into their vehicles and rushed back to the base. I had been watching the operation from a guard tower, so I had a bird's eye view. I noticed that the Iraqis, in their hurry, had left three of their own men on the streets. So much for accountability.

Regardless, the operations grew more involved, and the Iraqis finally began to take responsibility for a small portion of their own country. The development was encouraging. It proved that with the right amount of effort from everyone involved our idea of the New Iraqi Army could, one day, become a reality.

"If only this had occurred at the very beginning," I mused to myself.

This realization only acted as further salt in my mental wounds. Seeing what could be accomplished with adequate resources and the proper attitude from all partners involved in the advising mission, I felt I understood with greater clarity the many dire deficiencies that had plagued us from the beginning. Poor predeployment training, a limited number of advisers, an initial lack of interpreters, little to no logistical support, poor communications, a convoluted chain of command, cultural barriers, institutional resistance to a change in the mission, the adaptable insurgency, the Iraqis' nature, their philosophy, their culture—all of this came together to shake what was at one time my total commitment to the cause of building a new Iraq.

What now replaced that complete faith in our mission and our leaders was merely a series of questions. What were we doing in Iraq? What was the objective for the New Iraqi Army? How did the powers that be expect us to develop an entirely new army from scratch without the proper resources? Did anyone ask the Iraqis what they wanted? Did anyone take the Iraqis' culture into consideration when figuring out how long it would take to create a New Iraqi Army? What would happen if I told you it would take at least twenty—yes, *twenty*—years to develop a fully operational Iraqi army that can defeat any enemies and be self-sufficient? Was America prepared for such a commitment? Do any Americans even know what Insha Allah means and what the ramifications of such a philosophy are for the Iraqi people?

For me, this was already a devastating series of questions, and the list just kept growing.

How long did the American military have to create this New Iraqi Army? What was our timetable? How long did we have before the American people had had enough? What would happen then? Would we leave? Would the Iraqis remember the lessons we taught them, or would they revert to their old undisciplined ways? How many of them would walk away from it all? Would the New Iraqi Army simply scatter? Would the new Iraq simply collapse?

On one particularly brutal day in June 2005, with nothing but more questions coming at me, I decided to ask the most important question of all: When are we getting out of here?

THE RESULTS AND THE OUTLOOK

When are we getting out of here?

The question, of course, had a double meaning. It all depended on which "we" I was talking about. The drifters were going to leave Iraq, of that there was little question. Of course, during this tour we had gone long periods without even knowing to whom we belonged, so the day and time of our departure was an ever-moving target. In fact, right up until the last day rumors persisted that CMATT was trying to extend our tour for another three months.

Oddly enough, once we returned home we found out that we had stayed over a month and a half longer than we were supposed to. According to the military gossip network, all individual augmentees were supposed to serve only six-month tours. We stayed past our seventh month without anyone telling us we could go home. This was another slap in the face, but my face was too bruised from all the others for me to feel the sting.

We escaped Iraq only because we took our retrograde into our own hands. We continually asked our brigade advisers when our replacements would arrive. The new AST was our salvation. For many weeks speculation on their arrival ran rampant, and all sorts of rumors floated around. First we heard the new AST would arrive in a couple of days, then a couple of weeks. Then we heard it was in the country but not getting to Habbaniyah for another two weeks. It was as though someone was constantly taking the finish line and moving it away from us.

Even after the AST arrived, we had to force ourselves onto one of the freedom birds back to Kuwait. Our names were not on the flight's manifest. But we had been through too much to let that stop us. The drifters had learned never to take "no" for an answer.

The new AST illustrated three different issues. First, CMATT had sent another team of only ten members, all Marines. Where did this leave the sixteen members of the 1st of the 506th? As it turned out, they were pulled back to their original unit. This highlighted the flaw with the MiTT concept. The MiTT had been composed of two different teams, one from CMATT and one from the local American unit. How could the adviser effort have cohesion if the advisers were from different units and changed depending on where the Iraqi battalion was based?

Second, on a good note, the new AST Marines brought with them much better equipment. They had much better communications gear, more firepower, and more up-armored vehicles. Also, we heard that SKETCHY had been replaced by something called the Phoenix Academy. Language and culture training and other similar improvements were included in the curriculum at the new academy. All of this suggested that someone was actually listening when we sent our complaints up to the various higher commands. It was too late for us to benefit from the more-thorough training, but at least we had contributed to improving the mission.

Third, the new AST members behaved in a way that helped me gain perspective on how far we drifters had come. I witnessed their first tentative attempts at communication with the Iraqis, the first time they saw Iraqis walking holding hands, and their stares of disbelief at the pile of dirty water bottles stacked by the Iraqi Port-O-Jons, and all of this brought back memories from my days of adjustment.

On the military side of things, the new AST members were appalled at the force protection problems endemic to our side of Camp Habbaniyah. The officer in charge of the new team immediately slammed the setup and even extended his ire to some of our operations. The problem with his assessment was not that he was incorrect in his conclusions. Yes, Camp Habbaniyah had major problems: the neighboring towns were not completely under control, the base was not completely protected, the Iraqi leave policy sapped the combat strength of the entire battalion each and every month, and we were still dealing with occasional riots over pay or the food or whatever. So, yes, he was correct in his basic assessment. What he did not realize—what he could not realize—was how far we had come to reach even that level. He had no idea with what we had started. Only one with a drifter's perspective could look at the chaos of Camp Habbaniyah and marvel at the unbelievable progress we had made.

One could say that the discrepancy between the views of the incoming AST and our veteran team was all a question of context. While we had been able to train the Iraqis and have some effect on their behavior, the Iraqis had clearly had their own effect on us. The realization that context mattered to us Americans too was a good example of the way their thinking had penetrated ours. When one of the new AST members marveled that the front gate to the Iraqi side of camp was less than tactically sound, three of us drifters shrugged, smiled to ourselves, and then spoke in unison: "Insha Allah." When the new AST members looked at us with confusion, we had to share another laugh. It was as though we were looking in the mirror at ourselves from the past, when we were unfamiliar with the Iraqi world we were about to enter.

"Don't worry, you'll soon learn what that means," one of us counseled. In truth, I was still grappling with the phrase's full meaning. When it came to the divine, some things are not measurable.

What was measurable was the performance of the 9th Battalion, and that measure was an important part of the assessment of our tour. Consider, for a moment, the Iraqis' military fitness when we first met them. They could barely function on the fire team level. When they were first attacked, they reacted with total disregard for fire discipline. Their leadership was ineffective. Their Battalion Staff was not engaged in any of their operations. They shot wildly at night at imaginary targets. The American units they worked with were fearful of their recklessness. Finally, they went to the bathroom inside abandoned houses.

By the time we were ready to leave, the battalion commander and his staff were working with an adjacent American unit to coordinate joint operations. The Iraqis were also using terrain models and operations orders to plan and conduct their own independent company-level operations. They were patrolling and operating in an assigned sector of their own country and mixing with the local populace. They were developing networks to inform the civilians about the enemy and constantly seeking to find and kill that enemy. In short, they were learning to fight the insurgency. Not to mention, they stopped going to the bathroom inside abandoned buildings and used the facilities provided to them.

Toward the end of our tour, some of the Iraqis were assigned to move to nearby Ramadi to help a U.S. Army unit that was stationed on the east side of that volatile city. Once our Iraqis were in the city and operating for a few weeks, we received reports from some of the U.S. units working with them that the soldiers we'd trained were "shit hot." The Americans in Ramadi had never seen Iraqis who could operate so capably. It was a testament to our effectiveness as advisers and a clear indication of the results we could achieve.

After we left the country, Major Lawson and Captain Yamamoto received reports that the entire battalion was moved over to Ramadi. This move supported our decision to train the Iraqis in the fundamentals and not tailor the training to the specific region we were operating in. The plans for the Iraqis were always changing. Only a sound foundation would help them remain flexible enough to work in a variety of areas.

The move to Ramadi also provided a reminder of how far the Iraqis still had to go. While they were able to plan and operate on their own to some extent, they had yet to experience a long-lasting engagement with the insurgents. The attacks we had endured were always of the hit-and-run variety. In Ramadi, the enemy decided several times to stay and fight. The results were not pretty. The exact numbers of casualties were not released, but the 9th Battalion lost a great deal of their men to injury and death. The New Iraqi Army remained very much a work in progress.

I knew the deal. For every two steps forward, the jundees would take at least one step back. Even in those last few days the Iraqis did things to remind me of what we had started with. During the last week we were there, the Iraqis were moving their living quarters to a different part of the base. They wanted to move the Port-O-Jons as well, so a group of them decided to use one of the Nissans to transport one of the portable toilets. I was walking down the service road when I saw eight jundees lifting an entire Port-O-Jon onto the back of the pickup truck. The toilet unit stood high in the flat bed. The Iraqis jabbered back and forth, and I didn't need a translator to realize they were saying the toilet was standing too tall for them to drive off with it. What do you think they did to remedy the situation? That's right: they laid the Port-O-Jon on its back. What was the problem with this solution? The Port-O-Jon was full!

"Noooooo!" I screamed, but it was too late. They had already started to drive off. Human piss and watery shit were spilling out of the toilet as it lay on its back. It flooded the back of the Nissan pickup truck until it flowed out the back and splashed directly on the service road. The Iraqis left a long trail of human waste in their wake as they gleefully drove off.

When I ran up and screamed at them, they looked at me like I had three heads.

"What the fuck are you doing?" I yelled at an Iraqi lieutenant who was apparently supervising the operation. He didn't know why I was yelling, so I angrily pointed at the piles of shit that were now lying in the middle of the road. He finally nodded in understanding and shouted something to one of the jundees. The soldier came back a second later with one of the squeegee things they used to clean the tile floors in their rooms. He smiled and then started to scrape the shit off from the middle of the road to the dirt shoulder.

"See, Mister, clean," the Iraqi said with a cracked smile. He was so proud.

The sight of that Iraqi standing there with the squeegee reinforced a conclusion I had come to already: despite the progress we made in bringing military competency to a battalion of the New Iraqi Army, we were working against forces that might've been too great to overcome. Were they really learning from our routine and training regime? Or were they repeating what they saw in the hopes of pleasing their American partners? I was proud of our work, but my doubts lingered.

As yet more reinforcement of these doubts, the day before we left Camp Habbaniyah, the Iraqis prepared for another week of leave. The Iraqi main effort was still in full effect. Nothing could stop them from taking their vacations. Despite any professional pride I felt, I was not going to miss Iraq or its people.

We all gathered out in the courtyard and shook hands with the Iraqis we knew the best. I expected a touching farewell, and I was surprised by how little sadness or regret I felt. I tried to be polite and not show how elated I was to be leaving. Lieutenant Hamza, the Iraqi intelligence officer I had been working with, gave me a hearty shake and even a hug.

"Mulazem Awal Nevarra. You my friend." He smiled.

"You my friend too, Hamza." I replied. His grin grew.

Mohammed was next. We hadn't seen much of each other toward the end.

"Mohammed, be safe. OK?" I said, extending my hand. "Don't lose faith," I continued, surprising myself with the sentiment.

"I do. I do, Sir." He held his hand over his heart.

"Asalaam Alaikum."

"Alaikum Asalaam."

He was off the next moment, yelling at some of the less disciplined of his fellow Iraqis to get their act together and get on board the Leland truck that was going to take them on vacation. The trucks fired up their engines and lined up a in a single file.

Snoop was the last to come up to me. He looked like someone had killed his dog.

"It's going to be fine, Snoop."

"Yes, Sir."

"Who knows, one day you may be able to come over to the United States."

"Yes, I would like that, Sir."

"Then you can come and look me up. I take you out in New York City."

We looked at each other. I wanted to mean what I said. But we both knew this was going to be the last time we ever saw each other. We smiled politely, hugged, and then he was off with the rest of the leave convoy. The ten of us drifters waved the trucks on their way with huge smiles on our faces. It probably looked like we were smiling to wish the Iraqis good vacations. Of course, we knew the truth: we were leaving Iraq, and nothing could beat that.

As for when America was going to get out of there, that was still being determined. Based on the results of our time with the Iraqis, as I assessed them, I did not think we would leave anytime soon. Unfortunately, much more work still needed to be done. First, as previously mentioned, the Iraqis would have to become truly battle hardened. They would have to engage the enemy and learn from the engagements. None of us Americans knew exactly how all the Iraqis would perform during such engagements. Second, there was no guarantee that all of them would stay and fight. Desertions arising from the disastrous leave policy continued to sap the strength of the unit. Third, the Iraqi soldiers' problems with context continued to plague them every time they moved to new bases or new areas of responsibility.

None of this took into account the political situation. Would Iraq stay together as one country? If not, we'd have to say good-bye to the New Iraqi Army that contained all three ethnic groups. What about the connection between the new sovereign government and the military? How was that going to work? How was the Ministry of Defense going to support its military? Would it be able to provide supplies? Who would direct the Iraqi forces? Who would be in charge? What did the Iraqi government think of our effort to create an entirely new Iraqi military?

Finally, the most important consideration, could the Iraqis

reconcile the differences between the tenants of their faith and those of democracy? If they continued to believe every aspect of their lives was directed by God and only God, would they ever believe in the concept of government for the people by the people?

America would have to have the answers to these questions, which would provide a good picture of Iraq's future, before it could pull its troops out of the country. Based on my experiences as an adviser to the New Iraqi Army, I believed that we would have to stay for at least twenty years or, more likely, forever, if we wanted to make our conception of the new democratic Iraq work. In truth, the Iraqis whom the drifters lived, trained, and fought with were not going to save the country. Their children and their grandchildren, the young Iraqis who would grow up in a world without Saddam Hussein and without the brutal insurgents, would be the ones to change their country. The children would learn over time the true meaning of freedom and democracy. They could know a world where God was not the decider of all aspects of their lives, where free will and personal responsibility could be applied to achieving new heights. They could develop an outlook based on reason more than blind faith, an outlook based on hope.

Such a monumental undertaking required a level of effort and sacrifice that the United States as a country simply could not provide. The American people, back home, simply were not prepared for a fifty-year commitment. They had been prepared by our president and our Congress and our media to expect a short and decisive campaign.

Everything about the planning of our adviser mission supported my conclusion. The adviser mission was hastily pulled together with almost no planning. The first groups of advisers were thrown into nearly impossible situations with no clear direction and even less support. Going in, we had no understanding of the underdevelopment of the Iraqi military or the requirements for bringing that same military up to full combat effectiveness. Ultimately, Washington had no coherent plan and an objective that was way too ambitious if not outright ridiculous in its reach. The entire setup of our effort to start a new Iraqi Army from scratch was a recipe for disaster.

Afterword:
Home, with a Final Anecdote

So, there I was, walking back onto a C-130 plane. It seemed like just yesterday I had been walking off that same type of plane back in Baghdad. I was retracing my steps, walking backward in time. Only now, I was changed. I had seen the strangest of sights, met the most unique of people, and lived through one hell of a crazy time. An entire lifetime had been crammed into just under eight months.

I stepped into the belly of the freedom bird, strapped myself in, and waited to take off. The engines whirled to life. The ten of us—the drifters, the men I had gone into combat with—were seated across and all around me. The engines were so loud that we could not carry on a conversation. No words needed to be said anyway.

The engine roared with greater intensity as we began to accelerate down the runway. I half expected to crash before we took off. Everything about the deployment had taught me to expect the unexpected, to assume that God was more or less a prankster who did not care one bit about my feelings, hopes, or dreams. A pre-takeoff crash would have been the final irony. The last sick joke in this endless series of sarcasms. But the bird picked up speed, and I could feel the air tickling the wings' underbelly and lift the metal behemoth, which took us up into the sky at a steep angle. My stomach lurched up into my throat, but I didn't mind. I smiled broadly.

I caught a look from Major Lawson. We exchanged a knowing nod. Nothing needed to be said. We were on our way home. My long journey was over. My strange story had come to an end.

Some time later, I was at a family gathering, a homecoming celebration, and the usual question kept coming up: "So, how was it over there?" I heard the question over and over. In response, I would try to explain in depth all the craziness I had witnessed, but no one could fully appreciate it. I guess that is why I wrote this book. After the question was asked for the hundredth time and before this book was completed, I stopped going into great detail about my experiences. It was a waste of breath. Instead I told a short story that Captain Yamamoto had passed on to me before we parted ways.

An American officer, a major who had been assigned to another Iraqi battalion, was talking to the Iraqi logistics officer from that same unit. They were trying to figure out how many meals and water bottles the unit needed from the next shipment. The major had come up with one figure, the Iraqi officer with a completely different sum. The two went back and forth for a little while. Each was insisting that their own numbers were the correct answers. Finally, the American major had had enough and said, "I am a major in the U.S. Marine Corps. I have a master's degree in applied mathematics. You, on the other hand, wipe your ass with your own hand!"

This story best reflected our Iraq mission for two reasons. First, we were supposed to be there to win the hearts and minds of the Iraqi people. Obviously, that wasn't going quite as well as we would have liked. The Americans did not always use the right tactics or tone during their "advising," and the Iraqi soldiers behaved in ways that hindered the advising mission. They often disagreed with our counsel on matters such as military tactics and logistics, matters in which we were more knowledgeable. The second reason I found the story so symbolic of my wild ride with the New Iraqi Army was that the major was right—Iraqis did not use toilet paper.

INDEX

The abbreviation EN refers to Eric Navarro.

ABOUT THE AUTHOR

Capt. Eric Navarro was born in Brooklyn, New York, in 1975, and graduated from The New School University with a bachelor's degree in liberal arts with a specialty in writing. He was living in Manhattan on September 11, 2001, and decided to join the Marines the next day. He lives in Brooklyn with his wife, Dorothy, and remains in the reserves, ready to serve again should his country call. At the time of the book's publication, he will have returned to Iraq for a second tour. When he completes his second tour in Iraq he plans to attend New York University's Stern School of Business.